Johnson Beharry was born in Grenada in 1979. He joined the British Army in 2001, serving in the 1st Battalion Princess of Wales's Royal Regiment. He was deployed to Kosovo and Northern Ireland before being sent to Iraq in April 2004. Following his heroic actions on 1 May and 11 June 2004, he was awarded the Victoria Cross in 2005.

'A h⋯ ⋯day
Expre⋯

'Grip⋯ ⋯day
Telegi⋯

'Ren⋯ ⋯an's
odyss⋯ ⋯of
Gren⋯ ⋯Iax
Hasti⋯

'As v⋯ ⋯hat
Britis⋯ ⋯ing
mora⋯ ⋯ilt-
hood⋯

Barefoot Soldier

The Amazing True Story
of Courage Under Fire

JOHNSON
BEHARRY VC

with NICK COOK

sphere

SPHERE

First published in Great Britain in 2006 by Sphere
This paperback edition published in 2007 by Sphere

A CIP catalogue record for this book
is available from the British Library.

ISBN 978-0-7515-3879-3

Typeset in Bembo by M Rules
Printed and bound in Great Britain by
Clays Ltd, St Ives plc

Sphere
An imprint of
Little, Brown Book Group
Brettenham House
Lancaster Place
London WC2E 7EN

A Member of the Hachette Livre Group of Companies

www.littlebrown.co.uk

To my wonderful grandmother Isabella Bolah,
who passed away on 11 November 2002. You meant
everything to me. I love and miss you so much.
May you rest in peace.

And to Tamara. You know how much
you mean to me too.

CONTENTS

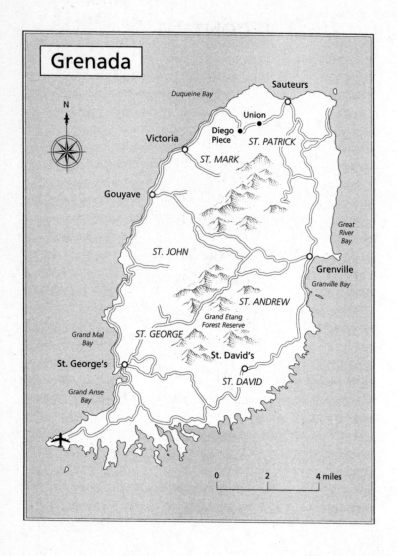

Grenada

N

Duqueine Bay

Sauteurs

Union

Diego
Piece

Victoria

ST. PATRICK

ST. MARK

Gouyave

Great
River
Bay

ST. JOHN

Grenville

Granville Bay

ST. ANDREW

Grand Etang
Forest Reserve

*Grand Mal
Bay*

ST. GEORGE

St. David's

St. George's

ST. DAVID

*Grand Anse
Bay*

| 0 | | 2 | | 4 miles |

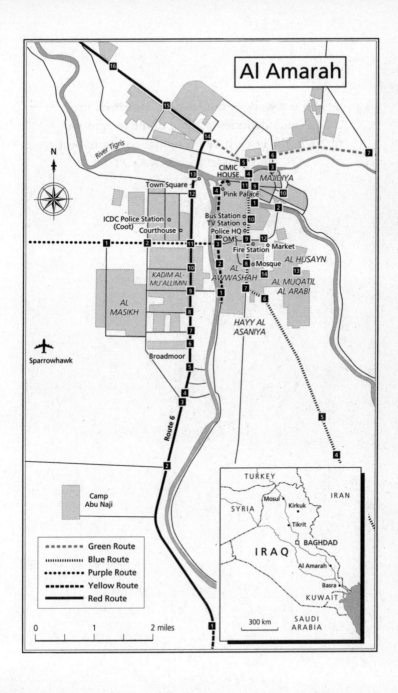

This is a work of non-fiction. However, the names and identities of some of the people and places in the book have been disguised to respect and protect their privacy.

Barefoot Soldier

PROLOGUE

I check my mirrors and wrench the steering column hard over, putting Whisky Two Zero into a neutral turn. We send up a shower of sand and grit.

The road we've just come down stretches into the distance. I floor the accelerator and watch our speed build. We're on a fast main road and traffic is light, but I need to keep a sharp lookout. There are pedestrians everywhere. Some stop by the edge of the road and stare at us as we roar by. Others carry on as normal as twenty-five tonnes of Warrior hurtles past them. I see kids wobbling on bicycles and old men on donkeys.

As I pass the work party by the street lamp, a couple of them wave. I stick my hand out of the hatch and wave back.

The contact area is a small town several kilometres to the south-east of Al Amarah. The road we're on will take us straight to it.

'OK, listen up,' the Light Infantry officer says. 'A platoon operating in convoy with an ICDC [Iraqi Civil Defence Corps] patrol has been ambushed.'

The army platoon has managed to extract from the contact area, the LI officer goes on, along with one of the ICDC Land Rovers, but this has been hit by small-arms fire, injuring two of its occupants. The other ICDC vehicle is cut off in the town and still under attack. The British Army platoon can't loop back to try to re-establish contact – every time they've tried, they've been engaged by mortars. They need a Warrior to go in for them.

A cluster of buildings – mainly single-storey – rises up on either side of the main road as we approach the contact area. I can see splashes of blue and green – clothes hanging on a line at the back of one of the houses.

The LI officer orders me to pull up on the side of the road while he assesses the situation. As I manoeuvre the Warrior on to the scrub we hear over the net that the army patrol has headed back to Abu Naji camp with their casualties. But the ICDC Land Rover is still missing.

'What now, Boss?' I say.

'I'm scanning the town now,' the commander says. 'Wait one.'

The sunlight is blindingly bright. The only movement I can see is a dog picking its way through a rubbish tip between us and the town. Then I turn and see a group of children running towards us. They're dressed in Arab clothing – long shirts that look like dresses – and are waving and shouting.

'Kids to our nine o'clock,' I say.

'Bloody hell,' the officer says. 'That's all we need.'

The kids reach the vehicle. There are four of them, no older than six or seven. They have no shoes on their feet and they're holding their hands out to me.

'They're shoutin', "*Bakshi*" – somet'ing like that,' I say.

'*Baksheesh*,' Jimmy says. 'It means money. Don't give 'em any.'

I look at the boy nearest to the vehicle. He is jumping up, trying to touch me. His face is filthy and he looks painfully thin, but he is grinning and seems happy enough. I reach into my pocket. I don't have money, but I do have a packet of chewing gum. I hand it to him and he runs off across the sand, chased by his mates.

'OK,' the commander says. 'There's still no contact with

the ICDC Land Rover, so we're going to go in and see what we can see.'

Keep your eyes peeled, he tells Jimmy and me.

As I ease Whisky Two Zero forward, Jimmy starts going on about the hatch again. I don't really see the problem. I prefer to drive with my head out anyway. It's better than hunkering down and using the day sight. But Jimmy doesn't like it at all. 'Fucking typical,' he says. 'My last day and I'm in a bloody deathtrap.'

There's nothing that can be done about it, the boss says.

We continue to move forward and then, as we close on the first group of houses, I reduce our speed. Behind me, I can hear Jimmy traversing the turret, sweeping the street either side of us for signs of life. But everything is quiet. It's a ghost town.

At a crossroads the boss suddenly commands me to reverse up. He's seen something off to our right. I come back and draw level with the crossroads. I glance right and see it too: a vehicle making tracks away from us. I squint against the glare; it's the Land Rover. The boss confirms it a second later. 'OK,' he says. 'Looks like they're safe and on their way back to Abu Naji. Might as well follow them, Beharry. Let's get out of here.'

I'm about to slip into drive when Jimmy yells, 'Jesus Christ, there's a bloke with a fucking RPG at two o'clock!'

The warning is so unexpected that instead of flooring the accelerator I turn to my two o'clock. There's a man down on one knee in the shadow of a wall. He's so close I can make out the check on his blue and white headgear and see the holes in his faded green combat jacket. And there's something on his shoulder. A black and brown tube, with a brown handle and grip.

'*Go, go, go!*' the boss roars.

'The fucking hatch!' Jimmy shouts.

There's a puff of black smoke and the RPG launcher kicks upwards as the round leaves the tube.

Less than a second has passed since the boss ordered me to move, but we're still not going anywhere. I'm frozen – not through fear but because I can't take my eyes off the rocket-propelled grenade that's coming towards us. I can see the cone-shaped warhead and the four little fins that keep it stable. I can see it rotating as it heads straight for us.

'Move!' the boss yells.

The RPG crashes into the armour plating to my left. My whole world stops. I know what these things can do. I'm waiting for the blast, the shockwave, the blinding, searing heat . . . Instead I hear a sound like a brick hitting a dustbin lid. The grenade bounces off the hull, then, almost in slow motion, down on to the ground. I watch it roll away, like a drink can some kid just kicked across the street.

I don't hang around to see what happens next. Flooring the pedal, I turn after the Land Rover and keep on going.

Fifteen minutes later we're back at Abu Naji. Jimmy is still shaking when he climbs down from the turret. He's also mad as hell about the state of his hatch, but when I have a go, she shuts just right, so I don't know what he's on about.

Unlike Jimmy, I can't get excited about what has just happened to us. It didn't feel real, and still doesn't.

I keep on seeing the RPG rolling along the road beside us. Maybe tomorrow they'll go back to throwing stones.

Later, as I'm sitting on the edge of my bed, Sammy and Campbell walk in. They went out on patrol, they saw the town, nothing happened. They ask me about my day. I tell them about my own little adventure. Over and over.

'What you t'ink happened?' Sammy asks. 'Why did the RPG bounce off the hatch and roll like that?'

'It was a dud,' I tell him. 'Somet'ing about it was mash-up.'

'There you go,' Sammy says. 'Lucky again.'

'Lucky?' I say. 'We've been mortared, the boss has been fired at – twice – and I get to stare down the barrel of an RPG launcher.'

'You wanted to be blooded and now you have been,' he says.

I suppose he's right.

The next afternoon most of C Company gathers in the tank park for a demonstration by the LI of how to make a house arrest. It's even hotter than usual outside. Sammy is standing next to me, fanning away the flies as we wait for the demo to begin. I can think of a lot of things I'd rather be doing, but I tell myself that it beats sandbagging, which is what we do when we're not on the road. Sammy is pissed off because we're not yet into our 'routine'. When you're 'in routine', he says, finding ways to beat the system gets a whole lot easier.

The only contact report at breakfast was two mortar rounds fired at CIMIC House. I'm starting to think things have gone quiet again when a Land Rover pulls up and an LI major jumps out. He runs over and pulls Major Coote, Mr Deane and a number of other officers out of the briefing.

They move into the shade of a Challenger 2 and listen to what the LI major has to say. I can tell by the look on their faces that it's not good.

A moment later they break up the demo and the LI major jumps up on to the front of a Warrior. He yells at us to listen up. 'There's a major contact going down right now in the centre of Al Amarah.' He cups his hands around his mouth so we can hear over the noise of a landing helicopter. 'It's serious shit this time and it's all happening at Yellow Three. A patrol got hit by a blast bomb as it drove past the OMS building. We have reports of a Land Rover being disabled and several casualties. The multiple is pinned down on the far side of the bridge at Yellow Three by sustained small-arms and RPG fire. Three further call signs have gone into the area to try to assist in an extraction and now they're bogged down as well. One of them was a Land Rover group led by the CO of 1PWRR, another by the CO of the Argyll and Sutherland Highlanders.'

Sammy and I look at each other. The centre of Al Amarah is at least fifteen minutes from the camp. Three, maybe four multiples are under attack, big time. And they include the CO, Colonel Maer.

'Go, Paki,' Sammy says. '*Fucking go!*'

I sprint to the tent, grab my helmet, webbing and SA80 and run back to the tank park. I jump up on to the hull of Whisky Two Zero and drop into the driver's seat. Mr Deane slides into the turret alongside an LI second lieutenant called Flanagan who is acting as our gunner. A couple of dismounts jump in the back – Big Erv and another LI man.

As I fire up the engine, Mr Deane's voice crackles on the net. 'Bee,' he says, 'you're going to have to pump the gas, mate. The old man needs our help. Get us there as quick as you can.'

'Roger, Boss.'

I release the handbrake, slip into drive and head for the gate. Broomstick's vehicle, Whisky Two Two, is right behind me. In my mirror I see a line of other Warriors kicking up a dust trail behind him. The whole company is heading downtown.

I turn left out of the gate on to Red Route, heading for Yellow Three. As soon as I hit the tarmac I stand on the accelerator and get Whisky Two Zero up to her max road speed.

Houses dot the scrubland either side of us. A camel nibbles at a dead bush in a dried-up ditch. Electricity lines criss-cross the sky and disappear into the heat haze.

A military transport plane comes into land at Sparrowhawk,

dropping flares as it sweeps over the outskirts of the town. A group of children stop playing football to watch it, shielding their eyes against the glare of the sun. As we roar by they wave and try to run after us, but we're going too fast.

We reach the junction where the road splits: Purple Route heading north-west around the perimeter of the city; Red Route running north, parallel to the river. Buildings start to loom out of the haze and so does the smell of shit.

'Hello, Whisky Two Zero, this is Zero,' the Ops Room fires up. 'Send your LOCSTAT.'

There's a faint crackle as Mr Deane switches to the battle-group frequency.

'Whisky Two Zero. At Red Four now.'

To our right I see a group of rusty gantries and cranes, and beyond it, sparkling in the sunshine, the slow-moving surface of the River Tigris.

We shoot past Broadmoor seconds later. So far there has been very little traffic on the road and I've been able to maintain a steady fifty miles per hour. Normally I'm able to take it a little higher. The heat always affects engine performance, but I'm worried about the power pack and make a mental note to check it later.

I look for the street lamp blown up by the roadside bomb – the point we reached yesterday – but it has gone. Ahead, as far as I can see, left and right, are alleyways and houses.

'Kadim Al-Mu'allimin,' Flanagan says. 'Better batten down the hatches.'

'Why?' Mr Deane asks.

'We're about to enter bandit territory,' he replies.

As I pull down the hatch cover I remember what Jimmy Bryant told me: the place we're heading for, the OMS building where the CO and the other call signs are pinned down, is filled with enough weapons to start a war.

The southern boundary of the Kadim Al-Mu'allimin

housing district is marked by a compound that is indicated on the map as a 'fuel farm'. As we pass a cluster of large, rusting tanks, the nerve-ends tighten in my belly. I've not felt like this since I was a kid.

I shift closer to the day sight. I can make out the water tower that Jimmy told me about, at the far end of the boulevard. A column of thick, black smoke rises high into the air beside it.

'Somet'ing's burning pretty bad,' I tell Mr Deane.

'Yeah, I see it,' he says.

Inside the Warrior I'm hotter than I've ever been in my life. Its sides seem to be closing in on me. Pretty soon I won't have room to breathe. I hate driving with the hatch down, but orders are orders, and when I look at the houses either side of the road, see just how close they are, how easy it would be for someone to shoot us as we go past, I figure that the LI guys know what they're doing.

'Whisky Two Zero passing Red Nine,' Mr Deane says.

In the day sight, the column of smoke starts to fill my field of view.

'Bee,' Mr Deane says, 'Lieutenant Flanagan is taking over from here. He knows the ropes. Is that understood?'

Understood, I tell him.

'You been downtown before, Beharry?' Flanagan asks.

'No,' I tell him. 'It's me first trip.'

'OK,' he says. 'In around four hundred metres we're going to hit the junction at Red Eleven, right by the water tower. You're going to take a right, which will line us up for the bridge. As you come over the river you'll see a two-storey building on your left with a mosque next to it. That's the OMS building. We're going to take a slip road off the bridge, loop back under it and take up position in an area of open ground out the front. There's houses and alleyways leading off to the south and west – and somewhere, in among them all, are the trapped call signs. Our job is to extract as many men as we can and fuck off back to Abu Naji. Is that clear?'

'Yes, sir.'

'Good lad.'

As we draw closer to the junction at Red Eleven, you'd never know there was a major gun battle going on.

A woman dressed in black makes her way down an alleyway to our right, struggling to hang on to two plastic bags full of shopping. A man carrying a door on his head stops and stares at us as we rumble past. A group of children watch us from a crumbling balcony. One of them is sucking a lollipop.

All we can hear is the growl of our diesel engine and the clank and squeak of tracks. I think back to what Mr Deane once said about situational awareness; how, as an infantryman with a distrust of vehicles, he hates to feel cooped up inside a Warrior. This must be doing his head in.

The houses either side of us are a mix of one- and two-storey buildings. Some have gardens out the front, others don't. Some are bordered by walls, others aren't. Electricity wires criss-cross the street like spider's webs. As we approach downtown, the city looks a complete fucking mess.

The water tower casts a shadow across the street. We've reached the junction at Red Eleven.

I check for traffic, but there are no cars anywhere, so I turn right and ease Whisky Two Zero on to Purple Route.

Ahead, just beyond the river, thick, black smoke billows up from under the bridge.

'*Keep going*,' Flanagan says, '*keep going . . .*'

As we rumble over the river I check my mirror. Whisky Two Two, Broomstick's wagon, pulls on to Purple Route behind me.

'There's a slip road on the right,' Flanagan says. 'You should see it any moment.'

I peer through the day sight. Smoke drifts across the bridge. 'Trust me, it's coming up,' Flanagan says.

I'm about to flick the day sight to passive night vision, so I can see through the smoke, but a breeze blows up from the river and the ramp suddenly appears.

I turn off the bridge, on to the slip road. We loop down and around to the right, coming back under the bridge, which carries on as a flyover into the east side of town.

A snatch with a jagged hole in its right side is burning out of control on the central reservation ahead of us. Beyond the long wheel-base Land Rover, to the left, is the mosque, and what I take to be the OMS building.

I move forward to allow the vehicles behind me to roll on to the area of open ground in front of them.

The CO comes over the net. He is down to two Land Rovers. The third has managed to extract from the contact area with a casualty to Abu Naji. I'm concentrating too hard on my surroundings to pay much attention to what is being said. All I catch is the fact that there's enemy in the OMS building, enemy in the mosque and enemy in the alleyways that feed into the square.

I hear the CO telling us to engage the OMS building. Seconds later Flanagan opens up with our chain gun. I watch a line of bullets hammer the front of the building and flashes of tracer punching through windows and hitting the interior walls.

'Enemy two o'clock to turret!' Mr Deane shouts.

I see bursts of fire from an alleyway, hear the rattle of our chain gun. I watch a line of bullets snake along the ground and bounce off the walls.

A man wearing blue jeans, a white T-shirt and a cloth wrapped around his head appears out of the shadows. Oh, God, a civilian, I say to myself. But at that moment, almost as if he's heard me speak, he stops and turns our way. I see a face, twisted by hatred. I also see that he's carrying a rifle, an AK47 . . .

'Gunman, Boss, moving left to right, three o'clock to vehicle.'

'I can't see a fuckin' thing!' Mr Deane shouts.

The gunman darts back through the doorway of a house. From the two windows on the floor above I notice little bursts of light and hear what sounds like stones pinging off our armour.

'There's enemy in that house, second floor, three o'clock to vehicle! They're firing at us!' I yell.

I hear the whir of the turret as it rotates, the *ratatatatat* of the chain gun.

The wall below one of the windows disintegrates in a cloud of dust.

Two Warriors shoot past.

Out of the corner of my eye I see one take up position at the top of an alleyway. Its turret trains on the OMS building and a line of tracer pours in through a window on the ground floor.

I catch movement off to our right and turn to see two men pushing a white Datsun saloon into the square. A head and shoulders bob up behind one of the windows and I get a glimpse of a black and brown tube . . .

'RPG! Behind the white car, two o'clock to vehicle!'

The figure behind the car stands up, steadies the tube on the boot and fires. The RPG roars away from the launcher, trailing a ribbon of smoke. It disappears beyond the field of view of my day sight.

Flanagan opens up and I see bullets punch into the side of the Datsun. The rear window shatters and the two people pushing it flee into an alley. I see no sign of the guy with the RPG.

I turn the steering column to the left and we neutral-turn

a fraction, enough for me to see where the RPG ended up.

There's a smoking hole in the wall of a house on the corner of an alleyway opposite the OMS building. In front of it is another wall running at waist height, parallel with the alley. I spot movement through the smoke between them. I flick to passive night vision as a figure in a camouflage shirt pops up from behind the wall, fires his rifle and ducks back down again.

He is followed a second later by another guy, who lets off a burst in the same direction.

'Boss, I can see our guys,' I yell over the net. 'To our ten o'clock.'

Flanagan is still firing in the direction of the OMS building.

'Got 'em,' Mr Deane says.

'What do you want me to do?' I ask.

'Reverse up. Get our back end tight against that wall, so they're shielded as they get in. Think you can manage that?'

No problem, I tell him.

I angle the nose around to the right, until the RPG hole in the side of the building slides into view in my mirror. Then I slip the vehicle into reverse.

Mr Deane talks to Broomstick in Whisky Two Two. Both wagons are going to go in and pick up the dismounts.

Bullets crack against the armour somewhere above my hatch. I slam on the brakes and we rock to a halt a few metres from the wall outside the house where the dismounts are holed up. Behind me, I can hear the crack of our chain gun again and, through my headset, Mr Deane still cursing his head off because he can't see a damn thing.

Right on the edge of the day sight's field of view, I see Whisky Two Two slide into position beside us.

'Fuck this for a game of soldiers,' Mr Deane says.

★

'I'm opening the hatch.'

If it's OK now for Mr Deane to open his hatch, I figure it's OK for me to. I stick my head out just in time to see Broomstick jumping off the turret of Whisky Two Two.

The two Warriors are just a few feet apart. Bullets ping and ricochet off Broomstick's wagon. Whisky Two Two's rear door is already open.

Dismounts start to roll over the wall and jump into the back.

Mr Deane fires his SA80 at the OMS building and I hear his bullets fly over my head.

I glance back. Chris Broome is yelling at the dismounts, '*Move, move, fuckin' move . . .*'

Soldiers continue to jump over the wall and pile into the back of our two wagons.

By now the enemy have got our range and bullets are flying off our armour.

Broomstick is standing in the gap between the two vehicles, still shouting at the dismounts from the Rover group to get a fuckin' move on. He ducks and curses as bullets fly past his head.

Mr Deane and Flanagan are still hosing down the OMS building.

'Is everybody in?' Mr Deane shouts.

'Yeah,' Broomstick yells back. 'Both wagons are packed out. You've got thirteen in the back of yours, including the CO from the Argylls.'

'What about the rest?'

'They're breaking out with the CO in the two remaining snatches from his Rover group.'

'Then we're outta here,' Mr Deane says.

'Boss, the door's still open,' a voice announces in my head-set.

'Who's that?' Mr Deane says.

'Erv, Boss.'

'Erv? What the fuck's the matter?'

'There's too many people back here. We can't shut the door!'

Broomstick is crouched between the vehicles.

'Chris?' Mr Deane shouts. 'Our door won't shut. Can you close the bastard from the outside?'

He runs around the back. I can hear shouting over Erv's radio; people are getting squashed.

Broomstick reappears and gives Mr Deane a thumbs-up. The rear door is shut. We're good to go. The trouble is, there's not enough room in the back of Whisky Two Two for Broomstick. I'm wondering what the hell's going to happen when a snatch drives past. Broomstick sees it too. He leaps out and flags it down.

The Land Rover screeches to a stop. Broomstick jumps in the back and they take off, heading for the bridge.

'*Beharry, go, go, go!*' Flanagan shouts. 'Don't let that snatch out of your sight.'

I hit the accelerator.

A Warrior is meant to take a maximum of seven people in the back. We have thirteen. They must be crammed to the roof in there.

I hear a lot more swearing and shouting over Erv's radio.

We drive up the ramp, back on to the bridge and take a left on to Red Route by the water tower.

Two hundred metres down the road, a gunman springs out of an alleyway and fires as we drive past. It's only when one of his bullets cracks off the turret and whistles past my ear that I realise I'm driving through bandit country with the hatch open.

Too late to close it now.

I step on the accelerator and watch the needle on the speedometer. I can barely reach forty-five. All I can see is houses stretching into the distance. This time, though, there's nobody on the street and no kids staring down at us from balconies.

Erv comes on the radio again; he sounds like someone is strangling him.

'Boss, it's hard to breathe back here. Can we stop so some of us can get out?'

'No,' Mr Deane says. 'We're still being shot at.'

'It's not me who's asking, Boss.'

'Who is?' Mr Deane asks.

'The CO of the Argylls – Lieutenant Colonel Grey.'

There's a pause. Then Mr Deane says, 'Perhaps you could politely inform the colonel, in the interests of his own safety, that he's going to have to bloody well grin and bear it till we're out of the contact area.'

Fifteen minutes later we pull up just inside the main gates at Sparrowhawk.

The back of Whisky Two Zero is like a furnace and Big Erv is worried that some of the dismounts are going to die unless we pull over and give them some air and water.

After everyone has piled out I see Colonel Grey take Mr Deane to one side. The CO of the Argylls is bathed in sweat. His face is pale and for a moment I think he wants to punch somebody. I can't hear the conversation, but by the time Mr Deane finishes talking with him, Colonel Grey's face softens and they end up shaking hands.

Fifteen minutes later, after we have all drunk some water and cooled down a bit, we pile back into the Warrior and head back to Abu Naji.

Back at camp the twenty-odd dismounts we extracted from Yellow Three gather around our vehicles to chat excitedly about the battle. Radio reports confirm that no one was killed, but we do have casualties, at least three, the most serious being Lance Corporal Kev Phillips, who's had a bullet hit his shoulder blade, then exit through the side of his neck. He's on his way to the field hospital at Shaiba and is expected to make a full recovery.

An officer appears and gets the men to ensure that their SA80s and Minimis are all clear of ammunition; the last thing anyone wants at this stage is a man killed by a negligent discharge.

As the dismounts head off towards the accommodation area to shower, change and eat, I can hear them whooping and high-fiving until they disappear around the side of a building.

'Bee?'

I turn. Mr Deane is climbing out of the turret. He has sweat and dust all over his face and he looks like he's lost a few pounds since the last time I saw him. 'You OK?' he asks.

'Yes,' I tell him, 'I'm fine.'

It's easier than saying I don't know what I feel. 'Exhausted' comes close. 'Drained' comes closer. But neither fully describes my emotions after what just happened.

'You did brilliantly, son,' Mr Deane says. 'Your driving was outstanding.'

'Thanks, Boss.'

'I mean it,' he says. 'What you did – manoeuvring the vehicle the way you did – took a lot of skill.'

'What I did weren't no different from the way Malloy drove,' I say.

Malloy is Broomstick's driver.

'Yeah, well,' he says. 'I'm proud of you both.'

He wipes the sweat off his forehead with the back of his hand and hops down to the ground.

'Listen,' he says, 'why don't you go grab a shower and a cup of tea? God knows, you've earned them.'

'If it's all the same, Boss, I'm going to stay with the wagon.

I want to make sure she's cleaned up and ready to roll for the next time. There's somet'ing not quite right with the power pack. I need to take a look at her . . .'

'I can send someone over to help you,' he cuts in, glancing at the sky. It's six o'clock, a couple of hours from sunset, but the heat is still unbelievable.

'That's all right, Boss. I'm OK. I rather be on me own.'

'Well, don't overdo it, eh?' he says, and turns to go.

'Hey, Mr Deane,' I call after him. 'You still rather be in a Land Rover?'

He pauses.

'Yeah,' he says eventually. 'Any day.'

But I see the smile on his face as he turns and walks away and I give Whisky Two Zero a pat just to let her know he doesn't mean it.

I hop down on to the ground and start to walk around the vehicle.

There are chips and nicks everywhere. I give up counting how many bullets must have struck us. The good thing is none of them has done us any damage.

When I get to the back of the vehicle I see that a light cluster is missing. I think it must have been hit by a stray bullet. But when I check the other one I see that's missing too. Somebody has unscrewed them. I remember the kids we ran into yesterday. Bloody hell, Johnson, I say to myself, while you're handing out gum, some kid's unscrewing your light clusters.

I can't help smiling. Not so long ago that kid was me.

PART ONE

Diego Piece, 1987

CHAPTER ONE

I'm leaning into the turn, one hand on the steering wheel, the other on the gear stick, as the Porsche starts to climb. This is the part of the journey that I like best. I've left the coast behind and I'm now deep in the hills. To my left there is a steep ravine. One slip, one careless movement, and the car will plunge on to the rocks.

Cars and buses crash on this road all the time. Only last week a van plummeted off the road to Gouyave, killing everyone on board. No one is sure how it happened. Some say that the driver was drunk; others that he swerved to avoid a sheep or a cow. My gran has her own theory. She says that the driver was possessed by an evil spirit and that it was the Devil himself that gripped the wheel and forced the van on to the rocks. My gran, my dad's mum, is full of stories about the bad things that happen on these roads. She tells them to scare me. She doesn't like me to drive; I'm too young, she says.

But nobody is going to keep me from getting behind the wheel of my brand-new Porsche 911 Turbo Convertible. I have 300 brake horsepower in the engine compartment behind me. I'm the king of the road. I can make the distance between Diego Piece and St George's in under twenty minutes. My record is nineteen minutes and twenty-seven seconds. The same journey takes some drivers an hour.

I keep my foot pressed to the accelerator and hear the

wheels spin. The blood rushes in my ears and my heart races. I press down harder on the pedal and the engine revs and whines. The air is warm. I've left the stench of the landfill behind. The landfill sits in the hills above the port and is so big and so deep that it is impossible to put out the fires that rage below its surface. They burn month after month, year after year. When the wind blows in the wrong direction you can even smell the fumes in Diego Piece.

But not today. Here I can smell the sea and the earth and the scent of a hundred different lilies and blossoms. I glance up at the bursts of yellow and red: ginger lilies, flamboyants, oleanders and bougainvilleas in full flower. Further back, I can see pigeon trees, silk cotton trees with their huge, thick trunks, blue mahoes and Caribbean pines, until the trees become so dense that I can see only the blackness of the forest.

When I'm not driving, this is where I like to go. There are streams where I can fish and deep burrows where Kellon and I can hunt for manicous and armadillos. Sometimes we spend all day in the forest.

Strands of elephant hair brush my face. The slopes rise vertically from the plantations. I can see jagged ridges and broken peaks through the gaps in the clouds. The mountains look like the teeth of a wild animal. The people of the village, my gran included, say that God made them this way for a reason: if you try to climb them, you will probably end up getting killed. But Kellon and I go climbing there all the time and nothing has ever happened to us.

People say all kinds of things. They can believe what they want. Some people I know have spent their entire lives in the village. They have never even been to St George's or Grenville. I want to travel. There's so much to see.

But I should be watching the road. I drop a couple of gears as I head into another bend and feel my heart miss a beat as the back of the Porsche lurches towards the edge. For an instant the rear-left wheel bites into thin air, then I correct the skid. I whoop with excitement and send another burst of power to the engine.

I accelerate past the bar, where the old men drink and play cards, past the Association, where the crops are brought to be weighed and bagged, past the school that I'll go to one day soon. I slow, because the bridge ahead is narrow and Lou-Jean is leaning over it, gazing at the stream below. I blow my horn so he knows I'm coming and he gives me space to pass.

Lou-Jean can't speak. He has long, matted hair like a Rasta. His teeth are blackened and broken and on very hot days he pants like a dog. There are always pieces of food smeared around his mouth. A lot of parents tell their kids that Lou-Jean will come to get them at night if they don't do as they're told.

I change gear and the turbo kicks in. I'm being cheered on by Devlin's builders, who are lined up along the scaffolding on the big house on the corner. Devlin is my cousin and owns the biggest building company in the village. Sometimes my dad works for him. The builders are my friends. Some days I go and watch them at work. They show me how to do stuff. I give them a blast of my horn.

Then I see something ahead: a shadow where the sunlight and the darkness meet. I hit the brakes and come face to face with an old woman standing in the middle of the road. I twist the wheel and slam on the brakes. My gran looks at me and shakes her head.

I know how much she loves me, but she doesn't understand. The only person who understands is my dad. He does some building work for a Grenadian who travels to England a lot and buys every car magazine there is. When he has finished them he gives them to my dad, who brings them home to me. My dad can't read, but sometimes, when he's not being angry, I sit on his lap, out on the porch as the sun goes down, and we go through the pictures together. I get my brother Jude to read out the models' specs. I like Jaguars, Ferraris and Maseratis, but the Porsche 911 Turbo 3.3, the fastest production car in the whole world, is the only one for me.

I put aside the cover of the rainwater bucket I've been using as a steering wheel and climb out of the tangle of roots at the base of the old cedar tree beside the porch of my gran's house.

The house is tiny, about twelve feet square, and sits in the middle of a clearing at the top of a hill that's so steep it's like a pillar of rock. Somehow it contains three little bedrooms – each the same size as the bed in it – and a kitchen. The kitchen is bare but for a stool and a small table where my gran sits when it is raining, and a cupboard where she keeps a few pots.

My grandpa, Cyril Bolah, built the house. Its base is secured to the rock with metal stakes, but some of them have come loose and when the wind blows the whole place creaks and groans like an old ship and moves another few inches towards the edge of the hill. The first time I felt this happen I ran into my gran's room and jumped into her bed. As she held me close and I listened to the beat of her heart, she told me how we Grenadians are blessed, because God has not sent a hurricane to the island since more than thirty years ago, when Janet swept through.

'They say God is a Grenadian, 'cos all the other islands in the whole Caribbean get hit by hurricanes 'cept us,' she said, stroking my head. 'We Grenadians is special.'

If the house that my grandpa built survived Janet, she said, it can survive anything. But to be on the safe side she hummed her favourite hymn, 'Blessed Assurance', and I can hear her humming it now.

From the woods below my gran's house, I hear my mother calling. I look back at my car. I can't wait to get in her again. I can't wait to tell my dad how fast she goes.

Nineteen minutes and twenty-five seconds from St George's to Diego Piece. Next time I'll beat that easily.

As I burst through the bushes my mother is standing on the porch, balancing Jade on one hip and Jeffon on the other. Jeffrey and Jemilla are both clinging to her skirt. Jemilla is sucking her thumb. Jade is crying. Jill is holding a plastic bag full of our clothes.

There are no lights on in the house and the shutters are closed. Some houses in Diego Piece are built on solid foundations and made entirely of brick. Some are built into the sides of hills and need pillars to support them at the front. Ours is the only house I know that is built entirely on stilts, in a dip where the stream floods when the rains come. When the wind blows and I'm lying in bed at night, I feel it swaying. It scares my little brothers Jeffrey and Jeffon, but it doesn't scare me. I pretend I'm in a boat, way out on the ocean, heading for distant lands.

The sun has already dipped below the hills. I hear the dogs whining. It's almost dark and everybody is waiting for me.

I rush to the edge of the porch. My mother looks down at me and I smile, but her expression doesn't alter. I touch her hand and it's cold. She doesn't even seem to know I'm here. I've only been gone thirty minutes, but it's as if the whole world has suddenly become a different place.

'What's the matter?' I ask. 'Where we goin'? Where's Daddy?'

'We have to leave,' she whispers in a voice that is so faint I can hardly hear the words. 'Jude, take hold of Jade. Jill, go back into the house and make sure the shutters are locked. Johnson, you carry the clothes. Everyone need to help.'

'Where we goin'?' I say again. 'Why isn't Daddy with us?'

'We need to hurry,' my mum says.

'Where's Daddy?' I ask again. 'I have to tell him about me car.'

Jill wrinkles her nose. She's always on my case. I can't do anything without her bossing me. 'What's he talkin' about?' she says to Jude.

'He pretends he's racin' a car in the roots of the old cedar tree up by Gran's,' Jude tells her. 'He races between St George's and Diego Piece. Each time he goes faster than the last. It's just a game.'

Jill pulls a face, tosses her head and turns on her heel. She goes back into the house.

'Where's Daddy?' I ask again.

Jude puts a hand over my mouth. 'No more questions,' he says quietly, 'I tell you when we get there.'

'Get where?'

'No more questions.'

Jill comes out of the house carrying the saucepan full of chicken stew and dumplings. I understand now. There will be no supper around the table tonight – no chance to tell Daddy about my 911 Turbo 3.3.

I drop the clothes bag and head into the house. I hear Jill cuss and tell my mum she's going after me, but Jude stops her. I run into the kitchen and pull the string that turns on the light. It's the only electric light in the house.

The room is long and narrow. There's a pile of clothes in the middle of the floor – the ironing that my mother does every night after we finish eating. Pots and pans stand unwashed.

I throw open the door to the bedroom. Light spills into the darkness. I run over to the big bed in the corner where all my brothers and sisters sleep. I kneel down and reach under it. Something runs across my hand – a cockroach or a spider –

and I pull back. Then I move around the bed and try again. There's nothing there.

I start to panic. Where can it be? My eyes fall on the straw mattress on the floor at the end of the bed, where I sleep. I turn it over. It covers a crack that's as wide as my hand. The crack runs from the outside wall to the middle of the room and through it I can see the pools of water below the house shining in the moonlight. A bad smell, like rotten eggs, rises up to meet me. I hear Jill and my mum calling.

I rush into my parents' room. There's no light from the kitchen and I have to grope my way to the far side of the bed, where my father sleeps. I run my fingertips across the floor boards. Nothing. I pick up the sheets and shake them. Something falls to the floor by my feet. I reach down and pick it up.

I've got it. *Motor*. The one with the picture of the 911 Turbo.

I run back the way I came, flick off the light and step back on to the balcony.

'A magazine?' Jill says. 'You went back for a magazine?'

'Leave him alone,' Jude says. 'It matters to him.'

She closes the door and bolts it. I tuck the magazine under my arm and pick up the bag of clothes. I hold it high so it doesn't drag in the mud.

Jude is first up the path. He lifts Jade and places him on his shoulders. My mother goes next, carrying Jeffon. Jemilla, Jill, Jeffrey and I follow. I can barely see over the top of the bag, but I know when we pass the noni tree from the cheesy smell of its pink, lumpy fruit. I look up and see the moon and suddenly I know I've been here before – on this path, in the darkness: Jude, Jill, Jemilla, Jeffrey, Jeffon, Mummy and me, all of us stealing from our own house in the middle of the night.

I hear a noise behind us; someone is following. I turn

slowly, but there's nothing there. The only movement is the ripple of the stream.

My nan – my mother's mum – and my mum's sister, Aunt Ena, are already waiting at my nan's house in the middle of the village. Nobody says a word as they open the door and show us in. The door shuts as quickly as it opens. My mum hands Jeffon to my nan. She sways and for a moment I think she's going to faint. But then she holds the edge of the table and steadies herself. Nan and Ena direct my mum, Jill, Jemilla, Jeffrey and Jeffon up the stairs. I'm about to follow them when Ena stops me.

'There's no more room upstairs, Treasure,' she whispers, 'but I fix a bed for you and Jude out back. You be nice and safe there.' She raises a finger to her lips. 'But you must promise, promise me, to keep quiet.'

She opens her eyes wide, pretending it's a game. But whatever this is, I know it's no game.

'Can you keep quiet?' Ena whispers. 'Not a sound?'

'Don't worry,' Jude says. 'He will.'

We step out into the courtyard. I hear my nan pull down the shutters at the front of the house. In the dim light at the back it's difficult to see where I'm going, but Jude seems to know the way. He takes my hand and moments later I find myself under the roof of the lean-to where my nan keeps her goat and rabbits. The goat bleats as we settle on to the bed of clean straw that my auntie has prepared for us. I hear scuffling sounds from the rabbit hutch.

I lie there not saying a word, just listening to the sounds of the village and watching the moon as it crosses the night sky. Dogs bark; I hear the distant sound of a radio. Inside the house, the lights stay off. Nan's home, normally alive with activity, is as quiet as the graveyard at the bottom of the village.

I reach for the magazine. There's just enough light to see

by. I flick through the pages until I come to the picture of the Porsche. It seems to gleam and come alive. Through half-closed eyes I can see myself sitting in her.

'Jude,' I whisper. 'You awake?'

He grunts. 'Go to sleep, Johnson.'

'I'm not goin' to sleep till you tell me what we doin' here.'

'Sleep,' he says.

I sit up and hit my brother in the ribs. He stifles a cry of pain and says, 'What you doin'? You crazy?'

'I'm goin' to scream and shout and punch the goat so the goat scream and shout too, unless you tell me why we here.'

'Keep your voice down,' Jude hisses.

'Tell me, then.'

'All right, all right. We here 'cos it's Friday.'

'Friday? What's so special about Friday?'

'Friday night is the night Daddy get paid.'

'So? Old Man Baptiste pay Daddy every week. What's so different about this week?'

Jude is five years older than me. He's at senior school in Sauteurs. He gets A grades in almost everything he does. He's my half-brother, but the fact we have different fathers doesn't make any difference to me.

'I want the truth,' I say. 'Tell me.'

For a long time Jude says nothing. Then he sighs. 'Do you ever t'ink about the house we live in?'

'It's our home. What's there to t'ink about?'

'Our house is only four years old, but the wood is old and rotten. Don't you ever wonder why our house is almost new yet it's fallin' apart?'

I shake my head.

'Do you want to know?' Jude says.

'I t'ink so . . .'

'You were the one who say you goin' to scream the place down if I don't tell you.'

'OK,' I say, 'I want to know.'

'After Mummy leave school she go to work in the Pool in Victoria – the place where the nutmeg go to be weighed, washed and peeled. She meet my dad, Lexan Williams, but the two of them split when I'm still a baby. Then Mummy meet a guy called Ken. He work at the Pool too. But when Mummy get pregnant with Jackie, Ken go to England – he have relatives there. When Jackie is born, Mummy write to Ken for money. But Ken never send her anything, so she go back to the Pool. She get my nan and Ena to look after me and Jackie and she work there all day. She work so hard it make her sick.

'But then she meet Daddy – your Daddy, my . . . new Daddy – and they take a room in a house down by the school. That's when Mummy she t'ink her life change. Daddy work hard. He work in the day for Old Man Baptiste and after he finish on the plantation he go an' work on a buildin' site, usually for Devlin. Daddy make more than seventy-five dollars a week. Mummy make a bit too. Life was pretty good then.'

'What happen?' I ask.

'One day the owner say he sell the whole house to Mummy and Daddy for five hundred dollars. Mummy and Daddy they save a bit and borrow the rest and soon the house is theirs – a great big house, with four bedrooms.'

I sit up straight. '*Four* bedrooms!' This is the first time anybody tell me this. *Four* bedrooms. This is as big as any house in the village, except for Old Man Baptiste's and the new one they're building on the corner.

'Shhh!' Jude puts his hand over my mouth. 'Two months later Mummy and Daddy find out that there are all sort o' problem with the house an' from that day they have not'ing.'

He waits a while and says, 'That's when he start drinkin'.'

'But everybody in Grenada drink . . .'

'With Daddy it was different. He always wait till Friday, the day he get paid, and then he go down to the store and he buy a big bottle of rum. And then he sit down and he play cards with the other guys and by the end of the night he lose a whole heap of money. The next night he go back again, drink another bottle and he lose a whole lot more. By Sunday there's not'ing left. This go on for week after week. But you know what Mummy do? One weekend she get a whole load of people together and she take that house apart, piece by piece. And everyone carry the pieces to the bottom of the hill where Gran lives and they build that house in the only place in the village they can – on Gran's land. A funny little scrap of land at the bottom of the hill that's good for not'ing 'cos the stream turn the whole place into a swamp.'

'But why can't we stay in our own house? Why do we have to stay at Nan's? So what if Daddy get a little drunk?'

Jude sits up. He leans on his elbow and looks at me. 'When Daddy start drinkin' on a Friday night he don't stop till Sunday night. That's why we have no money, Johnson. Daddy drink an' gamble away all the money he ever earn. An' when he drink he get angry – you seen him. Not just vex; he get really angry. That's why we have to move. Someone say they see Daddy comin' up the road with a bottle of rum. When he come home drunk, he hit Mummy. An' now Mummy afraid he goin' to start on us too.'

CHAPTER TWO

I get up as soon as the stars that I can see through the holes in the lean-to are gone. I've not slept much.

The things Jude said can't be true, I keep telling myself. My dad is a quiet man, who works hard. He has never had an easy relationship with Jude, because he is not his real son. So maybe, I tell myself, Jude is making these things up. But I've never known Jude to lie to me before.

All I want is to go home and see my daddy – to sit with him out on the porch, the two of us together, and leaf through the pages of my magazine. If I could just be with him I know everything would be all right.

But Jude has made it clear that none of us is to set foot back in the house until Monday, when Daddy goes back to work again. These are Mummy's rules. When my father starts to drink he doesn't stop until he has to go back to work. Jude told me the last time this happened, when I was three, my mother came back to the house to collect some clothes for Jeffrey and Jeffon, and my dad beat her because she woke him up when she tripped over a crate of Carib beer that was lying on the floor of their bedroom.

All we can do is lie low at my nan's until he drinks the house dry. If he passes by, trying to find us, my nan and Ena will send him packing. They're both strong women. And my dad knows that he owes Ena four hundred dollars. Even though he knows we're here, and this will make him angry, he's not likely to come looking for us. By the time Monday comes around he will have forgotten we were ever gone. That, Jude tells me, is how much my dad drinks. He drinks so much that he has no memory of it. As soon as he has gambled all his money away, by the early hours of Saturday morning, he goes back home to carry on drinking alone. And he keeps going till the last drop.

The air is heavy with the smell of damp earth and wet leaves. It has just rained and big, grey clouds roll down from the mountains. More rain is on its way.

A saffron tree, a lemon tree, an avocado tree and a five-finger tree grow in a clump ten feet from the porch of our house. In front of them is a little plot of sugar cane I planted with my mum. Between the sugar cane and the house is a big old nutmeg tree. My dad is always saying he will thin the trees because they cut out the light. He has been saying it for years, but they're still here. I'm glad, because I love these trees — especially the nutmeg tree. I fall asleep at night listening to the breeze through her leaves.

I creep forward as quietly as I can.

I catch sight of my dad through the bushes. He's sitting out on the porch in his favourite chair — the chair where we sit when we talk about cars and stuff.

My father is leaning back, tilting the chair back so his face is angled to the sun. He's smiling. He looks happy. I don't know what I expected; windows smashed maybe, or the sound of him in a rage somewhere inside the house. But he looks just the same. There's nothing different about him. He's not a monster. He's my dad.

Beside him is a small table and on the table are a bottle and glasses. I feel a tingling sensation in my stomach — the feeling I get when I hide with Kellon, when his dad is close but can't see us. I'm spying on my father. It feels strange. But I'm excited too.

I recognise the bottle. It's clear, with a black and white striped label. Even though I can't read I know that the red writing on the white part says 'Original White Rum'. Above it is the name of the maker: Clarke's Court. Clarke's Court is famous throughout Grenada. I've heard commercials for it on the radio. I know it's made from sugar and tastes great in punches.

It's the favourite drink of the guys who gather on the wall outside my nan's house, the limers, but I've never seen them drinking it with fruit punch. They pour it into tiny glasses – like the ones on the table – knock it back in one, then follow it up with a little water.

My father leans forward and his leg knocks against the table. For a moment he stares as it dances in front of him. Then he lunges, grabbing the bottle by the neck. The table falls and one of the glasses shatters. My father leans over and picks up the table. He tries to set it back on its legs, but it falls over again. I hear him cuss, and he has another go. This time he succeeds. He puts the bottle back, then gets down on his hands and knees and grabs the glass that hasn't broken.

He says something to himself, then, as if he's shooing away a fly, he brushes the pieces of glass from the balcony with the back of his hand. Then he holds his hand up and watches blood trickle down his arm. I figure that he'll go into the house and get a piece of cloth and tie it round his hand, but he just flops back into his chair and stares at the sky.

I take a step forward. My father is hurt. I want to help him.

A twig breaks.

The sound is so soft I hardly hear it myself, but it's enough to set off the dogs. They start to bark and howl from underneath the house. I drop to the ground. I've never liked the dogs. They scare me. We keep them to frighten away thieves. They're wild dogs, with a strong instinct for hunting.

'Shut up,' I hear my father say, but they still go on barking.

He gets to his feet and leans over the edge of the porch. 'Shut up!' he shouts again.

The dogs bark louder than ever. They're doing what they're trained to do. They know that somebody is in the trees. I think about running away, but I'm afraid my father will see me. I've heard the anger in his voice. I don't know what he will do if he realises I've been spying on him. He makes his way slowly down the steps, the bottle of Clarke's Court in his hand.

The dogs stop barking and slink into the shadows. One of them starts to whimper.

My father picks up a stick of wood and raises it above his head. I brace myself for the first blow. Then he lets the stick fall to the ground, drops to his knees and buries his face in his hands. He settles himself between the dogs. He's talking to them – talking to them like he talks to me.

A peal of thunder rolls up the valley. It starts to rain. The dogs lick my father's face.

The rain is falling hard now. Drops the size of cherry stones hit the ground around me.

I want to throw myself in my dad's arms. I want him to hold me the way I once saw Kellon's dad hold him.

But I don't. I turn and run. I run so fast I don't even notice the branch that whips across my head.

At the top of the path I stop and look back. Our house is painted green from top to bottom. Through half-closed eyes it almost vanishes against the shrubs, weeds and vines that tumble into our yard. The blinds are drawn and the house is quiet. I don't know where my father is now.

As I lay awake last night under my nan's lean-to, trying to

drive the picture of his crumpled face from my head, I told myself he's not a bad man. But thoughts I don't want to have twisted in and out of my mind. Some of these thoughts were memories: the bruises around my mother's eyes, the times I've seen her crying silently as she hangs out the washing in the cool, dark spaces under our house. Others were like a dream that hasn't broken yet, like when we left the house on Friday.

I've no actual memory of running from our house when I was little, but for as long as I can remember I've had a feeling of running from *something* – something I can't see or hear but which gives me the worst fear I've ever known – a fear that grips me in the depths of my belly.

I turn and break through the trees. The ground around my gran's place is completely flat, as if a giant has taken a machete and chopped off the top of the hill and hurled it into the sea.

The sound of singing reaches me from the other side of the house. To get there I have to dodge around the tiny vegetable patch where my gran grows just about everything she needs – saffron, celery, sweet potato, melons, pumpkins, gungo peas, tomatoes and cabbages – alongside the fruits that grow up here wild. There are carambolas – star-fruit trees – mammy apples, soursops, avocados, mangoes and pawpaws.

I like the soursop most, a fruit with a spiny skin that can grow as big as my head. My gran slices off the top with a sharp knife, then gives me the only spoon she has in the house, so I can scoop out the soft flesh. It's the closest thing in the forest to ice-cream.

I dart behind the house and check the shower, because sometimes my gran sings when she's scrubbing herself. The shower is a bucket with holes in the bottom that my grandpa rigged up in a tree. Fifteen years after my grandpa built it, it's still here and it still works. My grandpa died when I was a

baby and, though my gran swears she sees his ghost sometimes, the reality is, she's all alone.

At the base of the tree is a barrel that collects rainwater.
When my gran wants a shower she scoops water out of the
barrel, climbs a little ladder and slops the water into the
bucket. If you fill the bucket to the top you get a shower that
lasts about two minutes. It takes several trips to fill the bucket
to the top. This is easy for me, because I move with the speed
of a cat, but for my gran it's a different story. By the time she
fills the bucket with a second scoop, the first has drained away.

The best thing about the shower, I think, is the view. From
this side of the house you can see all the way across the sea to
Carriacou, the second biggest island in the Grenadines. Today
the air is so clear I can see large ships steaming past Carriacou
towards St Vincent.

I hear singing again – the first verse of 'Blessed Assurance' –
but now it sounds as if it's coming from the *front* of the house.
This is the trouble with the strange, magical place where my
gran lives: the wind can whip your words away, swirl them
through the branches of the big old trees and throw them
back at you from a completely different direction. My gran
says that this is the trees making mischief, but I'm too old to
believe in those stories any more.

When I was little, three or four, I used to come up here and
sit on my gran's lap, out the front of the house, where she
always sits when the sun goes down. She'd say, 'Johnson, what
you wan' to do wit' you life?' And I'd tell her, 'Gran, I want to
be a driver.' And she would say, 'What kin' of driver?' And I
would say, 'A racin' driver.' And she would say, 'Where you get
these ideas from?' And I would say, 'From my dad.'

And then she would tell me that when he was little my dad
was a dreamer too, just like me, his head filled with all kinds
of crazy ideas. She would sit with him under the boughs of
the big old cedar tree where I make my car and get him to

throw his wishes into the branches. Then she used to get me to do the same thing. When I told her I couldn't get my head around the idea of throwing wishes into a tree, she'd say, 'Everyt'ing has he and she place in the world and everyt'ing have a soul,' and she would hold my face in her hands as she said it. Then she'd nod to the tree. 'This old tree, she's a good soul. She's a wishing tree. I talk to her every day. Go on, make you wish.' So I used to close my eyes, scrunch them up really tight and throw my wish into the tree.

'What you wish for?' my gran would ask, and always my answer would be the same: 'I want to be a driver.'

I run round to the front of the house, but there's no one there. My gran has lit a fire on the rocks where she does her cooking. Water is bubbling away in a pot balanced on three large stones. Now I know she's close. I'm about to call to her, when her voice reaches me again, and this time I know where she is. There's a spot just below the house where she goes in the morning, often just as the sun is coming up; a piece of ground between her big old cedar tree and the mango, where you can see *everything* – the whole world – all at once: sea, valley, mountains, trees and sky.

She's standing with a brush in her hands, sweeping the leaves off the top of my grandpa's grave. My grandpa is buried in a raised tomb around three feet high, and it gleams white because every year my gran gets one of us – her grandchildren – to give it a fresh lick of whitewash. It's a job that she offers only to her 'fav'rit gran'chillun', but as she has a favourite grandchild from each of her nine children, there are quite a few she can call on to do the job.

My gran is very open about which of us are her favourites. But in my dad's case she says she can't make up her mind between me and Jill. We're both favourites. I notice, though – and this warms my heart when I think on it – that Jill doesn't ever get to paint my grandpa's grave.

I love my sister, but she's the one who likes to rule the roost. Most of my brothers and sisters just take it, but not me. Jill and I argue a lot.

The sight of my gran, and the sound of her voice as she sings, pull me up short. I can hear in the words of the chorus how much she still loves him:

> '*This is my story, this is my song,*
> *Praising my Saviour all the day long.*
> *Angels descending bring from above*
> *Echoes of mercy, whispers of love . . .*'

She thinks it describes how Heaven will look when she and my grandpa are together again.

I tiptoe away, back towards the house, and climb into the roots of the old cedar tree. I pick up the lid of the bucket and the stick I use as a gear shift.

Normally, when I close my eyes I can see the road ahead of me. But today, when I close them, even when I scrunch them up really tight, I can't see anything. The roots are just roots and the lid is a lid.

'Johnson?'

Even though she doesn't have a tooth in her head, my gran still manages to beam me a huge, radiant smile. Words can't express just how much I love her in this moment. I struggle to hold back my tears.

My gran comes and sits on the roots. 'Are you goin' to speak to me about it, chile?' she says.

'Speak about what, Gran?'

'Whatever it is that's vexin' you so bad.' She leans forward and touches the skin around the cut on my head. 'An' how you come by this?'

I shrug. 'It's nothing, Gran. Me an' Ansell have a fight, that's all.' Ansell is a cousin on my mother's side. My father's family are all of Indian descent; my mother is half-Indian, half-Negro. Ansell is always picking on me. I don't like him at all.

'Do you want to tell me about it?' my gran asks, arching an eyebrow.

'There's not much to tell,' I say, looking down at my feet.

'So how come you mammy not put a poultice on it?'

I see the look on her face and know that she's never going to leave this alone.

'You bes' come along,' she says.

I follow her into the kitchen. My gran walks slowly. She doesn't use a stick, but she probably should; every now and then she has to stop and catch her breath. Jude says she has a bad heart, but when I ask my gran about this she says there is nothing wrong with her; she's just getting old. I've no idea how old she is, but I've never seen anyone with so many lines on their face.

She reaches on top of her cupboard and brings down a small clay pot. Then she leads me back outside and sits me down on the rocks. Her poultice is filled with all kinds of herbs and leaves, and salt and sugar and rum. She scoops three fingers into the pot and starts to apply the brown, sticky paste to the cut. It smells terrible but feels cool and soothing on my skin.

'I ask you one mo' time,' my gran says. 'If you mammy see you yesterday, she'd a treated you sheself.' Again she looks at me. 'So where you were, Johnson?'

'I stay out late,' I tell her. 'I didn't see Mummy since it happen.' I pause. 'We stayin' by my nan's for a few days.'

I hope she doesn't ask me why.

I know that Daddy and my gran don't always get along. In the days when she used to come down the hill and see us, there were times when I saw the two of them argue pretty badly. My gran can be bossy when she wants to be (maybe this is why Jill is also her favourite, because Jill is just like her) and this can make my dad get pretty vex. In our house he wants to be boss.

Sometimes my gran goes to church. The rest of the time she stays here, looking after her garden and talking to my grandpa. If she needs anything she calls down and one of us will go get it. Maybe she doesn't know of my dad's drinking.

'Daddy get sick an' we have to leave the house so he can get better,' I say, choosing my words carefully. I can't bring myself to look at her. I stare at my toes instead. They're covered in little nicks and cuts from the rocks under the bridge. Luckily my gran's eyesight is too bad to see them, otherwise she'd have covered them in a poultice too.

'When he get sick?'

'Friday,' I say. 'Friday night.'

'An' that's when you leave the house – all of you?'

'Yes,' I tell her.

For a long time my gran says nothing. Sometimes we sit on these steps and watch the seabirds soaring on the breeze. Sometimes I just sit here alone, watching her cook or pick through her vegetable garden. My happiest moments are when we sit quietly on these rocks, the two of us together.

But this is a different kind of silence.

When she opens her mouth again, my gran uses a voice I've never heard in her before.

'Johnson, you listen to me now, an' you listen to me good. What are the three most important things in life? What am I always tellin' you?'

'Love, respect, honesty, Gran.'

'Love, respec', honesty,' she repeats.

The only three things you need in life. This is what she tells all her grandchildren. They're the very first things, I can remember her saying to me.

'An' now I want you to tell me the truth,' she says. 'The absolute truth.'

I raise my eyes to hers. I try to force back the tears, but this time I can't. And with the tears everything else tumbles out too.

When I tell her what happened down under the house, what I saw with my own eyes, my gran makes a sudden noise, like something catching in her throat.

'Gran?'

'It's not'ing,' she says. 'Don' pay me no min'.'

She gets to her feet and stares out across the valley. I feel a huge sadness in my heart. I've told her the truth. I've told her what I saw. But from the look I've just seen pass across her face, I know I've done a terrible thing. What will she do? Is she going to cuss me for saying these things? Is she going to tell my dad? If she does, *then* what happens? Will my dad ever speak to me again? Will he tell her that I've been lying? Then who will my gran believe?

I wish I had listened to Jude. I wish I had listened to my mum. I wish I had never gone by our house. I wish I had never seen what I saw. I gaze up into the branches of the big old tree in front of the house – the tree where I drive my car. What I've done is something that my gran's wishing tree can never, ever undo.

I wipe the tears from my eyes and sit up straight. Whatever happens, I have to face my punishment. This is all my fault.

I hear my gran sigh. She turns to me. 'Johnson,' she says – and I'm surprised to hear there is no anger in her voice – 'you know how much I love you, don' you?'

'Yes, Gran.' I'm so relieved I almost cry all over again.

She sits down and takes my hand in hers. 'There goin' to be a lot of strange stuff happenin' in the comin' days an' weeks,' she says. 'There goin' to be a lot of stuff you an' you young min' ain' goin' to understand. Things is goin' to get worse 'fore they get better. But I want you to know that everyt'ing's goin' to be all right. Everyt'ing goin' to turn out fine. I know this, 'cos I *seen* it. You know how you gran can see things, don't you, Johnson? You know how you gran can see stuff that's goin' to happen tomorrow an' next week an' sometimes beyon' that. I'm always here for you, no matter what happen. You understand?'

She touches my cheek.

'This place, this hill, will always be a safe place for you. Remember that. You promise me?'

'Yes, Gran, I promise.'

I say these words. The truth is, I don't know what my gran is talking about, but if she says everything will be all right, I know that it will be. I'm not in trouble. Nothing is going to happen to me. I'm safe. These are the words that stay with me.

CHAPTER THREE

Some days Kellon and I make kites out of sticks and paper and fly them from the top of my gran's hill; others we catch a lift on the trucks that take cocoa and nutmeg from the Association to St George's.

We jump off at Gouyave and head straight for the beach, where we sit on the rocks and while away the day catching fish and talking. We fish with a stick, some line and a bag full of worms and never come back empty-handed. In Grenada, whether you have money in your pocket or not, there is always something to eat.

Today Kellon and I are heading into the hills to hunt manicous. The manicou is a possum – it looks like a rat – and makes its nest in the roots of trees. My favourite meal is oil-down. Oil-down is the national dish of Grenada, a stew made of breadfruit, vegetables and meat soaked in oil. The meat can be pork or chicken or fish, and sometimes all these things. Wild meat is always best, though, and manicou in oil-down is delicious.

Kellon and I use his dog to find manicous and chase them from their nests. A manicou's nest usually has at least one entrance and one exit. Kellon's dog, Alby, is small and quick and has a great sense of smell. He races down one of the holes, while Kellon and I stand with our sticks above our heads, waiting for a manicou to appear. You have to be fast to kill a manicou, but Kellon, me and Alby make a good team. After one of our hunting trips we usually eat like kings for a week.

Today there's something else that we have to do on our way up the mountain. My cousin Ron has heard about our hunting trip and has had one of his ideas. Ron is several years older than me and Kellon and is full of schemes about how to make money. He has arranged to meet us at the shack that Ena owns in the woods above the village. His plan is something to do with the shack and something to do with manicous.

Ron really is determined to be a millionaire by the time he's twenty-five. I would say it's the most stupid thing I've ever heard, except my gran told me that we've already had a millionaire in the family – my Grand Uncle Bill. I had never heard about him before, but then I've never had too much time for family history till now.

My Grand Uncle Bill bought a truck off the owner of the plantation where he worked. The truck had been abandoned for years; nobody thought it would ever go again, so he got it dirt cheap. He bought it with some money he borrowed from a bank, and set about doing it up. It was the first bus on the whole island and became a huge success. By the time he died, my gran said, the bus had earned Grand Uncle Bill more than a million Grenadian dollars.

I've been spending a lot more time with my gran in the past few months, because my mum has been quite sick and my dad is hanging around the house a lot more than usual. Jill is doing most of the cooking and the cleaning, but everyone has their part to play; mine is always making sure that we have water from the standpipe. I'm eight now. My birthday recently came and went.

I've noticed a big change in my dad since the day I saw him under the house. He has never mentioned it to me, but he looks at me differently now and we no longer sit out on the porch and talk about cars. This, I think, is what my gran meant when she said that from now on things were going to be different.

I've seen the shack from a distance, but never up close. It's almost a ruin. The most solid thing about it is the floor, because it's raised off the ground by stone pillars that are supposed to keep the rot out. Only, one of the pillars has partly collapsed, making the shack lean at a crazy angle. Strands of elephant hair, the creepers that grow from the oldest trees, have dug their way in through the roof. There's a door, but it's hanging off its hinges.

As we get closer Alby pricks up his tail and his ears and squeezes between the door and the frame. There's a snarling sound from inside, then a rat – a real one, not a manicou – comes flying out, closely followed by Alby. Kellon tries to hit the rat with his stick and almost whacks Alby on the head instead. It puts Alby off his stride and the rat makes its getaway in a crack between two large boulders. We leave the dog to sniff around the base of the rocks. There's no sign of Ron.

'He be by shortly,' Kellon says, as he grasps the door and pulls. There's a splintering sound and the whole thing comes away in his hand.

Holding our hands over our mouths and noses, Kellon and I step inside. The smell inside is terrible. It's weird, too, how the floor leans, and I almost lose my balance. Light spills in from the doorway behind us and through the holes in the roof. The shack is bigger than it looks inside, but it has no windows. It was once used to store nutmeg, but the trees have all died and the jungle has taken over. The creepers have grown down the walls and spread across the floor, meeting in a knotted mass in the middle.

I touch the walls and they're damp. The smell, when I'm brave enough to remove my hand, is partly of rotten wood, but there's something else as well. A buzzing sound gives us some clue, but it takes Alby to find it. A cloud of flies rises from the tangle of vines that have crept in through a hole in the corner. We shoo them away, but I get a mouthful and so does Kellon. We spend the next two minutes spitting them out, then turn our attention to the stinking carcass on the floor.

'Armadillo,' Kellon says, giving its shell a kick. 'A good t'ing it hasn't been dead long.'

We use leaves and stones to pick it up and remove it from the shack. We drop it into a hollow between the roots of a tree and cover it with earth and stones. But the smell doesn't go away so easily, so we head outside and perch on one of the rocks, waiting for Ron.

At last we see him, swinging his long arms as he strides up the hill towards us.

'How long you been here?' he asks.

'Long enough to bury an armadillo,' I tell him. 'We find him in the shack.'

Ron pokes his head around the door and pulls it back sharply. The stink of death doesn't shift easily. But he seems more concerned by the state of the place than the smell. 'What happen to the door?'

'It fell off in me hand,' Kellon says. 'The whole place is a mess. What you wanna do with it, anyway?'

Ron gives us a big smile. 'We goin' to turn it into a farm,' he says proudly. 'You know how everybody round here love they wild meat. Well, we goin' to give them wild meat. We do the place up good, we put manicou in here and pretty soon they make a whole loada babies.'

'How do you know manicou make babies if you keep 'em locked up inside?' Kellon says.

'Sure they do,' Ron says. 'They breed like rabbits.'

'I never heard not'ing so stupid,' I say.

Ron is almost twice my age, but he looks like I just hit him with a sledgehammer. 'I never heard you talk that way before,' he says.

'Come on,' I say to Kellon. 'Let's go.'

'Wait a minute,' Kellon says. 'What get you so vex all of a sudden?'

'Ron only needs us 'cos he knows I's good at buildin' t'ings an' your dad has the tools,' I say.

'That's not true,' Ron says. 'We're a team. An' these is good ideas. We can all make money, an', God knows, Johnson, somebody in you family need to be makin' some.'

I glance up. 'What you say?'

'You know how much money you dad owe me mum in unpaid bills?' He's talking about my Aunt Ena, who owns the shop. 'More than four hundred dollars. An' you know what he do? Instead of feedin' he family, instead of payin' back me mum, he tips all he wages down his t'roat.'

Ron is standing around three feet away. He's at least two feet taller than me, but I launch myself at him. He's so surprised that he falls to the ground, with me on top of him. I reach for his throat. I'm so angry that it gives me a strength that would frighten me if only I stopped to think about it, but I don't. I have my hands around his neck and I start to squeeze.

But Ron's neck is big and my hands are small. It takes him less than a second to react. He doesn't punch and he doesn't kick. He just grabs my forearms and gently eases them apart. Then he throws me to the ground and gets to his feet. We stare at each other for a couple of seconds. He says nothing and nor do I. Then, like a wave that washes over me, the anger is gone and I'm left feeling so ashamed that I run off into the bush.

It's five minutes before Kellon and Alby catch up with me. 'What's the matter with you?' he says, as I carry on walking. 'Ron is you cousin; you favourite cousin . . .'

'Let's just go hunt manicou,' I say. 'I don't want no other worries today.'

Kellon says nothing as he falls into step beside me. I can still taste the shame of what I've done. Of all my cousins, Ron is the one I like the best.

I've never lost my temper before – not like that. Kellon's words still ring in my ears.

What *is* the matter with me?

CHAPTER FOUR

Jude has left for the bus that will take him to senior school in Sauteurs. After Jill has made breakfast she will head off to school too. She goes to the Samaritan Presbyterian School at the bottom of the village, where I will start in a few weeks' time.

Mummy is still sick in bed. No one knows what is wrong with her, but she has a fever. It's down to Jill and me to get Jemilla, Jeffrey, Jeffon and Jade ready for the day. When Jill goes to school, Jade will be looked after by my nan, while Jemilla and me stick around and keep an eye on Jeffrey and Jeffon.

My first duty is to get the water. The standpipe is opposite my nan's house, near the wall where the limers sit. The journey down is easy. Carrying two full buckets back up the hill is hard. The water comes out of the tap slowly and I pass the time counting the bottles that have been left on the wall from the night before.

This morning I count thirty-seven bottles of Carib and nine bottles of Clarke's Court.

Some days, if I'm up early enough, I catch Mack or George or Westy sitting out on the wall, still drinking, as they watch the sun come up over the mountains.

Wisps of smoke rise from the embers of the fire where the limers cooked their dinner. They sleep till the afternoon, then pass the rest of the day exactly as they passed the one before. The only breaks in this routine are when Ena puts her speakers out on the balcony and everybody in the village joins the party.

By the time I get back home my dad is at work.

As soon as he wakes he walks up the road to Miss Anne's place and puts her cow out to pasture behind her house. Then he goes and works in the fields. Some days he picks bananas, some days nutmeg or cocoa, sometimes all of these things. It depends on the time of year and what Old Man Baptiste has planned for him.

When he has finished he might put in a few hours helping Devlin deliver building supplies. Then he goes to the bar or out drinking with friends. We hardly ever see him and we don't have any money. No wonder my mum is sick.

Our breakfast is always the same: hot, sugary water and a piece of bread or, if we have them, crackers.

Jill is making dumplings to go with the bananas that we'll eat for lunch. She keeps prodding me and telling me what to do. But I know what I'm doing. We all have jobs around the house and I take mine seriously. Jemilla is the one who scrubs Jeffrey and Jeffon in the shower; I'm the one who feeds them.

'Johnson,' Jill says, 'what's the matter with Jeffrey?'

Jeffrey is leaning back in his chair, his face tilted towards the ceiling; his eyes are rolled back. I feel his forehead with my wrist. There's nothing wrong with him. He's tired, that's all. Last night Daddy woke the whole house when he tripped over the chair on the porch and fell through the front door, then tried to get into the big bed in our room, thinking it was his own.

I pick up Jeffrey and put him back on the bed. I watch over him till his eyelids grow heavy again.

When I get back to the kitchen Jill has finished preparing

the lunch. She places a large metal plate over the pot containing the dumplings to keep away the flies.

'We need water,' she says. 'Almost all the water is gone. Daddy will be vex if there's no water when he come home.'

'But I just go and get the water,' I say.

Jill makes a face. 'I done me duties, an' now I have to go to school. You still got t'ings to do. We need more water.' She dries her hands and calls out to Jemilla, who is hanging clothes on the line under the house. The dogs never bark at Jemilla; but they always bark at me.

The buckets feel even heavier this time, as I head back up the hill, and I have to stop a lot to catch my breath.

On the slopes above me are Old Man Baptiste's cherry trees. Old Man Baptiste is the richest man in the village. He has hundreds of them. Cherries make me think of my gran.

The one thing she doesn't have in her garden is a cherry tree.

I get an idea. When I take her water I'll also bring her some cherries. My gran loves her fruit. Cherries will make her feel better.

Old Man Baptiste has plenty of trees. When Kellon and I sneak into his orchard at night we always find a lot of fruit on the ground – fruit that will only rot if it's left there. The next day, when we ask if we can take the fruit home before it goes bad, Old Man Baptiste waves his stick at us and says the only way we can know there is fruit on the ground is if we have been in his orchard. He tells us to pick it from the bush or buy it from a shop and says if he ever catches us on his land he'll beat us.

Kellon and I come back at night, take what we can carry in our hands and pockets and then make sure we leave as many bite marks as we can in the fruit that is still on the trees. Old Man Baptiste knows it's our teeth that have been in his mangoes and plums, but he can't prove it.

The way I see it, there's not much love, respect or honesty in Old Man Baptiste, so everything he gets he deserves.

I tip the water out of one of the buckets and hide the other in the long grass. The road is empty. I dart into the orchard. I creep through the trees until I'm in the middle, surrounded by Old Man Baptiste's ripe red cherries. I jump up, grab hold of a branch and swing into a tree. I pick the cherries as fast as I can and drop them into the bucket beneath me. In next to no time the bucket is half full. It's time to go.

As I drop to the ground I lift my head and see a pair of legs, bare from the knee down. My heart starts to pound. But it isn't Old Man Baptiste; it's my father. In his left hand he's holding a bottle of Carib. In his right is his belt.

A look of rage spreads across his face.

He takes a step towards me and raises his belt.

My father has never, ever hit me before. 'Daddy, please . . .' I cry.

He starts to tell me he's been looking for me all over the village, but I know this isn't true. He must have been lying in the grass, drinking his beer somewhere nearby, and seen me as I crept into the orchard.

'The cherries ain' for me, Daddy,' I say. 'I pick them for Gran . . .'

'You's a t'ief,' he says. 'Me son is a t'ief.'

He's so drunk he can barely get the words out. In the space of a few seconds I weigh up my choices. I can either stay here and get a whipping or I can make a run for it to my gran's. Even though she's sick, my dad would never dare head up to her place when he's drunk. She would cuss him something rotten and if my dad is scared of anyone it's her.

I drop the bucket and run.

The belt buckle whooshes past my ear. I reach the edge of the orchard and look back. My father is still on his feet, but swaying. He has managed to hold on to the Carib. I can't see the belt any more.

I run as fast as I can and don't stop until I reach my gran's little house. The door is open. It always is. I tiptoe inside. I don't want to wake her if she's asleep. But the bed is empty. Maybe she has gone to the toilet or maybe she has wandered down to my grandpa's grave.

I go round the back of the house and call out her name. I stop and listen, but hear nothing except for the wind in the trees. Now I start to worry. I know that my gran is not well. What if she has wandered off and something has happened to her? Maybe she has taken a fall? Maybe she has broken a leg? What if she's hit her head?

As I start down the path that leads to my grandpa's grave, I see some movement out of the corner of my eye. I turn and it's Jemilla. She's standing at the top of the path.

'Johnson,' she says, 'come quickly. Mummy needs you.'

'But Gran . . .'

'Gran's not here . . .' She starts to cry. 'Please, Johnson. Come quickly.'

She turns and hurries back down the path. I follow her. Jemilla runs fast and I don't catch her till she gets to our house. I no longer care about my dad. My gran is gone. Something is very wrong.

I run into our kitchen, but nobody's there. There's no one in our bedroom either. I hear voices coming from my parents' room. I open the door. The blinds are drawn, but there is light streaming through the cracks. My mother is propped up in bed. Lying next to her are Jeffrey and Jeffon. Jemilla is standing by the door, wiping the tears from her face. There's someone standing beside her. A woman. I can't see her face.

'Come here,' my mother says weakly. She pats the bed beside her.

I sit down.

'Yes, Mummy?'

I wait. My mother draws a breath. Her lungs wheeze.

'Gran is sick,' she says. 'They come and take her away jus' now in an ambulance.' She touches my hand. 'She goin' to be OK, Johnson, but it will take a while before she be better. She need rest.'

'It's her diabetes,' Jemilla blurts. My little sister is only seven, but she's smart and clever, like Jude and Jill. She picks up a lot. I know that my gran has a bad heart and that there's something wrong with her blood. Maybe that is what diabetes is.

My mum's fingers curl around mine. 'The doctors come and take a look at me too,' she says. 'They don't like what they see. They want to make some tests in the hospital. That's why your Auntie Abigail is here.'

Abigail.

I turn. My father's sister takes a step forward. 'Hello, Johnson,' she says. Her voice is cold. It always is. She's painfully thin. The only time she brightens up is when she's around Ainsley, my cousin. But Ainsley isn't here. He must be at home with Harrison. I have a really bad feeling.

'You be goin' to stay with your auntie for a while,' my mum says. 'Till everybody be better.'

I don't know whether she's talking about herself, my gran or my dad – or all three. It doesn't much matter. My world is falling apart.

I bite my lip. Whatever happens, I'm not going to cry in front of my brothers and sisters. And I'm certainly not going to cry in front of Abigail. I'm gripping my mum's hand like a vice. I want to let go, but I can't.

'Why can't I help Jill and Jemilla?'

My mum touches my face. My nan and Ena can only cope with so many extra mouths, she says. The house is full as it is. Jude will stay with his grandparents – his father's parents – in Victoria. My nan will look after Jade. Jill will do whatever she can, whenever she can, to look after Jeffrey and Jeffon, but when she has to go to school Jemilla will step in. Ena still has to run the shop.

Turning to Abigail, my mum says thank God we have the love and support of my dad's sister at this difficult time.

Abigail takes a step forward and puts her hands on my shoulders. 'Come, Johnson. When we get home you and Ainsley can play. And then, when school starts, you and Ainsley can go to school together.'

'It will only be for a short time,' my mother says. She sits up, takes my hand and presses it to her cheek.

'But why me? Why me?' I say.

My mother has no answer. She falls back exhausted and closes her eyes.

Abigail's hands are still on my shoulders. I feel them tighten their grip.

'Go and get your t'ings,' she says. 'It's a long walk to Red Mud.'

The walk from Diego Piece takes an hour, and we do not say a word to each other the whole way. Abigail walks at an amazing pace and doesn't stop – not once. But she has shoes and I don't. And she has an umbrella and I don't.

'Let's be clear about somet'ing right away,' she barks, as soon as we walk in through her kitchen door. 'You are me brother's son and I'm takin' you in 'cos this is a bad business, a very bad business. I want to help you mammy any way I can. Everybody can see how terrible she sufferin'. But there's rules in this house, Johnson Beharry, an' I won't tolerate no disrespect. Is that clear?'

'Yes, Tan Abigail.'

Abigail's house is smaller than ours. It has one bedroom, a kitchen and a sitting room. Given how my auntie is, I'm surprised by the state of the place. There are unwashed dishes in the tub by the window and a thick layer of dust under my feet. I can see Harrison through a crack in the bedroom door. He's asleep on the bed.

'I may not live in Deego Pee,' Abigail says, 'but I know people there. I talk to them. I know how you's disappearin' into the bush all the day long, lookin' for rats an' mice an' Lord knows what else up in them hills. There'll be no runnin' off for as long as you's here under me roof. Is that clear?'

'Yes, Tan Abigail.'

Ainsley asks his mother when I can come out to play.

'First t'ings first.' She produces a sack – the kind they use down at the Association for bagging up cocoa and nutmeg – and points to the floor on the other side of the kitchen table. This is where I'm to sleep.

Then she tells me what I have to do to earn my keep. I must get into a routine. She starts to go through the list.

There are animals that need feeding before the rest of the house wakes up: a cow, a donkey, a goat, a rabbit and a cockerel. When this is done I must prepare breakfast, wait for Abigail, Harrison and Ainsley to wake up, then sit down and eat myself. Afterwards I will wash the dishes, clear everything away and sweep the courtyard.

'Can we play now?' Ainsley asks.

Abigail shakes her head. 'Go wake you father.'

Harrison appears a minute later, rubbing his eyes. 'Hey, Johnson,' he says.

We shake hands. Harrison is tall and easy-going, but I'm wary of him. He leads me and Ainsley outside. There's a large nutmeg tree in the middle of the courtyard. I feel a stab of longing for home; it reminds me of the nutmeg tree that stands outside our house.

I already know that Abigail hates leaves. Harrison points out the brush that I'm to use to clear them: a bunch of twigs tied with twine around an old broom handle. It's so old I'd be better off picking them up with my hands.

Harrison moves on. At the back of the yard is a lean-to. The lean-to is divided into pens. In the first pen is a donkey, in the second a goat and in the third a cow. The cow provides milk. The goat's milk is turned into cheese. Harrison doesn't say what the donkey is for. His fur is patchy and one ear flops down over his face. He looks too old and tired to carry anybody. I ask whether he's a pet.

Harrison laughs. A pet! Each animal has its job to do, he says. He owns a plot of land up in the hills where he grows fruit and vegetables. The donkey carries him up the track and the produce back down. They have a cockerel too. He's all that's left of a load of poultry after a wild dog got into the yard a few months back. Abigail, Harrison and Ainsley were out at the time, but a neighbour saw what happened. They have a rabbit and that got attacked by the dog as well.

Ainsley grabs my hand and shows me the rabbit in his pen. Half of one of his ears is bitten off and one back leg is mash-up. He hops with a limp. The rabbit only survived, Ainsley tells me, because of the cockerel.

'The cockerel?'

'When our neighbour hear all the commotion, he come around to find the cockerel fightin' the dog,' Harrison says. 'The neighbour say the dog lose an eye, 'cos of the way the cockerel go at him.'

'And what's goin' to happen to the cockerel?'

'Abigail is waitin' for a good time to cook him,' he tells me.

'And the rabbit?'

'We get another rabbit so he make babies,' Ainsley says.

I look around me at the state of the yard. I can see where Harrison has put chicken wire to stop dogs getting in over the gate again. The wire is held up by two thin sticks and looks like it will blow over in the next storm.

The rabbit run is also in a bad way. The frame has been pegged to the ground with stakes, but if a dog wants to get in, it can dig under it.

The donkey ee-aws so loud that Ainsley jumps.

Then the cow and the goat start. Next the cockerel crows. In a second the whole place has gone completely crazy. Even the rabbit starts jumping around, throwing himself at the walls of the run.

From inside the house Abigail yells and Harrison runs over and smacks the donkey and the cow until they stop hollering. He whacks the goat too, but it doesn't make any difference. The goat only stops when Ainsley gives him a potato.

'Abigail, she hates the noise,' Harrison says. 'Jus' make sure you feed 'em nice an' speedy. An' if that don't work, give 'em a whack.'

He shows me the shed where he keeps the dried grass for the cow and the donkey; and a bin full of slug-eaten cabbage, carrot and sweet potato for the goat and the rabbit. I spend the rest of the morning picking up leaves and doing the house-work. By the time I've finished washing the dishes and getting water from the standpipe, the tree has dropped more leaves and I have to sweep the yard again.

Ainsley and I get some playtime in the afternoon. We go out into the road and kick a football around. I've never been into football much, but Ainsley loves to play and he's a good kid, so I don't complain.

When we sit down and eat – the first time that I've stopped all day – I think about my family. I worry about my mum and my gran and wonder whether they're OK. I think about Jill, Jemilla, Jeffrey, Jeffon and Jade at my nan's. If only I were with them, I know I'd be able to help. Instead I'm here, looking after Abigail and her family. It makes no sense.

After dinner I clear away the dishes and wash up. Then I help Harrison settle the animals for the night. Since the dog got in, there isn't a whole lot to do. The cockerel goes into the pen with the rabbit; the donkey, the cow and the goat pretty much look after themselves.

I watch Harrison check the bolts on the gate. 'You know that a wild dog could get in again and kill the baby rabbits and the new chickens you goin' to get,' I say.

'You think?' he asks me, giving the wire above the gate a shake.

'I'm just thinking out loud,' I tell him.

Harrison looks at me. It's too dark to see his face, but I can almost hear the thoughts running through his head.

'You like to fix things, don't you?'

I could fix his whole yard up pretty good, I tell him.

'That's cool.' He wanders back into the house.

I go to bed that night holding the hammer from the bag of tools that Kellon's dad gave me before I left Diego Piece. Kellon's dad knows I like to make things and the hammer will be a comfort to me, he says. I have to use my clothes as a pillow and the sack prickles my skin, but if I concentrate really hard I can hear the sound of the wind in the nutmeg tree and this helps me to get to sleep.

Abigail comes back one day to tell me that my mother is in hospital in Victoria with a sickness called meningitis. The doctors say she's lucky, as meningitis can kill. She'll be back in Diego Piece in a week.

Meanwhile my gran has left the hospital and is resting up with my Aunt Jane. The doctors have given her medicine for her diabetes, but have told her that she needs to take things easy, as she has another kind of sickness on top of the diabetes: high blood pressure. I ask Abigail what this means and she says it can place a strain on Gran's heart. This is why she needs to take things easy.

Jane is Abigail's sister. Sometimes I wonder how. Jane has a smile as big as her heart and she hugs each and every one of us whenever she comes to visit. She lives in a place called Annandale on the edge of St George's and helps her husband Chris run a car-repair yard. I thank God that my gran is in good hands. It helps me to look on the bright side.

Soon my mum will be back in Diego Piece and when my dad comes to his senses and stops his drinking, she'll go back to him. This is what I tell myself when I lie awake at night, listening to the wind as she moves through the branches of the nutmeg tree.

CHAPTER FIVE

The class is packed with desks and chairs. There's one small window and although it's wide open, the air is so hot and sticky – so still – I feel as if I can't breathe.

I'm seated in the middle of the room, halfway between the wall and the window and halfway between Mr Sweeny's desk and the back of the class. I tug at the neck of my T-shirt and stare out of the window. From my desk I can see the base of the hill that leads to my gran's little house. Seeing it makes me feel better.

I'm in a state of shock. For years Jude and Jill have been telling me how much they love school, but I'm wondering which part they can possibly mean.

I would like to sit next to Kellon, but I can't. Instead I get to sit by a girl called Roxanne, who comes to school with exercise books and a pencil case that's bulging with pens, pencils and crayons. She keeps staring at something under her desk. When I catch her eye she looks away quickly and smiles, as if she's doing something wrong and doesn't want anybody to know about it.

After a while I realise she's staring at something under *my* desk, not hers. I look too, but the only thing I see is my two bare feet. I look around and finally understand what Roxanne is looking at: I'm the only child in the class without shoes.

When she stares at my feet again I dig her in the ribs. I do it with my elbow and barely touch her, but she cries out like a baby. Mr Sweeny, who is drawing on the blackboard, snaps his head around.

Who has made a disturbance in his class?

There's laughter from behind me. Mr Sweeny reaches into his pocket, produces his strap – a short piece of leather with a grip at one end – and brings it down hard on the edge of his desk. Roxanne jumps. Then she starts to cry. The class goes very quiet. Mr Sweeny has already told us that he won't stand for any nonsense. Troublemakers will get the strap across the palm of their hand. Those that make trouble a lot will get sent to Mr Mark, the headmaster, and Jude says he has a strap that hurts even more.

Roxanne's tears splash across a picture of a house she has drawn on the cover of her exercise book, smudging the ink and making it run.

I put my hand up. 'I did it, Mr Sweeny,' I say. 'I make her cry out.'

'What is your name?' he asks.

Johnson, I tell him.

'Your last name, boy?'

'Beharry, sir.'

Mr Sweeny puts his piece of chalk down. He takes off his glasses, rests them on the edge of his desk and stares at me. 'What did you do?'

'I dig me elbow into her.'

'Why?' he asks.

I've nothing to say. I'm not going to tell Mr Sweeny that I dug my elbow into Roxanne's ribs because she's staring at my bare feet.

'I don't know, sir.'

Let's see what you *do* know, he says, and beckons me to the front of the class with his long, bony finger.

'What is this?' he asks, pointing at the shape that he has just drawn on the blackboard.

It looks like a sweet potato, but I know that if I say it's a sweet potato everyone in the class will laugh and then I really am in trouble.

'It's our island. It's Grenada, sir.'

Mr Sweeny nods. He looks pleased. 'And how big is our island?' he says.

I know that Diego Piece is near the top, in the north, and that St George's, the capital, is close to the bottom, above what looks like a little tail sloping into the sea. I know it can take an hour to drive to St George's along the narrow, winding road that leads from Diego Piece through Victoria and Gouyave to the capital and that the bus can sometimes take twice as long. I'm interested in the time it takes to reach places.

When I used to race my Porsche along that road in the roots of my gran's cedar tree, Jude and I used to argue about the fastest time a car could make it to St George's. When I told Jude I'd done it in less than twenty minutes he laughed at me.

'It's twenty miles from the top of Grenada and it's ten miles across,' I tell Mr Sweeny.

He nods again and manages to look even more pleased. The incident with Roxanne is forgotten. He asks me to sit down.

As I take my place Roxanne checks that Mr Sweeny is facing the blackboard, then she sticks her tongue out at me from behind her exercise book. I take no notice and stare out of the window again. It's a bright, cloudless day – perfect weather for hunting manicous or armadillos. I glance at Kellon and see that he's doing the same.

Up on the hill that leads to my gran's house the tops of the trees are blowing in the breeze that drifts in from the sea. I can see boobies and gulls floating on the currents of air. Kellon and I could be up there, flying his kite. Down here in the valley there is still not so much as a breath of wind. There's no air in the classroom either. The back of my throat is dry.

When I look back at the blackboard I see Mr Sweeny has drawn lines across his map, dividing the island into six parts.

Does anyone know what these are? he asks.

Several children put their hands up. I don't, even though I know the answer: they're the six parishes that make up the island. I can't see the point. I can get all this from my gran and from Jude and Jill. I know that St Andrew's, on the eastern side of the island, is the biggest parish and that we live in the smallest, St Mark's. I know that Queen Elizabeth II of Great Britain is also the Queen of Grenada, but because she doesn't live here we have to have a prime minister, a Grenadian, to rule over us. I know that Grenada, Carriacou and Petit Martinique are the three main islands of the Grenadines and that Grenada is far and away the largest. I even know that ninety thousand people live on the island. I know that we're very lucky, because Grenada, being at the southern end of our ocean, the Caribbean, gets very few hurricanes and that God, who sends the hurricanes, must be a Grenadian, because the last one we got, Hurricane Janet, was more than thirty years ago, when my mum was a little girl. I know the power of a hurricane, because my mum has told me how she remembers seeing sheets of galvanised steel and whole roofs flying through the air as she fled from her house to a neighbour's.

I know that nutmeg and cocoa are the island's main crops. Almost all my relatives have been involved in picking and delivering these crops, one way or another, ever since my great grandfather, Joseph Gunpot, arrived in Grenada from India a hundred years ago.

The exceptions were my Grand Uncle Bill, who became a

millionaire from setting up Grenada's very first bus company, and my Aunt Jane and Uncle Chris, who own a garage on the outskirts of St George's.

I'm quite certain that my Grand Uncle Bill never attended a day of school in his life.

And I know for sure that Uncle Chris never learned how to fix a car by sitting in a classroom.

One way or another I will do everything I possibly can to get out of school.

School is for Jill and Jude. It's not for me.

One day Kellon and I are playing cricket during break when I spot Jill sitting at the base of a grassy bank, her head in her hands. I recognise the red ribbons in her hair.

I run over. When she looks up, her face is wet from crying. 'Oh, Johnson,' she says, 'where have you been?'

My first thought is that I'm in trouble with Mr Sweeny or the headmaster, Mr Mark, because yesterday I bunked off school, playing with my new friends – Stephen, Gregory, Dexter and Joshua in their den in the woods above the school. They've shown me and Kellon a way of getting out of lessons: by volunteering to work in the kitchens for a roly-poly cook called Mavis. After we're done in the kitchens we take off into the woods and hide out in the den – a cave at the bottom of a rocky outcrop – where nobody notices we're missing. Or so I thought. Now, suddenly, I'm afraid. 'What is going to happen to me?' I ask.

My sister frowns and wipes away her tears. 'What is going to happen to *you*? Nothing is going to happen to you.'

'Then what are you talking about?'

'It's Mummy,' she says. 'She just stop by the school.' She buries her face in her hands again.

I put my arm around her. 'What is it?'

'Oh, Johnson . . .'

Now that my mum is back from hospital, there are too many people at my nan's for my aunt to be able to cope. My father is still drinking, so going home is out of the question. But my mother, brothers and sisters have to live somewhere.

I think back to the day of our hunting trip; the day that Kellon and I met up with Ron at the shack. It wasn't fit for manicous. But tonight, and as far into the future as I can see, that's where my family will be living.

In assembly the next morning, after we have sung two hymns, we listen to Mr Mark talk about the importance of kindness and how the two things he won't tolerate at the Samaritan Presbyterian School are rude, inconsiderate children and bullies.

Since Stephen, Gregory, Dexter and Joshua are none of these things I wonder whether this is why Mr Mark turns a blind eye to the fact that they hardly attend class. Even so, Kellon and I walk into Mr Sweeny's class expecting him to be waiting with his strap. But he's not. The only person who asks about our absence yesterday is Roxanne. Then she goes back to writing big, loopy letters in her exercise book.

Mavis walks in during the first class after break. She asks for volunteers and several kids stick up their hands, but Mavis ignores them and chooses me and Kellon.

Outside the class we thank her and she says there's nothing to thank her for as long as we do a good job, just like yesterday.

We promise we will.

There are ten children in the hot, smoky kitchen, but Stephen, Gregory, Dexter and Joshua aren't among them, so I figure they've got word that they're in trouble and have decided to stay away until the heat dies down and Mr Mark offers them one of his truces.

As soon as we finish the dishes I tell Kellon that I'm bunking off the for the rest of the afternoon. I'm not even going to stop and have lunch.

'For the whole day?' he says. 'For that we get a loada shitty trouble.'

'I don't expect you to come with me,' I tell him. 'In fact I feel happier doing this on me own. I don' want you to get into trouble with you dad and mum.'

'Is it about what Jill tell you yesterday?'

I nod. 'I gotta know that me mum, me brothers an' me sisters are all OK.'

Kellon keeps watch as I make my way to a hole in the fence. I give him a wave, then I'm into the bushes. I pick up the bag with my tools I have hidden and, checking there are no teachers around, run up the road.

As soon as I can I dart into the bush and begin the hard march up the side of the hill.

On the way it starts to rain. By the time I reach the shack I'm soaked through. I stop twenty feet away and stare at it. It looks the same as the day Kellon, Ron and I left it. Somebody has tried to fix the door hinges, but because they haven't put it on straight, it doesn't shut properly. The roof has been patched, but the shack still leans down the hill and I can smell the rot.

I walk up to the door and ease it open. I hear a rustling noise. My heart is beating so hard I can hear it. I peer into the darkness. The light reaches across the floor. There's something in the corner, in the shadows. I take a step inside.

Voices come at me from all directions.

'Johnson!'

'It's Johnson, Mummy!'

Jemilla springs at me. I turn to see Jeffrey and Jeffon leaping to their feet. They rush me – Jemilla from the front and my brothers from the side – and because of the slope I lose my balance and fall.

Before I know it, I'm pinned to the floor by all my brothers and sisters – Jemilla, Jeffrey, Jeffon and little Jade – and for a magic moment I forget about my dad and his drinking, my Auntie Abigail, my mum's meningitis and school. I even forget I'm in the shack.

I hear my mother's voice, low and urgent, telling us to be quiet. I turn and see her. She's hunched in the corner, her legs drawn into her chest, her arms around her knees. She's shivering.

I rush over and we hold each other. She strokes my hair and I stroke hers. We say nothing. We don't need to. When I first saw her I thought she was sick. But she wasn't sick, she was frightened. They thought I was my father.

I think I have it bad, but I don't. If anything, I'm the lucky one.

CHAPTER SIX

I've no idea how old Old Man Baptiste is. He could be sixty or he could be a hundred. People can't remember a time when he was young. He seems to have been old and bad-tempered for ever. His body is thin and short, his skin looks grey and he has a patchy white beard. Long hairs sprout from his nostrils and ears. His round glasses, sunburned forehead and beak of a nose give him a look of Mahatma Gandhi, who we're learning about at school.

But Old Man Baptiste is interested in the rewards of this life – he's only out for himself.

I find him in one of his nutmeg plantations high above the village, cussing a worker for damaging one of his trees. I can see no sign of damage, but Old Man Baptiste, with his funny, high-pitched voice, is ranting about the growing cycle of the nutmeg; how it takes five years or even six to tell the sex of a tree, how only the female trees bear fruit and how none will grow for at least two years after the male trees have been identified and separated from the female ones.

'My trees are precious – more precious than any cow, sheep or goat – and this is how you treat them,' he bellyaches, before turning on his heel and nearly walking straight into me.

'You . . .' he says. 'Are you come to steal my damn fruit?'

Old Man Baptiste doesn't frighten me. I guess it would be

different if I depended on him for my living, like most people in the village, but I don't. I smile and shake my head.

It's all I can do not to say something that will make his blood boil. He breaks every one of my gran's golden rules. He loves no one, except himself, and he respects no one, not even himself. Which is why he doesn't have, and never will have, *my* respect. But today, for the first time in my life, I need Old Man Baptiste, so I tell myself: be careful.

I've thought about this moment for days. What I will say. How I will say it. I've gone through it with my cousin Ron; he knows about making money, he knows how to deal with Old Man Baptiste. Ron tells me that I will need to enter what is known as a negotiation.

I look Old Man Baptiste directly in the eye and tell him I want him to give me a job.

He laughs. A couple of nearby fruit pickers risk *their* jobs by stopping what they're doing and listening in.

'Give me one good reason why I should employ you. You're a child – and you savage my trees when my back is turned.'

'Mr Baptiste, sir,' I say, 'I can give you many good reasons.'

He stands there, sneering at me. 'Go on then.'

'First, you should know that I'm a hard worker. When I come here I will not sleep and I will not skive.'

'Well,' he snorts, 'that *will* be something of a novelty. Everyone says they will work hard, but nobody knows the meaning of the word. Every damn one of you ends up skiving. You're all the same – you want money for nothing.'

'Second, I can climb any tree in your plantation without a ladder.'

'That I do believe! You're in and out of them the whole time, stealing my fruit.'

'I don't drink rum or beer,' I tell him, 'so I will never get drunk and damage your trees.'

'But you've *already* damaged my trees,' he says. 'You and that friend of yours leave bite marks in my fruit. You think I don't know?'

I look him straight in the eye. 'That's another good reason why you should give me a job. If you give me a job I will stop leaving bite marks in your fruit.'

'But this is blackmail!' Old Man Baptiste shouts.

I'm not a hundred per cent sure what blackmail is. It never comes up in discussions with Ron. But if blackmail is about getting what you want, whatever it takes, then I guess he's right.

I start to feel nervous. I think I might be close to getting what I want.

'The most important thing,' I tell him, 'is, if you give me a job I will work for no money.'

His eyes narrow. 'If you don't want money, what do you want?'

'I want a pair of shoes.'

I've never owned a pair of shoes in my life. If I have shoes I can save fifteen minutes when I walk from Red Mud to Diego Piece. If I have shoes I can sweep Abigail's yard, the job I hate most, in half the time. I won't have to pick thorns and splinters out of my feet every ten seconds. I've worked it all out in my head. I need to be able to spend as long as possible helping my mum at the shack.

In the last week Ron, Kellon and I have turned the place around. We have re-hung the door and built up the broken pillar so that the shack no longer leans down the valley. We have plugged all the holes in the roof, and the place has started to dry out.

'Shoes?' Old Man Baptiste says. He's not laughing now. He's trying to see where the trickery lies. 'What kind of shoes?'

'Four weeks' work for a pair of flip-flops,' I tell him.

I can see Old Man Baptiste making calculations in his head. 'A pair of flip-flops will take six weeks' work.'

The best thing I've learned since I've been at the Samaritan Presbyterian is the meaning of the word 'truce'. This is what I'm offering Old Man Baptiste, and he knows it.

He holds out his hand.

I tell him that there is one more thing. It will cost him nothing, but I can't do without it. I need six large empty crates. The kind he uses to box up his fruit.

I remember one last thing Ron told me. I tell Old Man Baptiste I will accept the flip-flops as payment when I've finished my six weeks. But the crates I need now.

Ron said Old Man Baptiste would understand. In business it's what is called a 'down payment'.

Old Man Baptiste's thin, bony hand is still outstretched. I put my hand in his and shake on it.

In the weeks that follow I get up, feed the animals, clean the house, sweep the yard, make the breakfast and get Ainsley ready for school. I attend two, sometimes three classes in the morning, then work in the kitchens until lunch.

As soon as I've eaten I take off up the hill and hang in the cave with Gregory, Stephen, Dexter and Joshua, who are starting to spend so little time at school they may as well not be there at all. Nobody seems to care whether I'm there either. Abigail is only interested in Ainsley and Mr Sweeny is happy as long as there is order in his class. Everyone around me is too wrapped up in their own problems to know what I'm up to, and this suits me just fine.

Joshua is keen to show me how to make something he calls a 'bazooka', but for the moment this must wait. There's something else I need to build first – a surprise for my mum's birthday.

I've stashed Old Man Baptiste's crates in the den, right at

the back of the cave. They're all damaged in some way, but it doesn't matter. I'm making her a bed, in two three-foot sections, with legs at each corner. This way I can carry them to the shack one at a time. When I get there I will screw the two sections together and nail down the slats that support the mattress.

It's starting to take shape. I can't wait to see my mum's face when I give it to her.

After about forty minutes' work on the bed I run up to the plantation. I work there for an hour, sometimes two, picking cocoa and nutmeg, then rush back to school to collect Ainsley and walk him home.

After six weeks, as we agreed, I go to Old Man Baptiste and ask for my shoes. On Friday – payday – he hands them over: white flip-flops with red straps and red soles. My first pair of shoes. I want to tell everyone, but I tell only Ainsley, on condition that he doesn't tell his mum. If Abigail sees my flip-flops she'll want to know how I came by them. And then the whole story will come out – school, skiving, my deal with Old Man Baptiste; everything.

I'm exhausted, but it takes me a long time to get to sleep. There is a lot to think about: the bed, my shoes and another piece of good news – something that Abigail let slip over dinner. My gran is coming home in two weeks' time.

I can see light at the end of my tunnel.

The next morning Abigail sends me over to Diego Piece to pick up some shopping from the store at the bottom of the village. Thanks to my new shoes the walk between the two villages is no longer a hardship.

But when I get to the store the sports bag that I hand over is filled with so much stuff – milk, tins of meat, butter, rice, sugar and flour – that I can hardly lift it.

After several attempts I work out that if I put the bag on my back, with one of the straps on my forehead, I can go a couple of hundred yards before I have to stop and rest. But in the high heat every step becomes a struggle and it's several hours before I make it back to Red Mud.

Before I get to the door I take off my flip-flops and tuck them into the waistband of my shorts, under my T-shirt.

Abigail is out in the yard. I slip my flip-flops inside my rolled-up bedding and put the bag of shopping on the kitchen table.

In walks Abigail, followed by Harrison and Ainsley. She's holding a broom and sweating. She's in a foul temper; clearing up leaves is her least favourite job.

'Where you been?' she yells. 'It's been three hours since you been gone.' She goes crazy about everything – the state of the yard, the fact that she, Harrison and Ainsley are starving because they've been waiting for me.

I try to tell her that the shopping was heavy and I could hardly lift it, but she tells me to be quiet. I'm lying, she says. I gotta be.

'You been skivin'. I just know it. You and that friend of yours. Skivin' when you uncle, you little cousin an' me are goin' out of our minds with hunger.'

I know better than to argue with Abigail when she's in one of these moods. It's better to say nothing and wait for it to blow over like a passing storm.

She opens the bag.

A vex kind of look passes across her face. She picks up the bag and carries it to the back door, where she holds it up to the light.

'Come here,' she says quietly.

My blood runs cold.

I walk over to her.

Suddenly Abigail grabs the back of my neck and forces my face into the bag. One of the jars has broken and molten butter has gone everywhere. The sugar and flour bags have split open. Everything except for the tins is ruined.

'How did this happen?' she screams. 'How?'

I can't think. But as her grip tightens on my neck it comes to me. When I stopped and rested one time, I must have set the bag down too quickly. If a rock was underneath, it would have smashed the jar.

I pull myself away and rush to the other side of the table.

Abigail runs after me. She screams for Harrison and Ainsley to do something, but they just stand there, as shocked by her anger as I am.

Abigail knows she can't catch me. No matter how quickly she moves, I always manage to keep the table between us.

She picks up my bedding and lashes it across the table like a whip. It misses me but hits the table and splits, sending something flying across the room. One of my shiny red and white flip-flops lands with a plop at Harrison's feet.

Everybody stares at it. Then they look at me.

There's nothing I can do except stand and watch as Abigail plunges her hand inside the sack. With a look of triumph she holds up the other shoe.

She asks in a low and trembling voice exactly how I've come to own a bright, shiny new pair of flip-flops.

I stand with my hands behind my back and say nothing; there's nothing I can say.

Abigail decides that I must have stolen the flip-flops; that I'm a dirty, rotten t'ief.

I hold my breath, but Ainsley springs forward with tears streaming down his face and throws his arms around me. 'He not a t'ief,' he shouts at his mother. 'Johnson work hard for he shoes. He pick fruit for Old Man Baptiste and Old Man Baptiste pay him wit' a pair of shoes.'

Ainsley knows the whole story. It doesn't take too much longer for everything to come out.

Abigail hands my flip-flops to Ainsley with a warning that if he dares give them back to me he'll find himself in as much trouble as I am.

Then she says that she, Harrison and Ainsley are going to Diego Piece to replace the food I've just ruined, and to order some 'galvanised'. They need a new roof for the lean-to, because when it rains, water pours through the holes, soaking the donkey, the cow and the goat. I know it is the feed they're thinking of, not the animals.

After they leave I stand by the nutmeg tree, watching a huge bank of thunderclouds roll up the valley.

Suddenly the heavens open. The rain lashes down and soon I'm standing in my bare feet in a huge puddle. Leaves float on the water like tiny boats. I watch them swirling this way and that as they're blown by the wind.

Abigail doesn't want to find a single leaf on the ground when she gets back. This was her parting shot to me as she left the house.

I walk over to the animals. Water is pouring through a hole in the roof on to the donkey's head. I look at him and he looks at me.

I put my arms around his neck and bury my face in his fur.

I tell him how sorry I am and how much I will miss him.

I tell him I have to leave and that I hope he understands.

It's my mum's birthday. I will present her with the bed, then break the news that I've left my aunt's for good. Abigail is not my mum's sister; she's my dad's sister. My mum used to say that the drinking is like a sickness with my dad. I will tell my mum, maybe the sickness that makes my dad drink comes out in a different way with Abigail.

Either way I'm not going back.

An hour after I walk out of Abigail's house I reach the den. Stephen, Gregory, Dexter and Joshua are nowhere to be seen.

I sit for a while in the mouth of the cave as another storm cloud passes overhead. One more time I go over what I'm going to tell my mum. I can make myself useful in the shack. I can wash clothes, I can cook, I can help Jill and my mum look after the little ones. I can even bring in some extra money by working for Old Man Baptiste.

I pick up the pieces of the bed, one on each shoulder, and set off towards the shack.

As I approach it I know something is wrong. Normally either my mum or Jill is outside doing the washing or cooking a meal. Today everything is quiet and the door of the shack is shut.

I put the pieces of the bed on the ground and push the door back. The shack is empty. It isn't simply that there is nobody inside; there is *nothing* inside. No clothes. No food. Everything that was here two days ago is gone.

All my life, thanks to my gran, I've seen the forest as a magical place, but now, surrounded by the rocks and the trees, I see it differently. My imagination runs riot. Maybe somebody came up here and killed my family. Or maybe the spirits of the forest – the manitou – took them.

Stop it, I tell myself. What would the spirits of the forest want with my brothers' and sisters' clothes?

If Jill was here she would remind me that I'm nine years old – old enough to use my brain. So think, Johnson, *think*.

I sit down and think, and the answer pops into my head. If anybody knows what has happened, it will be Ena.

I pick up the bed and set off down towards the village.

CHAPTER SEVEN

As I break through the trees Diego Piece is spread out before me. Sunlight races across the rooftops, chasing the clouds' shadows away. People are gathered around the standpipe and some of the limers are already ranged along the wall, smoking and drinking. The limers spend their whole lives there. They while away the day, drinking, smoking, cooking and eating. One of them, Mack, is lighting a fire in the oil drum they use as a cooker.

Ena is sitting at her table in the shop, jotting down sums on a piece of paper. She looks up and sees me standing in the doorway.

'Johnson,' she says, 'what in the worl' you carryin'?'

I put the pieces of the bed down. My shoulders hurt where the wood has dug into my skin. 'Where's Mummy?' I ask. 'Where's everybody?'

She replies, like it's the most natural thing in the world, 'They're at home, Treasure.'

'Home? You mean, me gran's place?'

'No, Treasure,' she says. 'Your home. Nobody tell you? They move back in las' night. They back with you daddy again.'

Ena is still talking as I pick up the bed and start to run up the road. I focus on the base of the hill at the top of the village. The pieces of bed knock against each other, making a clack-clack sound as I run. I ignore the laughter of the limers and the pain in my shoulders where the wood digs into my skin. Soon I no longer feel the weight of the bed or the splinters in my feet or the heat of the sun on my head.

I cut through the trees, dodging the sharp thorns that reach out towards my bare legs.

Ahead I hear laughter – the laughter of my brothers and sisters. I stop as I reach the edge of the trees, the place where I once stood and watched my father collapse in a drunken heap under the house.

What I see now helps me to rub out the memory of that day.

My father is standing on the balcony, surrounded by his children. He's holding Jade in his outstretched arms. He's tickling Jade and Jade is laughing. Jeffrey is holding one of my father's legs and Jeffon the other. They're standing next to the chair where I used to sit with my dad and leaf through the pages of *Motor* magazine.

Through the window I can see my mother moving around the kitchen. Jemilla and Jill are in there too – I can hear Jill bossing my little sister as they help my mum with the cooking.

As I step out of the trees Jeffrey and Jeffon see me and come tearing down the steps.

They ask what I'm carrying and suddenly I feel really stupid. My mum has the best birthday present she could possibly ask for – she's back home. She has no need for a bed. She and Daddy already have one.

'You built that?' Jeffon asks.

I nod.

'Why?' Jeffrey asks. 'Why did you build a bed?'

It's a simple question, but I don't know what to tell him. My family is here – they're back *home* – and nobody told me.

Watched by my father, I climb the steps, dragging the bits

of the bed with me. I walk through the kitchen into our bed-room. I set down the pieces and tip my tools on to the floor. I'm fixing the two main sections together with the first screw when I hear the door open behind me.

The wood is hard and the screw goes in with difficulty. I grit my teeth and twist the screwdriver. My father says my name, but I don't stop what I'm doing; I don't turn around. I don't want to talk to him. I don't want to talk to my mother. I don't want to talk to anyone.

All I want is to get the bed finished.

It's no longer my mother's bed. It's my bed. This is where *I* will sleep.

'What are you doing?' my father asks. 'Johnson . . .?'

I say nothing. I carry on working.

'I ask what you're doing . . .'

Still I carry on.

'Johnson, look at me when I talk to you.'

I turn round. I can feel tears behind my eyes. I taste them in my throat, but I'm not going to cry. This is my home. My bedroom. My bed. I'm *not* going to cry.

My father is in the doorway. Abigail is standing next to him.

The sight of her kills the urge in me to cry. I turn back to the bed. If I can just finish it, I tell myself, there will be no cause to send me back to Red Mud.

'What are you doing here?' Daddy asks. There's anger in his voice now.

'I's not going back,' I say, as I twist another screw into the bed frame. 'Me brothers and me sisters are all here. This is where I goin' to stay.'

'You're goin' back to Red Mud with Abigail,' my father says.

I look at the bed. The screws have gone in well. The frame is sturdy. Now to put the slats across, ready for a mattress.

I reach into the bag and take out the bundle of planks, but before I can undo the string that ties them together my father walks across the room and pulls me to my feet. He twists me round, gripping me by the arms so I can't move. He starts shouting at me. He knows everything, he says, everything. He knows that I've been skiving off school, he knows I've been working for Old Man Baptiste on the sly when I should have been studying. He says I've abused my aunt's hospitality and brought shame on him, my mum, my brothers and my sisters because of it.

You're going back to Red Mud, he says, and that's that.

He's going with Abigail and Harrison to see a friend who has some galvanised. His friend is going to sell it to Abigail. It will take an hour to do the deal. After that Abigail, Harrison and Ainsley will set off for Red Mud and I will follow them with the galvanised. Carrying it on my own is my punishment. Every step that I take between here and Red Mud will make me think about the suffering I've caused.

I listen to him, but say nothing.

What is there to say?

The dad I used to know is gone. When I saw him on the porch with Jade in his arms and Jeffrey and Jeffon by his legs, I thought he was back. But he's not.

He releases me, turns on his heel and slams the door behind him.

I sit down on the corner of the bed and stare out of the window. The rain clouds have blown out to sea. I can see sunlight on the wet leaves of the palm tree on my gran's hill. If only, I think. If only.

I hear whispering outside the door. It opens a crack and there is my mother. She has Jill, Jemilla, Jeffrey and Jeffon by her side. The boys cling to her skirt. My sisters look as if they want to scoop me up and hold me. But I don't move and nor do they.

My mother comes and sits on the corner of the big bed. My brothers and sisters settle down beside her.

'Did you make this?' she asks, pointing at the bed.

I made it, I tell her. I can't bring myself to look at her as we speak. I stare at the floor.

'Did you make it for me? For my birthday?'

I make it for myself, I tell her. Nobody else.

My mother puts her hand under my chin and raises my face to hers.

'Johnson . . .' she says. 'Johnson, don't be vex with me . . .'

'Who else is there to be vex with?' I say to her.

'Listen to me . . .' I can see that she's fighting back her tears. 'There are too many people under this roof. Too many mout' to feed. Your father has promised he stop his drinkin', but you know, an' I know, my beautiful son, that he's not the man he used to be. He's different. There is an anger in him. An anger that is quick to rise, an', when he lose he temper, there's no tellin' what might happen, what he might do. I don't know how t'ings goin' to work out here, I don't. But I have to try, Johnson. I have to give it a go. Raisin' a family in that shack . . .'

Her voice trails away. A tear rolls down her cheek.

'But I want to be with you,' I say. 'I want to help.'

She takes my face in her hands. 'I know it can't be easy livin' with Abigail. I know how much you want to be with us . . .'

'Then why can't I be?' I say. 'Is it 'cos of something I do? Is it 'cos . . .?'

I don't want to finish what I was going to say. But I don't have to speak the words. I already know that the look in my eyes is plain for my mum to see.

'You must know,' she says, 'that I love you more than life itself. You must always remember that.'

'Then why am I the one – the *only* one – of all me true

brothers and sisters who can't live under this roof? Why am I the one who has to be sent away?'

My mother puts her arms around me and pulls me to her.

''Cos out of all of me sweet darlin' children,' she whispers in my ear, 'you are the one I can trust – I can rely on – to get through this.'

In the end I agree, not because my mum thinks I'm the one who can look after myself, but because of a feeling I get that my dad will punish her, not me, if I don't do as she asks. I promise on the condition that I can finish building the 'little bed', as my mother calls it, and that this is where I will sleep when the time is right to come home.

When I'm done I set it at right angles to the big bed and screw it to the wall. This is where it will wait for me till I'm back again.

Twenty minutes later I go outside. Abigail, Harrison and Ainsley have already left for Red Mud. The piece of galvanised is leaning against the noni tree halfway up the path. My father is nowhere to be seen.

Jill, Jemilla and Jeffrey help me to lift it on to my back. The sun has made it very hot. The galvanised burns me through my T-shirt. I have to pour some water over it to cool it down.

'Let me help you, Johnson,' Jeffrey says. 'Let me come to Red Mud with you.'

'Just keep the little bed warm for me till I get back,' I tell him. I pat him on the head and he smiles.

I hoist the galvanised on to my back and take a few steps up the hill. I don't get more than a few feet when I feel the weight of it shift. I try gripping harder, but it keeps on sliding and I end up with two cuts across the fingers of both hands for my trouble.

Blood drips on to the path. I set the galvanised down.

When Jeffrey sees the blood he says he's going to go inside

and get Mummy, but I tell him not to. My mother has enough on her mind already. Instead I tell him to look for an old piece of rag while I work out how I'm going to carry the galvanised.

I go down under the house, where my father keeps all kinds of scrap. The dogs bark and snarl, but they're leashed to their post and can't get me. I find a long piece of string and wrap it around the top of the galvanised.

I remember seeing a picture in a book that Jude brought home from school. It was about Ancient Egyptians, Greeks and Romans. Jude tried to tell me about the Romans, how long their empire lasted, and which countries they conquered, but the only thing that got my attention was how the Romans built things. My favourite picture was of something called a siege tower – a huge building on wheels the Romans used for smashing down walls. The picture showed how Roman soldiers used to protect themselves from their enemies' arrows by hoisting their shields on to their backs and linking them together to form what they called a 'tortoise'.

This is what I do now.

By wrapping string around the top of the galvanised, I turn myself into a Roman soldier with a shield on my back. When Jeffrey comes back with a piece of cloth, I tear it in half and wrap it around my fingers. Then I grip the string and pull the galvanised on to my back again. The string bites into the cuts, but the cloth makes the pain bearable and stops the flow of blood. I say goodbye to Jeffrey again and set off up the path.

Ten minutes later I approach my nan's house. The limers on the wall laugh and joke about the strange-looking armadillo that wanders past them. I'm already tired and thirsty, but I can't stop and drink at the standpipe because I know the limers will continue to ask me all kinds of questions about what I'm doing and where I'm going, and I'm not in the mood to give answers to anybody.

I press on, trying not to think about the journey ahead, but because I know about time and distance part of me is calculating how long it is going to take me to get to Red Mud. I've walked only a quarter of a mile and it has taken me twice the time it normally takes. At this rate I will not be in Red Mud till after dark and this worries me because I've never much liked the dark.

The road is lined by tall trees. I try to think of the forest as the good place my gran says it is, but I know that there are bad spirits there as well as good ones; that my gran never talks about them because she doesn't like to scare me.

I call on my gran now to give me courage and strength, because I can feel all mine draining through my feet with every step I take.

I talk to her as if she were next to me and imagine what she would say.

'Keep walking, Johnson.

'One step at a time.

'Keep walking.

'Don' look back . . .'

Suddenly there is a loud bang – something has hit the galvanised right next to my head.

I peep out from under it in time to see Ansell, arm raised, another stone in his hand. He's standing beside a big mahogany tree. He must have been hiding, waiting for me, picking his moment to hurl the stone. The noise as it hit the galvanised almost gave me a heart attack.

He drops the stone and stands there, staring at me, his hands on his hips.

'Well, if it ain' me little cousin,' he says, the scar on his face twisting his smile.

'Go away, Ansell,' I say. 'I's not in the mood.'

'Meeting up with you friend Lou-Jean?'

I say nothing. The last time we met, I was playing under the bridge, and it was Lou-Jean, the village idiot, who came to my rescue. Ansell would never forget being shamed by someone like Lou-Jean. But here we're in broad daylight, in the middle of the street. *Keep walking.*

'What's with the galvanised?' he yells. 'You buildin' a car?'

I turn round and walk on. A second later there's another crack on the galvanised.

'Or maybe you buildin' a house for you mammy,' he shouts after me. 'I hear she be needin' one. Even somet'ing you build gotta be better than that shack she livin' in.'

I stop and turn round. 'Me mother ain' livin' in any shack,' I say. 'She at home with me dad, me brothers and me sisters.'

'But not you,' he says. 'How come?'

I walk on.

'What's the matter, Johnson?' he shouts. 'Manicous and Lou-Jean the only friends you got?'

I want to turn and fight, even though I know Ansell will cream me, but I hear my gran's voice telling me to keep going.

As I head down the hill Ansell keeps throwing stones. Every time he hits the galvanised he laughs. His laughter rings in my ears even after I round the corner and his stones can't reach me any more.

My feet hurt, my hands hurt and I'm hot and tired and thirsty.

And I've not even left Diego Piece. I have another two hours of this to go.

I pass the bridge and wonder if Lou-Jean is somewhere below. Part of me would like to slink down under the bridge and live in Lou-Jean's world of water and shadow. Lou-Jean may be crazy, but he has a good heart. Living with Lou-Jean would be a million times better than going back to Abigail's.

Up ahead, on the right, is the big house with the scaffolding. Except, when I look up from under the galvanised, I see that the scaffolding is gone and the house is finished. This tells me how long it's been since I last walked along this road.

The house is the biggest in the whole of Diego Piece. It's three storeys high and has balconies on every floor. There's a lawn at the front and a tarmac drive that sweeps up from the big double gates to the door.

Outside the door is a Land Rover and beyond that I can see a lush, tended nutmeg plantation. As I approach, two dogs appear from behind the Land Rover and throw themselves at the gate, barking and snarling at me. I hear a woman's voice telling them to be quiet.

I look at the house again and spot her on one of the ground-floor balconies.

She's sitting on a grand chair with cushions and a high back and has a magazine in one hand and a long glass of fruit punch in the other.

The thing I really notice about her is the huge pair of sunglasses.

She's old enough to be my grandmother, but with her black hair and sunglasses she looks very different from my gran. There is something . . . I try to think of the word . . . glamorous . . . about her.

My dad once showed me pictures in a magazine of a Grand Prix race that happened when he was a kid. He was always telling me about the famous drivers from those days: Graham Hill, Jackie Stewart, Jim Clark.

The woman on the balcony reminds me of the women with big sunglasses who stared back at me from the pages of that magazine. The women that hung out with Graham Hill, Jackie Stewart and Jim Clark.

Glamorous – that's how my father described them.

That is how the woman on the balcony seems to me.

Although I can't see her eyes, I know she's watching me, because her sunglasses follow me down the hill.

'Little boy,' she calls out, as I draw level with her. 'Where are you going?'

I tell her that I'm going to Red Mud.

'With no shoes?'

'I ain' got no shoes,' I say. 'I owned a pair of shoes for a day, but now me little cousin Ainsley's got them. It's lucky for him we the same size.'

She smiles and sets the magazine down. 'You're taking that piece of galvanised all the way to Red Mud?'

I tell her I am.

'Who are you?' she says. 'What's your name?'

It's Johnson, I tell her.

'Johnson who?'

'Johnson Beharry.'

'Well,' she says in a voice that sounds almost as if she's talking in her sleep. 'Isn't that extraordinary?'

She calls for someone to sort out the dogs. A tall thin man, old enough to be my grandfather, appears. He whistles and the dogs come to him. He grabs them by their collars and takes them inside. Then he strolls down the drive and opens the gate.

I'm standing right outside. The galvanised is still on my back.

We look at each other and the man smiles. He has the kindest face I've ever seen.

'Do you know who I am?'

I shake my head.

'My name is Hammond Beharry. I'm your grand uncle. You must be Florette's boy.'

I nod my head.

'Florette's mother is my sister,' he says.

I want to tell him that I like his house, and I *really* like his Land Rover, but I never get the words out. Everything starts to swim before my eyes; the sky goes very dark, my legs turn to jelly and I feel myself falling.

CHAPTER EIGHT

I'm sitting in a chair and looking at a woman with big sunglasses. We're outside, on a balcony. A fan is beating gently above my head.

The woman hands me some fruit punch and I take it. I notice that my hands are shaking.

'How are you feeling?' she asks.

I touch my head. 'I'm fine, I think . . .' I look around me. How did I get here?

'You fainted. You need to drink, Johnson. You're dehydrated.'

Dehydrated.

I need to drink.

I have a vague memory of standing outside the big house on the corner and seeing a glamorous woman with sunglasses.

This woman.

I remember walking in through big iron gates and talking to a tall, kind-looking old man with a bald head.

A Land Rover outside the house.

Then nothing.

'I'm your cousin, Johnson,' the woman says. 'Some people call me Babby, and some call me Syie. I'm married to your Grand Uncle Hammond.' She holds out her hand. 'Welcome . . .'

We shake hands. 'Thank you for the fruit punch,' I manage.

Her husband, Grand Uncle Hammond, comes and stands behind her.

'That was a big piece of galvanised you were carrying,' he says. 'Are you feeling better?'

I nod and knock back the fruit punch in one go. Cousin Syie asks Hammond to get me some more, then she asks to see my hands.

I unfurl the pieces of cloth that are tied around my fingers. They're covered with dried blood. I try to open my fingers, but I can't. It's as if they're still wrapped around the string I fixed to the galvanised.

Cousin Syie takes off her sunglasses and studies the cuts. She looks at my grand uncle, then she turns to me.

'We need to put something on your hands, some medicine,' she says. 'You won't be walking another step this evening, young man.'

'But Cousin Syie,' I tell her, 'I have to deliver this piece of galvanised to me aunt.'

'Then Hammond can put it in the Land Rover and take it to her himself. You're not going anywhere. You're exhausted.'

'But Cousin Syie,' I say, 'my aunt will . . .'

She puts her fingers to her lips. 'Follow me.' She leads me by the arm into the kitchen.

I've never seen anything like it. There's a cooker, a fridge, a sink with taps, shelves filled with plates and glasses and, on a table in the corner, a television.

Cousin Syie washes my hands with cold water from the tap and puts some disinfectant on the cuts. The disinfectant stings terribly, but my cousin says that's a good sign. It means the medicine is working.

She takes me into the sitting room and sits me down on a long settee. Across the room is the biggest television I've ever seen. Underneath it is a video. I get down on my hands and knees and look at it.

'I seen a TV before,' I tell her. 'But I never seen a video, 'cept in magazines.'

'Maybe you'd like to watch something . . .'

'I never seen a movie neither,' I say.

She asks me what I'm interested in and I tell her I like cars. She opens a cupboard and scans through a whole bunch of videos till she finds the one she's looking for. It's a movie called *Beverly Hills Cop* – one of her son's favourites. She puts the video into the machine and presses 'Play'. She says I'll like it, because it has some great car chases. In the meantime she's going to make me a sandwich, while Hammond takes the galvanised to my Aunt Abigail in Red Mud.

I watch the movie, but never get to the part with the car chase.

The next thing I know, I'm waking up in a bed with sheets, in a strange room. I pinch myself, because at first I think I'm dreaming.

Then I remember the day before: the empty shack, the walk to my parents' home, my dad, Abigail, the galvanised, Ansell and the big house on the corner . . .

I get out of bed. I hear talking and follow the sound down a big open staircase.

Grand Uncle Hammond and Cousin Syie are sitting at the kitchen table.

Cousin Syie says good morning and asks what I would like to eat for breakfast.

'*Breakfast?*' I say.

I've slept for almost thirteen hours.

Over breakfast Cousin Syie and my grand uncle tell me their story.

She's a first cousin to my mother and Hammond is my mum's uncle. Everyone is connected to everyone else in some way in the village and even though they spent very little time in Diego Piece, they kept in touch with my mum and knew she had grown up and had a family.

When Hurricane Janet struck in 1955, Hammond and Cousin Syie had only been married eight years. Their children were very little. Hammond was a farmer and Janet wiped out all his nutmeg trees. Everything they had was destroyed.

'Hammond had no idea what he would end up doing,' Cousin Syie says. 'He just knew that going to the UK was our only hope of starting again.'

Hammond went on ahead and sent for Cousin Syie and the children as soon as he was settled. After a lot of looking he found a job as a chef, and that's what he did for more than thirty years.

'The moment the children were all in school, I went out to work, joining Hammond in the same catering business,' Cousin Syie says. 'We worked all the hours God sent. We bought our own house in London and, as the years passed, saved enough money to start building this house.

'Though we're Grenadians by birth, we feel we're also English – our children were all raised in the UK and are now all settled there. With our three kids in England, and with their children – our grandchildren – settled there too, I have to divide my time between the UK and Grenada.'

Hammond has come back to farm again. He loves farming.

'That you were sent to us is a miracle,' Cousin Syie says.

I'm not sure I understand.

She takes my hands in hers. 'How would you like to come and live with us, Johnson?'

'With you? But, I . . .'

'We've spoken to your mother. I went to see her this morning.' She pauses. 'It's OK, Johnson, she told us everything.'

'There's no need for you to go back to your aunt in Red Mud,' Hammond says.

'When I'm in England, which is a lot of the time, Hammond is here on his own,' Cousin Syie says. 'He gets lonely. But you can be with him. You can help him on the farm. Your mummy says you like to farm.'

'I do a bit of work for Old Man Baptiste,' I say.

'We will clothe you and feed you and look after you,' Cousin Syie says. 'You'll be safe here, Johnson. What do you say?'

There is nothing to say.

It's like my Cousin Syie said. It's a miracle.

The first thing Cousin Syie and my grand uncle do is take me out to buy clothes and shoes in St George's. We go in Hammond's Land Rover. Sitting in the back, watching him work the gears and the steering wheel as we twist and turn on a road that I've only ever seen before from the seat of a bus or in my imagination, I tell myself I'm in Heaven.

The Land Rover smells of oil, leather and rust. It's more than twenty years old, but it works just fine and will last another twenty years at least, Hammond says, which means he will be dead before it is. He chuckles to himself as he says this, and Cousin Syie tells him not to be morbid. I ask what morbid means and she says it's when you dwell on bad stuff, and I tell her that that's not my way, that my gran taught me always to look on the positive.

Cousin Syie tells me this is a really good thing and that she would like to get to know my gran better.

'She be comin' back from me Tan Jane's place in Annandale any day now,' I tell her. 'I miss her so much, Cousin Syie.'

She turns round and looks at me. 'It's important for you to know that you can visit your family any time you like,' she says. 'We want you to feel at home, but you must never, ever feel that you're a prisoner. You must see your mother, brothers and sisters whenever you like. You must go and visit your gran. All we expect – all we ask – is that you tell us where you are so we don't worry about you. I've promised your mother that we'll take the best possible care of you.'

'There's one other thing,' Hammond says.

'Yes, Grand Uncle?'

'Your mother tells us that you don't like school. Is that correct?'

Yes, I tell him. I don't care for school at all.

'Getting an education, Johnson, is the most important thing in the world. Anybody who is anybody in this life always has an education.'

I stop watching the road. A small alarm bell rings in my head. 'How can something be good for you when it makes you sick?' I say.

Cousin Syie laughs. 'Nobody gets sick from school, Johnson. You might not like school, but it doesn't make you ill.'

'But it does, Cousin Syie. When I'm sittin' in the classroom I can't breathe. I feel sick.'

'You have to attend school,' Hammond says.

Cousin Syie touches Hammond's arm. He stares straight ahead.

She turns to me. 'You'll have proper clothes and shoes. We'll pay your lunch money. That will make a big difference to the way you feel about school. There won't be any more times when you go hungry, Johnson. Those days are over. Being hungry can make you feel ill.'

'But I'm not hungry. I eat every day 'cos I work in the kitchens. They feed us in return for the work we do. Doin' stuff with me hands, even if it means doing the washin' up, is better than sittin' in a classroom.'

'There will be no further need to work in the kitchens,' Hammond says.

He keeps looking straight ahead and grips the wheel so tight I can see his knuckles go white.

'Promise me you will give it a try,' Cousin Syie says.

I take a deep breath and nod.

We pass the landfill site and Cousin Syie holds a handkerchief over her mouth and nose. We pass by the big cement works, then wind our way past the sports stadium, up over the hill where the cemetery is and then down towards the port and the town centre.

High on a rock overlooking the town is Fort Rupert.

It was there, Hammond says, that Prime Minister Maurice Bishop, God rest his soul, was murdered by his arch-rival Bernard Coard, which gave the Americans their excuse to invade the island in 1983. You were three at the time, he tells me, too young to remember a whole lot about it.

But I remember one thing – the sound of helicopters. And whenever I hear a helicopter, I think of sweets. My brother Jude told me that people tell stories about the Americans flying around dropping sweets. But Jude swears the Americans never dropped any sweets on Diego Piece and he never actually met anyone, anywhere, who saw sweets fall from a helicopter, so it must be a shed-load of crap.

Cousin Syie coughs into her handkerchief.

Hammond tells me there's another word for it – *propaganda* – and that it must work, because if Grenadian kids like me get a good feeling whenever they think of America or, in my case helicopters, then that's the proof of the pudding.

Hammond wasn't in Grenada at the time of the invasion, but he tells me that Grenadians loved Maurice Bishop because he cared for them, really cared for them, and there's plenty of people in Diego Piece who wouldn't have homes if it weren't for him.

When I ask how come, Hammond says that Maurice

Bishop, God rest his soul, came up with a scheme where the government paid for wood or galvanised if you needed to build a house but didn't have the money, and you could pay the money back at twenty dollars a month, which seems like a lot to me, but Hammond says is really nothing. When Bishop died, the scheme died too, because a lot of the paperwork – details of who the government gave wood and galvanised to – got destroyed in the invasion. As a result, thousands of Grenadians ended up getting their houses for nothing.

When I tell Hammond that this would never have happened if Maurice Bishop had lived, that people would still be paying his government twenty dollars a month, he says I'm missing the point. Maurice Bishop was a good man and if I go to school I'll learn about him and a whole lot more.

We spend the morning going in and out of shops and I come away with T-shirts, shirts that have buttons and long sleeves, shorts, long trousers and Reeboks – shoes that are white and have laces. I pass the time on the journey back learning how to tie a bow on my knee.

Hammond is right about something. The clothes and the shoes make me look forward to school. I can't wait to show off my Reeboks.

'Gran!'

I burst through the trees and run around her vegetable garden. I've run all the way and my heart is pounding. She's humming 'Blessed Assurance', the hymn that is always on her lips when she thinks of my grandpa.

She opens her arms wide. Even though I know she has had diabetes and high blood pressure, I throw myself into her arms and let her cover me with kisses.

'How's me fav'rit gran'child?' she says, as she squeezes me tight.

'Gran, Gran,' I say, 'you're not goin' to die, are you?'

She laughs. 'I's not goin' anywhere. I's jus' fine.'

There's so much to tell her I don't know where to begin.

'Come on,' she says. 'Let's go an' watch the sun go down.'

We walk around the side of the house together, past the shower that my grandpa made and the bucket in the tree. The sun is already half in the ocean. Between the sunset and my gran and I are the blue-green waves, sea birds riding across the sky, ships steaming to and from St George's, the islands of Carriacou and Petit Martinique – and the smudge on the horizon that is probably St Vincent.

'I missed this,' my gran says.

'Me too,' I say.

'T'ings got worse, but now they better – ain' that right?' she says.

I close my eyes and think back to the last time I saw her and try to picture in my mind's eye all the things that have happened in between.

I try to see Abigail and the shack, the school that makes me feel sick, the flip-flops I owned for a day, all kinds of bad stuff, but the pictures don't come. Instead I see the things I made, Kellon's dad, the tools he gave me, the yard that I made good, the donkey, and his friends: the goat, the cow, the rabbit and the cockerel. I see my brothers and sisters, Hammond and Cousin Syie, and my brand-new Reeboks.

'You won't believe what's happened to me,' I tell her.

'Well,' she says, 'we got all the time in the worl' to talk about it.'

The sun slips below the horizon and my gran gives my shoulders a squeeze.

'Look at the state of me garden,' she says.

She has been away for months. The grass is as tall as my knees and there's a lot of fruit that's fallen on the ground.

'I'm sorry, Gran,' I say, 'I shoulda look after it for you.'

'Never min',' she says, and kisses the top of my head. 'We get it lookin' perfec' again in no time.'

She gets to her feet and wanders into the bushes on the edge of her vegetable garden.

When she reappears she's clutching a knife in one hand and a large green fruit covered with spines in the other. She sits down beside me and lops off the top of the soursop. Then she pulls two little spoons from the folds of her apron and hands one to me.

She doesn't say anything. There is no need. The soursop is my favourite fruit and my gran is back in her little house at the top of the hill.

We sit on the steps, the two of us, eating from the same fruit, the sky darkening around us.

My gran is right. She always is.

Everything has turned out just fine. And we've got all the time in the world.

CHAPTER NINE

Kellon, Joshua and I decide we're going to build a car out of planks of wood and some ball-bearings we scrounge from a pile of old farm machinery on Old Man Baptiste's plantation.

We build a box four feet long and eighteen inches wide for us to sit in, then attach it to a chassis. The chassis is made out of wood bound together with string and some of Kellon's dad's special glue, which he makes out of boiled fish bones.

Next we put on the wheels. The back axle is fixed; the front one is hinged and attached to a rope, so we can steer it left and right.

I hammer two strips of tyre rubber on to the mudguards over the rear wheels. To slow down, all I have to do is stand on them.

To begin with, Kellon, Joshua and I sneak off to the den during break and I do what I can before the bell goes. After a couple of days I start to lose track of time, stop fretting and take most of the rest of the day off.

I get a bit of hassle from my new teacher, Mr Narine, but there are fifty people in his class and he can't keep track of everyone. Besides, he's my cousin, and I reckon he's going to cut me more slack than Mr Sweeny.

Stephen, Gregory and Dexter don't care much about

building things and stay out of our way. Stephen says there's a name for what we're building – it's a dog cart, not a car.

Thanks to all the hours we put in, we're able to finish our dog cart in under a week.

The weekend is three days away and we all agree we can't wait that long to test her out. We drag the dog cart up to the top of the road and climb in.

Kellon sits in front, where he'll do the steering. Joshua sits in the middle. I stand at the back, so I can control the brakes.

At first she goes slowly. But as we round the corner by my nan's house, we start to really pick up speed – we're suddenly going twenty miles per hour, maybe twenty-five.

The limers raise their glasses and give us a huge cheer. The dog cart makes a noise that sounds like we've got firecrackers under our wheels. My feet start to vibrate. I can feel my insides shaking.

People run out of their houses to see what the fuss is about. I worry that Hammond might come out too, but with the wind in my face and the dog cart performing better than I dreamed, I'm not stopping for anybody.

My job is to control the speed. As we head for the next turn I press my foot on the mudguard. There's a bit of a smell, but the brake does the job and we go into the turn at the right speed.

I hear a scream from Kellon and he jumps out. He lands on his feet and barrels into a stack of boxes stashed beside the road.

Then I see what he saw: the radiator grille of Old Man Baptiste's Toyota pick-up; it's fifty feet away and powering up the hill. I can make out the top of Old Man Baptiste's bald head. He doesn't know he's about to kill us; he doesn't even know we're here.

It's too late to do what Kellon did; it's too late to jump. Joshua grabs hold of the rope. If he steers to the left we'll come off the road before Lou-Jean's bridge; to the right there is the narrowest of gaps between the Toyota and the rocks that rise up the hillside.

Joshua veers to the right and Old Man Baptiste hits his brakes.

Oh God, I say to myself, we're goin' to die here.

I close my eyes and a picture of my gran pops into my head.

Time stands still. I feel myself floating. I look down and see that I'm above the road. I can see the dog cart and I can see the pick-up. I can see us in the dog cart.

Joshua is doing what he can to steer for the gap between the car and the hillside. We're a second away from Old Man Baptiste's wheels. I try to close my eyes – I don't want to see this – but my eyes are already closed and I can't turn the picture off, so I look up and find my gran's hill and focus with all my might on the wishing tree instead.

Suddenly the sound comes back on – I hear the screaming of the tyres, the rattle of our wheels, the roar of the pick-up's engine . . .

'Woo-hooo!' Joshua yells.

I open my eyes. Somehow – I've no idea how – we've made it through the gap without a scratch on us or the pick-up.

I turn to see Old Man Baptiste skid to a halt outside Ena's shop. I keep watching as he opens the door and hurries inside. Then we're round the next corner and on to the last straight stretch of road before it bends and forks: left past the school and the Association, right towards Red Mud.

The road is starting to level out. I feel our speed dropping off. I've got water instead of muscle and bone in my legs.

I look at my hands and they're shaking.

'Was that Old Man Baptiste?'

It was, I tell him.

'Where is he now?'

I've no idea. We almost died back there.

'We gotta do that again,' Joshua says.

I don't say anything. Old Man Baptiste stopped at Ena's shop. Why?

The answer comes to me a moment too late – a second before we come out of the turn and Joshua and I are faced by a line of teachers.

Ena has a phone. Old Man Baptiste used it to call the school.

I jump on the brakes and the dog cart judders to a halt six feet from Mr Mark.

He's standing in the middle of the road, his right arm out-stretched.

My instinct is to run into the bush, but Joshua is never going to get out in time. Besides, we built the dog cart together, we faced death together; we might as well face this too.

Ten minutes later, after six whacks from Mr Mark's strap, I'm frog-marched into Mr Narine's class and paraded in front of his pupils.

'I've had it up to here with you,' he says, hitting his hand against the side of his head. Mr Narine is a quiet and patient man. It's really something to see him blow his top.

'You and your friends terrorise this village with your stupid pranks and games when all the time you should be at school. I take pride in my work; pride, I tell you.'

'I'm sorry, Mr Narine,' I say.

'This is a great school, with a great principal and many dedicated teachers. When you skive, you insult them and you insult me. Is that what you want?'

'No, Mr Narine.'

'Good,' he says. 'Because the next time this happens I'm calling the police. Now, you have a lot of work to catch up on. End-of-term exams are approaching. If you don't put the effort in, you will be straight off to Mr Mark again. And he, I've no doubt, will do what I should have done long ago – he'll tell your uncle and guardian, Hammond Beharry, exactly what has been going on.'

I've never liked Clarice Kotchway. She's twice the size of any other kid in the class and is always bossing people around. She tries to get kids to join her gang and those who don't, like Kellon and I, she either picks on or works on the other kids so they turn against us.

It sounds silly – she's a girl and I'm a boy – but she's afraid of nothing and nobody. If there is one person in the Samaritan Presbyterian I'm always going to have a showdown with, it'll be Clarice.

A few days after my talk with Mr Narine he tells us to get on with some homework in class while he leaves the room for a few minutes.

My pencil breaks and seeing as Sheldon, who sits next to me, isn't in class today, I open his desk and borrow one of his.

Clarice spots me and says she's going to tell Mr Narine, because – and these are her words – I's a t'ief and t'iefing is somet'ing she can't abide.

The only people who ever call me a t'ief are my dad and Abigail and when Clarice adds herself to this list my blood boils over and I yell at her that she can go jump in the land-fill. Clarice goes red in the face and lunges at me. She tries to grab the pencil, but only succeeds in taking a deep gouge out of the back of my hand with her fingernail.

I'm still short and skinny, even though I'm eleven now. Clarice, though, is the size of one of the WWF wrestlers I saw Hammond watch on the TV.

I look at the blood coming from my hand and Clarice says, would you like some more, because there's plenty more where that came from?

When she scratches me again something in me snaps and I punch her in the belly – at the exact moment that Mr Narine walks back into the classroom.

After break I'm summoned to Mr Mark's office. As I walk through the door the first person I see is Clarice. Behind her are Mr and Mrs Kotchway and next to them is Grand Uncle Hammond, looking serious.

Mr Mark is standing behind his desk with Mr Narine beside him. I glance at Mr Narine, but he can't bring himself to look at me.

'You know now why you're here,' Mr Mark begins. He comes around from behind the desk and stands between me and the others.

I look at Clarice, who is rubbing her stomach and smirking at me.

Mr Mark talks over the top of my head, as if I'm not there. 'The thing that surprises me, that upsets me, as I'm sure it must upset you,' he says, addressing my grand uncle, 'is that I know Johnson to be a good boy. All right, I grant you that he doesn't like his studies very much, but he seems so . . .'

He searches for the right word.

'. . . well, angry,' he says.

'He has not had an easy life,' my grand uncle says simply.

'Nor have his brothers and sisters,' Mr Mark says. 'Yet his brother Jude and his sister Jill were both exemplary pupils at this school and both passed with very good grades into secondary education.'

'Please, just take it from me that this will not happen again,' my grand uncle says. 'The holidays are almost upon us. I will deal with this.'

'Be that as it may,' Mr Mark says, 'we have to make an example of him.'

Mr Mark then does the thing I least expect him to do: he

sends me home for the last few days of the term to, in his words, 'ruminate' on my sins.

Hammond and I don't speak for the rest of the day. I go up to my room while he wanders up to the nutmeg grove. When I look out of my window I see him walking between the trees, his hands behind his back. I realise how much I've hurt him.

Later he knocks on my door and asks me to come down to the grove to help him. He needs me to do the thing that I do best: climb into the high branches to get the fruit that he can't reach with his ladder.

As we walk from the house I tell Hammond how sorry I am.

'This comes from hanging around with those friends of yours, skiving all day long, doing nothing . . . The Devil finds work for idle hands, Johnson. Do you want to end up like Mack and Joseph and Westy?'

Like the limers? I ask.

Like the limers, he says.

I tell my grand uncle that that's not how I see things at all. 'I wasn't skiving. I wasn't doing nothing, Grand Uncle. I promise.'

He looks at me, surprised. 'Then what were you doing?'

'I was buildin' things, doin' stuff. There's a difference.'

He shakes his head. 'This is how it starts, Johnson. You tell one little lie and it grows and grows. There's no difference. Skiving is skiving.'

'A lie?' I say.

'You lied to me. You made me a promise and you broke it. This is what hurts me most.'

He lets out one of his deep, long sighs.

'I've thought long and hard about what to do,' he says. 'How to fulfil my promise to Mr Mark that I would take some appropriate action over this.'

I'm not sure what 'appropriate action' means, but I've a bad feeling it is going to hurt a lot more than all the ruminating I've done in my room.

'I've spoken to your mother,' Hammond says. 'I've also been on the phone to your aunt. We all think it would be a good idea for you to go and spend the holidays with her.'

I feel utterly crushed. The one thing I never expected was that Hammond would send me back to Abigail.

'But me Aunt Abigail don't have a phone,' I say.

'I'm not talking about Abigail,' he says. 'I'm talking about your Aunt Jane.'

It takes me a moment to get my head around this.

'Me Aunt Jane? In Woodlands?'

'You're always telling us how much you like cars,' Hammond says. 'Well, perhaps you should find out what it is like to live, eat and breathe them for a while.'

My Aunt Jane and Uncle Chris own a vehicle repair shop on the edge of St George's. My gran stayed with them when she was recuperating from her high blood pressure and diabetes. I don't know Uncle Chris too well, but I love Aunt Jane.

'I don't know what to say,' I tell my grand uncle.

'Get this out of your system,' he says, 'because when you come back here again, you'll be straight back into school. Is that clear?'

'Yes, Grand Uncle.'

And this time, he says, no skiving, no liming, no sneaking off into the woods to build things. Just good, honest work.

CHAPTER TEN

Grand Uncle Hammond drops me off at the edge of St George's, where the main road meets the track that leads to Aunt Jane and Uncle Chris's garage. I can smell petrol and exhaust fumes alongside the stink of sewage.

I ask Hammond if he wants to come and say hello to Aunt Jane and Uncle Chris, but he says he's got to be getting on back to Diego Piece. There is nutmeg, cocoa and banana to pick. He'll come back in two weeks, he says, to take me home. He slips the Land Rover into gear and makes a U-turn.

Vines and creepers crawl through the rusty skeletons of cars and trucks on either side of the track. Beyond them I can make out the upper storey of the house my aunt and uncle built when the business started to take off and they moved from Annandale.

Tan Jane waves as I step aside to let a bright-red dumper truck limp past, its engine misfiring badly. She bounces up the track towards me, a big smile on her face, arms outstretched. Hot on her heels are my little cousins: eight-year-old Leesha, six-year-old Kim and five-year-old Nadia. A little way behind them are the toddlers: Ken, in a bright-orange T-shirt and no trousers, and the baby, Chunks, who is wearing nothing at all. I put down my bag and Tan Jane gives me a big hug.

'It's been a long time . . .' She takes a step back and looks me up and down. 'My, so tall now.'

After she has given me something to eat and drink, she sends me off to tell Chris it's four o'clock; he has to be at the bank before it closes. They're so busy they need a second repair bay, and must get a loan to build it.

She makes it sound as if money grows on trees, but I know it doesn't. It took a lifetime for my Grand Uncle Bill to make a million out of his bus; Chris and Jane are still in their thirties, and don't look like millionaires to me. Hammond said this is because they only charge people who can afford to pay them, and I can't make out whether he thinks this is a good thing or a sin. My grand uncle has all the things he has – his house in England, the house in Diego Piece, his nutmeg grove and his Land Rover – because he worked hard and saved hard. Chris and Jane just take life as it comes.

I find Chris behind the repair shop. His head is under the bonnet of the dumper truck that coughed and spluttered up the track behind me, but I know it's him because he's wearing a white suit that I remember from my last visit. He steps back, shakes his head at the bare-chested man who's sitting in the cab and signals for him to turn off the engine.

Chris is the best mechanic on the island. He's tall and lean, has pale skin and green eyes, brown, curly hair and a neat goatee beard. He doesn't look much like a Grenadian, but his accent is as thick as any on the island.

He turns, gives me a big smile and a high-five. 'Johnson, my brother, how's t'ings?' he says.

'Not bad,' I say. I can't take my eyes off the black handprints and smudges on his trousers.

The bare-chested man jumps down from the cab. He's not much taller than me but I guess he must be in his mid-fifties. He has long hair, a bulging belly and trousers that are held up by a piece of string.

He's joined a moment later by a guy around half his age in a yellow T-shirt.

'Good doctor-man, speak to me now,' the bare-chested man says to Chris. 'What is the problem with me pride an' joy?'

Chris scratches his head. 'Could be the injector, or could be a loss of compression caused by the valves or the pistons or both . . .'

Injector, compression, valves, pistons. I feel my blood pump a little faster.

'When will you know?' the bare-chested man says.

'When I take a look at her, Roger, my friend.'

'But you jus' take a look at her.' Roger spreads his hands, a vex look on his face.

'I mean, I need to give her a proper look,' Chris says. 'Roger, your pride an' joy, she's sick. I need to strip down she engine to tell you what the problem is.'

Roger bends down and puts his head in his hands.

'But we's needin' our pride an' joy now,' the man in the T-shirt says quietly.

'She can't wait till tomorrow?' Chris asks.

Roger sighs and starts to tell Chris how much trouble he's in and how only his pride and joy can save him. He needs her to pick up a big shipment of galvanised from the steel works and it has to be tonight because he's already spent the money he received from the builder who placed the order but he knows the night foreman at the steelworks and the night fore-man has said he can have a shipment of galvanised for free because the night foreman owes Roger a big favour but Roger has to pick it up during tonight's shift because after tonight the foreman won't be on duty for another two weeks and Roger needs the galvanised now.

Roger finally breathes in like a drowning man. 'It has to be tonight,' he says. 'Or I's a dead man.'

'We's dead men,' the man in the T-shirt adds.

As Chris starts to peel off his jacket I remember why Tan

Jane sent me over here. I make a big noise clearing my throat. Everyone looks at me.

'Uncle Chris,' I say, 'Tan Jane, she ask me to remind you about the bank.'

Chris's expression goes blank. 'The bank?' he says. 'The bank . . .'

He turns to the bare-chested man. 'Roger,' he says, 'this is me nephew Johnson. He stoppin' by us for a few days.'

I hold my hand out, like I've been taught by Grand Uncle Hammond.

Roger hesitates, then shakes it. 'Me friends call me Indian.'

'Indian Mahan is me main man,' Chris says. 'Anyt'ing I need, any toolin', any parts, bits an' pieces, anyt'ing . . . Indian, he can get it for me.'

Chris nods at the guy with the T-shirt. 'An' this is he nephew, Edmund.' He claps them on the back. 'No man had a better team.'

'An' the dumper truck . . . is their pride an' joy?' I ask.

'The dumper truck is an old Bedford and it is a total pain in me backside,' Chris says.

'Chris, good doctor-man,' Indian says, 'please don't talk about me pride an' joy this way.'

Chris shakes his head and rolls up his sleeves.

'What shall I tell Tan Jane?' I ask. 'About the bank?'

Chris glances at the sky. The garage sits in a bowl of land with wrecks of houses clinging to the hillsides. The sun is slipping towards the ridge behind the repair shop. It will soon be dark.

'You bes' be tellin' her that I go to the bank tomorrow, 'cos Indian an' Edmund an' their pride an' joy got a problem that have to be fixed.'

Indian is so relieved he walks over and gives Chris a hug. I turn to go, but Chris calls me back. 'You ever scrap an engine?'

'Me? No. Never.'

'You like to learn how?'

I tell him I would like nothing more in the whole world.

'Go tell Jane,' he says. 'Then come back here straightaway. We got us some work to do tonight.'

My job in this business, aside from learning how an engine comes apart and goes back together again, is to clean the parts that Chris hands me. The best thing for cleaning is diesel fuel and he sends me to open up the office, where he keeps the keys to all the vehicles.

I open the door and turn on the light. I expect to see something like Mr Mark's study, with a desk and paper on it, but there is no desk and no paper, only engine parts. They're everywhere – on shelves, on racks and spread out across the floor. Some are old and dirty, others are new and still in their boxes. I spot a big red phone on the floor, partly covered by an oily rag; it's the only thing that reminds me that this really is meant to be an office.

The keys are hanging from a line of hooks on a piece of hardboard pinned to the wall. I look for the set with the football key ring, put them in my pocket and lock up again.

Back in the repair shop, Chris and his chief mechanic, Coxy, have hauled a block and tackle over to the Bedford and are fixing chains to the engine. Coxy has two missing front teeth and dreads, and is wearing an old blue boiler suit but no shoes. Indian and Edmund are watching them nervously. Indian keeps staring at his watch.

Chris leans over the engine and undoes a set of bolts with a wrench. When he comes up for air I hand him the keys.

He points through the open doors – past Chunks, who is paddling in a puddle of oily water – to a vehicle that's parked up on the far side of the yard.

He tells me with a smile on his face that she's a Seddon Atkinson, a garbage lorry with a mash-up Perkins Diesel engine in her.

'Why you laughin'?' I ask.

It's just funny, he says; it's just Grenada. 'The government go and buy a whole load of second-hand garbage trucks, but 'cos they old an' cheap, they find out they can't get up an' down the hills. An' what's St George's built on?'

Hills, I tell him.

He hands me the key with the football ring and asks whether I know how to siphon a tank. I nod. I've seen it done. He gives me a can and a length of clear plastic tube. I walk over to the Seddon Atkinson, unlock the fuel cap, stick the tube into it and suck till I get the taste of diesel in my mouth. I put my finger over the tube to stop it flowing back into the tank, spit the diesel out and feed the end of the tube into the can.

By the time I've filled the can the engine is already out of the Bedford and resting on Chris's workbench. He pours half the diesel into a bucket, hands me a bristle brush and tells me to watch, wait and listen. He starts by removing the rocker cover, the exhaust manifold and the injector pump. Coxy holds the light and hands Chris the tools when he needs them.

Meanwhile Indian and Edmund roam about in the background like a pair of restless animals. It's starting to get dark and by now Indian is muttering the whole time about what the builder will do to him if he doesn't get him the half a ton of galvanised he's promised him by tomorrow. 'I's just goin' to have to take the truck and lie low somewhere for two weeks,' he says. 'Not'ing else for it. If I go home the builder find me an' kill me.'

'Where can you lie low in Grenada?' Chris says. 'Everybody know everybody.'

'An' everybody know you by your pride an' joy,' Coxy says. 'You got the only bright-red truck on the island.'

Indian has no answer to this.

It's almost midnight before the engine is back in the Bedford and Indian and Edmund are in the cab, ready to burn over to the steelworks so Indian can pick up his galvanised and save his arse from the builder who is otherwise going to kill him.

For the next week I hang around getting my hands dirty as Chris and Coxy work on the Seddon Atkinson. Chris is putting in a brand-new engine – a Cummins 180 diesel, supplied on the cheap by Indian, to replace the original Perkins.

Once the Perkins engine is out, Chris gives me an open-ended spanner, a ring spanner, a socket set, a paintbrush and a can of white paint and tells me to take it to pieces and number each part.

He gets me to lay out the parts on a piece of newspaper, like he did when he was teaching himself, then he tells me to reassemble it, using the numbers as my guide. If I get stuck, he comes over and helps me. He wants the engine to be back together again when Hammond arrives to take me back to Diego Piece next week.

Meanwhile he not only fixes up the Seddon Atkinson with a new Cummins diesel, but also replaces the old, mash-up automatic gearbox with a reconditioned high-low manual gearbox that Indian drops off as a thank you for getting him to the steelworks in time to pick up the galvanised. The builder is happy and Indian lives to fight another day. He and Edmund are now spending a lot of their time hanging around the repair shop.

With so much work going on, and the promise of more garbage trucks to fix up with new engines and manual gear-boxes, Chris and Jane have persuaded the bank to loan them that money. Work on the second repair bay will begin after I return to Diego Piece.

One morning I'm chasing after Chunks, who keeps running off with pieces of the carburettor that I've laid out on my workbench, when Chris calls me over to the office. A client of his, a driving instructor called Breezy, has broken down by Grenville, and it sounds like a burned-out clutch, so the vehicle can't be fixed on the spot. Chris asks if I'd like to go out in the tow truck.

I've never been to Grenville, the largest town on the east coast, but I've seen a map; I know the journey like the back of my hand: the bridges, the hairpin bends, the gorges, the descents and the climbs.

'What you doing?' Chris asks me.

I realise that I've been talking to myself all along.

It's foolish, I know, I tell him, but it's something I used to do when I was a little kid. Most of the time, I don't even know I'm doing it.

Doing what? he asks.

I tell him about the times I used to travel between Diego Piece and St George's on the bus with my mum; how I used to memorise the trip, every last detail of it, so I could replay it later in my mind's eye when I sat under my gran's cedar tree in my Porsche 911 Turbo 3.3.

Chris listens. I expect him to laugh, but he doesn't. 'From now on,' he says, 'don't look out the window. When we're in this truck I want you to look at me. Not me face, but me hands and me feet. Watch what I doing. Watch how I work the wheel, the brakes, the clutch, the gears. If you want to know how to drive, it's time you learned good an' proper.' He smiles. 'And here's another tip I goin' to give you. Get rid of them shiny white Reeboks and practise drivin' in you bare feet.'

When we get to Breezy's place, a small, single-storey house built into a bank next to the main road on the outskirts of Grenville, Chris parks up and heads across to a brown Datsun sitting under a galvanised lean-to, its bonnet open. Breezy is in the driver's seat, his window down, smoking a cigarette. He's as old as my grand uncle at least, with grey hair and the blackest skin I've ever seen.

I slide over, take hold of the steering wheel and try to turn it left and right, but it's stiff and barely moves. I kick off my Reeboks and try to work the pedals. The only way I can reach them is by sliding right down, with the edge of the seat in the small of my back, and this is how Chris finds me when he comes back to connect Breezy's Datsun to the tow bar.

I'm still fiddling with the carburettor the next day when Chris comes over and drops two blocks of wood on to the bench beside me. Each block has a hole drilled in it and a piece of string through the hole.

'They for you feet,' he says. 'Tie them on. Then see if you can reach them pedals.'

I rush over to the tow truck, climb in the cab and do what he says. I tie the blocks of wood to my feet and set them on the pedals.

Chris is standing by the door when I look up. 'They fit?'

They fit perfect.

I decide that the best place to practise my gear changes is in Breezy's Datsun, which is fixed now and awaiting collection. I'm still practising when I see Breezy ambling up the track towards the garage. He and Chris have a short discussion and Chris hands over his keys. I open the door and slide off the seat. I forget that I still have the blocks of wood on my feet and for a moment I feel stupid as I stand beside the car, trying not to lose my balance.

'Where you think you goin'?' Breezy says.

I start to apologise, but Breezy waves it away. 'Get back in,' he says. 'You goin' for you first drivin' lesson.'

I can see Chris over Breezy's shoulder, stroking his beard, a big smile on his face. He catches my eye and gives me a thumbs-up.

He's done a deal with Breezy: for fixing the Datsun's clutch, Breezy will give me two hours' free driving instruction. There's six days to go before I head back to Diego Piece, so this, I work out in my head, means twenty minutes each day.

My first lesson starts now.

As I settle back into the driver's seat, my heart is racing. Breezy squeezes his body into the passenger seat and hands me his key.

'How old are you?' he asks.

Eleven, I tell him.

He shakes his head and tells me that if I put a single scratch on his car he will chop me up in tiny pieces and put me in the oil-down he's preparing for dinner tonight.

I put the key in the ignition and turn it. The Datsun's engine coughs into life.

Breezy glances anxiously at the blocks of wood on my feet and starts telling me what to do. I act like I'm listening, because it's Breezy's car and I know I should be grateful. But I want to tell him that I've been practising for this moment as long as I can remember; that I may be a kid but I know what to do; cars are my whole life.

I say nothing, because Breezy looks stressed already, and right now I don't think he really wants to know about my Porsche 911 or the dog cart or what Chris has taught me or all the practice that I've been putting in on his Datsun with the engine off.

I dip the clutch pedal, slip into first gear and set the accelerator, just as I've seen Chris do it; then, slowly, I lift the clutch and feel it bite into the gear.

I feel it in the way Chris told me to feel it, through the vibrations that come up through the pedal, through the block of wood on the sole of my foot, through my skin, my bones.

'Handbrake,' Breezy says.

I release the handbrake and increase the revs. The car lurches forward on to the track, and Breezy grabs on to the dash.

We start to roll towards the entrance to the repair yard, bumping and grinding over the potholes, and now we're on our way I realise I've got a problem.

Being able to reach the pedals is one thing, but I'm too short to get a proper view over the bonnet. I don't want to admit this to Breezy – he's worried enough already – so I carry on, navigating by the trees and wrecked vehicles that mark the edge of the track.

I press down on the clutch and move up into second gear. I get a rush of warm air over my face through the open window. We're bouncing down the track and I'm about to move up into third gear, when Breezy suddenly lets out a cry that pierces my eardrums.

'In the name of God . . .'

I hit the brake as hard as I can and the vehicle shudders to a stop. Breezy jumps out and runs round to the front. I kick the blocks off my feet and stand up so I can see over the bonnet. There, in front of us – maybe three feet from the radiator grille – is Chunks, naked as the day he was born, his thumb in his mouth. When he sees me his whole face creases into a smile.

I open the door and get out. I scoop Chunks into my arms and he gurgles with delight. Breezy's just standing there, shaking his head and cussing to himself.

'Wh-what you t'ink you doin'?' he screams, as I carry my little cousin back to the car and open the rear door.

'I's puttin' Chunks in the back,' I tell him.

'Why?'

'So we can carry on with me lesson.'

'After what just happen?'

'Sure,' I tell him. 'Now we know where he is.'

Breezy doesn't see things the same way. 'The lesson is over,' he says.

He opens up the door, reaches into the back, picks up Chunks and hands him to me.

My little cousin and I watch the brown Datsun drive away, trailing a cloud of grit.

When Breezy comes back the next day we make sure that Chunks and the other kids are safe inside the house with Jane. We head to the end of the track, where there's a big turning circle, and I drive round and round, straining to keep my feet on the pedals and my head above the dashboard. But after ten minutes, just as I'm starting to make some really good gear changes, Breezy looks at his watch and announces that he's got to go and pick up someone he's teaching in St George's.

Exactly the same thing happens the following day, this time after only five minutes. On the third day Breezy tell me he's going to have to cut down on the lesson again, because he can't afford the petrol. I get two minutes of his time and no more. It's expensive, he says, trundling around the repair yard and the turning circle in low gear.

I tell Chris, thinking that my uncle will step in on my side, but he says he can't force Breezy to make good on his promise. I have to accept what I can in the way of driving time and be grateful.

On the day Hammond is due to collect me, Chris takes me out into the yard and points at the Seddon Atkinson. He's holding a set of keys in one hand and my blocks of wood in the other. 'If I done me job right,' he says, 'the new gearbox will work smooth as silk – an' she's got power steering.'

He places the keys in my hand.

'Me? I goin' to drive her? I ask, amazed.

He nods. 'I need to take her for a test. Make sure the new engine and transmission system work OK. I seen the way you drive with Breezy. I t'ink you ready. She all yours.'

'But I . . .'

'You want me to change me mind?' Chris says.

I shake my head and start walking towards her. With her cab so high off the ground, and her huge garbage bin and crushing system, the Seddon Atkinson always seems like a monster to me, and now I know I'm about to get behind the wheel she looms over me like my Grand Uncle Hammond's three-storey house.

I break into a run, then tell myself that this is not so cool and drop back to a walk. When I reach the Seddon I turn around. Tan Jane has come out of the house and is standing in the middle of the repair yard. She's got Chunks and Ken on her hips and Leesha and Nadia by her side. When I catch her eye she smiles.

Everyone has come out to watch me. My aunt and uncle must have been discussing this for a while. And when they look at me I see something else. They're proud of me. As proud as they are of their own kids.

Chris opens the door. He slides on to the passenger side, making room for me. I strap the blocks to the soles of my feet and he puts the key in the ignition and starts her up. The Cummins roars into life.

'Manual gearbox, exactly the same as Breezy's Datsun,' he says. 'You all set?'

I place the blocks on the pedals. Because the cab is high off the ground, I get a better view through the windshield than I did in the Datsun.

'All set,' I tell him.

He releases the handbrake. I press down the accelerator and start to raise the clutch. Slowly, like a great ocean liner, the Seddon Atkinson begins to move.

Out of the corner of my eye I can see Chris stroking his beard. I daren't look at him, but I know he's smiling.

I concentrate with all my might on what I'm doing and the way ahead. The track is a long way down. As I pass the repair yard Jane and the kids cheer and wave.

When we get to the turning circle Chris tells me to go around it and stay on it till I get the hang of the power steering. On my third go round he tells me to build up a little speed, then slip her into second.

I can't believe the power of this vehicle – the power of the 180-horsepower Cummins diesel. I wish I'd known about the Seddon Atkinson when I was little, when I played in the roots of my gran's cedar tree.

'Next go-around, take a right,' Chris says.

'A right?' A right turn will take me away from the repair yard, towards the road.

Chris waves his hands – go on, she's all yours.

I take a right and press on till I get to the junction. It's a Saturday and traffic is light. I indicate and ease the Seddon Atkinson on to the road.

Unlike Breezy, Chris isn't nervous at all. He puts his feet on the dashboard and offers soft words of encouragement. That's good . . . hold her steady . . . drop down a gear for the corner . . . perfect . . .

After a mile we turn and head back.

Just as we reach the track, Hammond's Land Rover comes round the corner. I follow him into the yard and park up behind him. He doesn't see me get out of the driver's seat, which is probably for the best. There are certain things Hammond isn't yet ready for, and the sight of his grand

nephew behind the wheel of a ten-ton garbage truck is definitely one of them.

It has been the best two weeks of my life and though I'm
sad to be leaving, I know how lucky I am, because I have
another home here.

CHAPTER ELEVEN

As the years pass, my visits to the repair shop act as a safety valve, keeping me in school and stopping me from falling out with my grand uncle. I keep the blocks of wood in my bedroom to remind me that, no matter how suffocated I feel in class, Chris and Jane are only a bus ride away from the Samaritan Presbyterian.

Each time I go to Woodlands I saw another inch off the blocks. By the time I turn thirteen I no longer need them to reach the pedals.

A year after he finishes the second repair bay, Chris builds a spray shop. Business at the garage is booming and I'm a part of the team. I carry out repairs and help Coxy with the spraying. I sit in vehicles under tow and move trucks around the yard.

In my early days there, some of Chris's neighbours asked him about the trucks tearing around the yard with no one at the wheel. Local people are very superstitious, so Chris had to tell them. They're not so scared now. An eleven-year-old at the wheel of a dumper truck is a whole lot better than a manitou.

I used to get five dollars a day, but now that's risen to ten. I'm making a fortune, but the most important thing is, I'm learning; I'm learning about business and I'm learning what it is to be a part of a family again.

In my last year at the Samaritan Presbyterian, almost all the children who started school with me in Grade 7 have now moved on to secondary education.

Joshua, Stephen, Gregory and Dexter left school as soon as they could. I see them in Diego Piece, hanging around by the standpipe, waiting for the moment when they will be invited by the limers to share their space on the wall.

Jude is working as a cook in St George's and Jill is at home helping to look after Jade, who is now at the Samaritan Presbyterian. All my other brothers and sisters have gone on to school in Sauteurs.

My dad hasn't stopped his drinking, but my mum has learned how to live with it. I'm still with my Grand Uncle Hammond and Cousin Syie, and I always make my visits home when I know my dad isn't going to be around. The only good thing about his drinking and gambling is that I know where he'll be on Friday night – down at the bar at the bottom of the village, blowing his week's earnings.

In the last three years Mr Narine has remained my teacher. Even though he knows I'm never going to be a model student, the fact that I'm honouring my side of the bargain – the deal I struck with my grand uncle to attend school without causing any trouble – has made him feel, I think, that his struggle to educate me hasn't been a complete waste of time.

I say goodbye to him when the summer term finishes, just before my sixteenth birthday.

'You still set on being a driver?' he asks as we sit together in his empty classroom.

Kind of, I tell him. Only trouble is, there's not much money in driving.

Money isn't everything, he replies, and I tell him I know that – I've seen it in the way that Chris and Jane work, and I've seen it in the way that he works too.

I see tears in Mr Narine's eyes. I know that his daughter,

my cousin Carol, has not been well – my mum says she has a cancer – and I wonder how you carry that worry in your heart and continue to teach a class of forty kids, day in, day out, when half of them don't even want to be there.

Through the open window the sun bathes the top of my gran's hill. The sight of it makes me say to Mr Narine something I never, ever thought I would; that I will miss this view. He tells me that your schooldays aren't called the best days of your life for nothing and I smile and tell him that now he's going too far. But I know that if it hadn't been for him, my Grand Uncle Hammond and Jane and Chris, I wouldn't be here at all, and I hold out my hand and thank him.

'So what are you going to do?' he asks.

I tell him that my plan is to put aside enough money to buy a garage by the time I'm thirty and that my first step on the road to achieving this is to accept a job as an apprentice panel-beater at a body shop owned by a guy called Kennedy in Sauteurs.

Mr Narine smiles and wishes me luck and I turn and walk from the room.

Although Kennedy pays me nothing, there are advantages to working for him. I learn quickly and the job is over by lunchtime, leaving me free to make money in other ways – mostly as a carpenter, building cupboards and shelves on local building sites – and at Chris and Jane's garage at weekends.

I don't mind putting in the hours, and soon find I'm pocketing more than a hundred dollars a week. A hundred dollars a week in our family – in most families in the village – means rich, but the only thing I spend my wages on is clothes; I don't mean just any old clothes, I mean the best that money in Grenada can buy. I wear Levi jeans, Ralph Lauren polo shirts and Nike trainers. Because I work hard, I take pride in the way I look.

The trouble is, not everybody sees things the same way.

The summer I turn sixteen my world turns upside down. First my cousin Ron is killed and then I get an infection that prevents me from working anywhere near a garage – probably for the rest of my life, if the doctors have their way.

Ron is killed when a boulder the size of a house detaches itself from a cliff and falls a hundred feet directly on to the bus that he takes to get to work in Sauteurs. His mother, Ena, and his brother and sister, Ali and Nesha, are devastated. We all are. Weeks later I get a fever, caused by an extreme allergic reaction to the paint used in Chris and Jane's spray shop. The doctors tell me if I go near the place again, it will more than likely kill me.

In the weeks and months after Ron's death, Ena, Nesha and Ali surround themselves with their friends and relatives. There's drink and music as usual, but things aren't the same. I don't think they ever can be.

When they close the music down – sometimes at one or two in the morning – Nesha and Ali head for a club called the Arena in Grenville. They're doing their best. They're trying not to do much thinking.

Me, I can't stop thinking – thinking about my cousin and the life that I've lost. I try my best to be a part of it all, but I always feel I'm on the outside, looking in.

I'm strolling back to Hammond's after another night on the wall, killing time with the limers, when a beaten-up Honda pulls up in the darkness beside me. The car belongs to a friend of Nesha, a decorator called Lexie who has a gold stud in his nose and gloss paint in his hair. Nesha is in the passenger seat, and three girls, her friends from Victoria, and Ali sit in the back. 'We's goin' to the Arena. D'ya wanna come?'

I look at my watch. It's close to one o'clock and I'm already heading for a showdown with Hammond. Since Ron's death and the news that I can't go back to work at Chris and Jane's, I've stayed out later and later, breaking my grand uncle's curfew time and time again.

Some nights, when the drinking and the talking go on till dawn, I don't even bother to go to bed. I wander up to my gran's, fetch her water from the standpipe, then head down to the Association and catch the bus to Sauteurs. Thanks to Kennedy, at least I'm working.

But panel-beating is a whole world away from mechanics. A whole world away from driving. And driving is my life.

'My brother,' Ali says. 'Get in.' He throws open the door and I squeeze into the back.

Grenville is twenty miles away and the road is winding and full of potholes, but we make it there in half an hour because Lexie is a fast driver.

The Arena is a house with a courtyard out the back where there's a tree filled with coloured lights. A guy working a turntable sits behind an upturned crate in a corner, under the open sky. We dance where we can and run for cover when it rains.

Tonight the place is packed. I get a Coke from the bar – an old fridge with a big lever handle manned by a guy who keeps change in his hat – and walk outside. One of the girls who came with us, Tania, glances up at me and smiles. I like the beat of the soca, and I would like to ask her to dance, but I don't want to make a fool of myself, so I stay put, standing on the edge of the courtyard.

Ali turns up with a Carib in each hand and stands next to me. He and I take the same bus from the Association each morning. I get off at Sauteurs and head for Kennedy's garage; he takes another bus to Grenville, where he work as a painter and decorator. Ali knows Kennedy and Kennedy is mean, he says. Kennedy will do anything to keep me on as an apprentice so he doesn't have to pay me.

'Forget cars,' Ali says. 'You know you can earn good money paintin' and decoratin', 'specially if you good. I seen the way you work, Johnson, the way you build t'ings. There ain' many people in Diego Piece who have what you an' me have. We should team up. Go into business, build our own houses, get rich.'

I smile. When he talks this way he reminds me of Ron.

'T'ink about it,' he says, and thrusts a bottle of beer in my hand. 'But right now, drink this and ask her to dance, my brother.'

I look at the bottle. I'm sixteen years old and I've never let a drop of alcohol pass my lips. I look from the bottle to Tania. Then I look at Ali.

'My brother,' he says, putting his hand on me shoulder, 'it's just a beer.'

He clinks his bottle against mine. 'Johnson, you have to loosen up. Take things easy.' He nods in Tania's direction. 'She likes you. But you won't get anywhere by sitting on that bony arse of yours.'

I raise the bottle and drink. It's bitter and cold. I feel it going to work. By my second Carib, I start to get used to it. By my third, I actually like it. By my fourth, I'm ready to dance.

CHAPTER TWELVE

Cousin Syie – Babby as we all call her – is home with Hammond again after being back in England and she has brought their son Raymond, his wife Irene and my cousins – her grandchildren, Darren and Gavin – with her.

I really like Raymond, Irene and my cousins. Irene is petite and pretty with a bright smile. She works as a nurse in England and dotes on her children; she has a soft spot for me too, maybe because Gavin and I are so alike.

After I've helped Hammond prune his orange trees, Irene takes me to one side and asks how I'm doing. She knows I've been hit hard by the chest infection and she has an idea. 'Come and see us in London,' she says. 'Darren and Gavin would love to show you around. You would love it, I know you would. It would do you the world of good to get away. Think about it.'

But I'm having too good a time with Ali, Nesha and the crowd that they hang with to give serious thought to anything else. I've also taken Ali's advice; I'm working less at Kennedy's and more as a painter and decorator.

As the bus bounces along the road to work, Ali asks me how things worked out with Tania.

'Who?'

'The girl at the Arena. That night we all go in Lexie's car.

She liked you and you liked her. Don't you remember, my brother?'

I've danced with so many girls since then and drunk so many beers I struggle to remember anything about that night, or any other.

Ali puts his arm on my shoulder. 'Johnson, my brother. Remember what I tell you. Life is for living, but everything in moderation.'

'Sure,' I say.

'Take it easy, my brother.'

The next night I'm sitting on the wall opposite my nan's, sandwiched between the limers and Nesha and her friends.

Westy and George are passing shots of rum across me to the girls and the girls are pouring them into a jug filled with fruit punch.

For the first time in months the boom-box is back on the balcony above Ena's shop. Ena is in the street, swaying to the music, dancing on her own. I watch her, drinking my beer and wondering which of the girls will come with us to the Arena, when Ansell joins us. He has started bleaching his hair and there are rips in his T-shirt. He high-fives Joseph, Westy, Mack and George; he's now a full member of their brotherhood. He hardly ever works; his girlfriend brings in the money for the rum he drinks and the weed he smokes, as well as looking after their three kids.

He leans forward. 'Johnson,' he says, 'you lookin' sharp, my brother.' He gestures with his glass to my jeans and Nikes. I know he's been drinking long before he got here.

'How many pairs of them trainers you got, brother?'

'Two,' I tell him. 'These and me Reeboks.'

'Your gran' uncle buy 'em for you?'

'No,' I say. 'I bought them myself.'

'Seein' as you got two pairs, then maybe you could see your way to givin' one pair to me, your cousin, who's in need of some shoes right now.' He laughs, raises his rum glass and clinks it against Westy's.

'How much money you make now, Johnson?' Joseph says.

'How much money *you* make?' I ask him.

Ansell, Joseph, Mack, George and Westy all laugh.

'Serious, for real,' George says. 'A hundred an' fifty a week? Two hundred?'

'That's me own business,' I say.

'Everyt'ing we have here,' Ansell says, 'we ready to share wit' you. Ain' that right, my brothers?' He nudges George, who produces a bottle and a shot glass from behind the wall.

'I got me a beer,' I say. 'Thanks.'

'Johnson don' drink rum,' Ansell says, leaning forward again so he can catch the attention of the girls. 'He not ready yet to be a man.'

'Leave him alone,' Nesha says. 'He's only just left school.'

I tell her I left school last year. I will be seventeen next month.

'Maybe he don' like the taste,' Mack says.

'How can a son of the soil not like the taste of pure white rum made an' bottled here in Grenada, from our own sugar cane?' Mack says.

I've had enough of this. 'I'll take a drink,' I say to George. 'I don't got no problem with rum.'

'All right,' George and Westy say. 'Respec', man.'

George passes me two shot glasses. The first he fills with rum, the second with water.

Everyone is watching me. I put the glass of rum to my lips.

'Drink her back in one,' Westy says. 'Then chase her down with the water.'

I tell him I know what to do. I expect the rum to burn my mouth and my throat, but it is sweet and cool. It doesn't burn at all. I put the glass on the wall and wash the rum down with some water. I close my eyes, and start to breathe in through my nose and out through my mouth. The tension and the pressure lift. When I open my eyes again, Westy has refilled the glass. I pick it up and drink.

'Respec', man,' Westy says.

I put the glass back down. Respect . . .

Me, Ali, Nesha and her friends leave for the Arena at midnight. The next thing I know, I wake up in my bed, the room spinning. When I close my eyes the sickness rushes like a wave from my head to my belly. Pictures flash in front of my eyes: the striped label of a bottle of Clarke's Court; the winding road from Diego Piece; lights pulsing at the Arena.

I manage to clamp my hand to my mouth as the vomit shoots up my throat. It seeps into my nose and through my fingers. I make a lunge for the door, but as I open it I throw up on the floor. My grand uncle is standing across the corridor. For a moment our eyes meet, then I run as fast as I can to the toilet. I don't have the strength to close the door behind me. I fall forward and spew my guts into the bowl.

I'm leaving the house to go to Ena's two nights later when I run into Hammond on the drive. He's carrying a basket full of oranges, bananas and plums. Since Babby, Raymond, Irene, Darren and Gavin went back to England he has spent all his spare time in the grove behind the house. He even takes a torch up there and tends to his trees in the dark.

I leave the back door open for him and the light from inside the house shines on his face.

'Where are you going?' he asks.

'Out,' I reply.

He looks at me with his big, sad eyes. 'Where did we go wrong, Babby and me?'

'I don't know what you talking about,' I tell him.

'What more could you want, that we haven't already given you?'

Me, Irene, Gavin and Raymond pose for the camera beside the Grand Etang, the volcanic lake in the centre of Grenada. The picture was snapped during one of Irene and Raymond's frequent visits to the island.

Gavin, me and Raymond cool off in a rock pool in the hills above Red Mud.

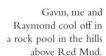

Me and some friends heading out on a trip to catch crayfish; Gavin is second from the left, I'm on the far right.

The yard behind Hammond's house. I'm on the left; Hammond's faithful old Land Rover is in the background.

A view from an upstairs balcony at Hammond's house, looking out towards one of the banana and nutmeg groves.

My Gran's passport picture – the only photo I have of her. It was taken a couple of decades before she died, but it captures the way I remember her. It stays with me, in my wallet, wherever I go.

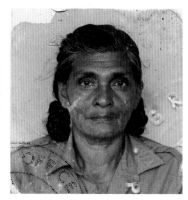

A typical scene in Diego Piece. The house in the foreground is Ena's – before it was knocked down and replaced by the home and shop where she lives now.

Chances are I'm bunking off school in this picture. That's me on the bike and Kellon on the right. The wall is where the limers usually sit, across the road from Ena's.

Slipping into some bad habits soon after I arrive in England. My life is starting to slide out of control again at this point. That's a bottle of Clarke's Court pure white rum in the foreground.

Working on a wall outside Irene and Raymond's house in Hounslow. Gavin and Darren are on the right. I'm never happier than when I'm building something. Check out the dreads.

Saying goodbye to my dreads the night before I head off to join the army. Irene watches as I get a tidy-up.

Getting ready for an inspection at Catterick.

Showing a healthy disrespect for authority in a break during my first field exercise; training, October 2001.

Preparing oil-down, Grenada's national dish, during the trip I made to the island at the time of my Gran's funeral.

Six weeks into my training at Catterick and I'm skinny as hell. By now I have a pretty good idea I'm going to make it as a soldier. My life is back in control; I'm happy again.

A typical scene from the suburbs of Al Amarah. Many of the buildings are old, the streets are chaotic and dirty and the sanitation leaves a lot to be desired – as does some of the local transport.

A patrol returns to the main gate at Abu Naji at sunrise. It became increasingly dangerous to take snatches – our long wheelbase Land Rovers – into Al Amarah as our mission unfolded. On the right, are some Warriors on QRF.

Iraqi youths surround a burned-out snatch in the aftermath of my first proper engagement – the day we deployed to rescue the CO's Land Rover group in downtown Al Amarah.

A snapshot of what we were up against – Iraqi militiamen armed with rifles and RPG-7s outside the OMS building before Operation Waterloo.

I don't need this right now, I say to myself, and carry on walking towards the gate.

'Enough of this,' Hammond says. 'Look at me, Johnson, when I'm talking to you.'

The sharpness in his voice, something I've never heard before, stops me in my tracks. I turn.

'You're staying in tonight,' he says. 'No more of this. You're shaming yourself. You're shaming your family. And you're shaming me.'

'Shame?' I say. 'Where's the shame in what I do?'

'The drinking, the girls, the partying, Johnson. It has to stop.'

I tell him I'm not a child. I'm no longer at school. I'm making my own way now.

'While you live in this house,' he says, 'you will obey my rules.'

Then it's simple, I tell him. I'll no longer live in this house.

I turn and walk down the drive. I open the gate, step into the road and glance back through the wrought-iron bars.

My grand uncle is standing in the light from the back door, his two dogs at his feet, his shoulders slumped.

Our eyes meet and the look on his face takes the sting out of my anger. Hammond is alone now – Babby will be in England for several more months.

I turn my back on the house, knowing that Grand Uncle Hammond is still watching me. One of the dogs lets out a low howl.

I feel ashamed, but I can't turn back.

The air is thick and damp and filled with the sound of crickets. I head up the hill. TV screens flicker in darkened rooms on either side of me. I smell roasting meat, spices, breadfruit, bananas and coconut milk; I hear music and laughter. The guys are cooking oil-down on an open fire on the corner by the standpipe.

Westy, George, Mack, Joseph and Ansell have been there, as usual, since the early afternoon. Ansell holds a piece of meat on the end of his knife and turns it in the flames.

I can see Ena, eyes closed, the pain of losing her son written all over her face, among the group of people dancing in the street.

'You want to stop and eat? We get us some manicou today,' Joseph says.

I thank him, but move on.

I reach the pathway that leads to our house. I brush past the noni tree. The smell of rancid cheese from its fruit hangs heavily in the air.

There's laughter inside. Jeffon and Jade chase each other between the rooms. I realise how much I miss them. The way they're playing tells me my father is not back.

I pull back the door and step inside. Jeffon and Jade stop their chasing game and stare at the person who has walked through the door. Then Jade's face breaks into a big smile. 'Johnson!'

He throws himself at me. The others rush over too.

It's good to be home again.

CHAPTER THIRTEEN

A three-quarter moon shines through the window above my head. I know that my father will be working himself into a fury as he weaves his way up the hill. I switch the radio off and listen. I no longer hear my mother. My father must not know that she has been crying. Seeing the misery he causes just makes things worse.

The little bed groans under my weight. She might have supported me perfectly when I was nine, but she struggles now. It's hard to believe she has survived all these years.

I hear the dogs barking. I count the seconds, a cold feeling in my stomach.

A shout.

My father is abusing our neighbour, a nice man in his sixties, out on his balcony enjoying a quiet drink.

There's a loud crash as my dad kicks in our front door. To get to the main bedroom – where my mother is waiting – he must go through ours.

I roll over, my heart in my throat.

My father is still on the porch. He hurls a final string of insults at the man next door. The walls of the house are so thin he could already be in the room with us.

Jade sits bolt upright in bed. I don't know if he's awake or dreaming, but he starts to cry.

I hear a voice telling my father to shut up. It takes me a moment to realise it belongs to me.

There's a terrible silence, the kind of silence that comes between lightning and thunder. Then, with a roar of rage, my father bursts into the room, nearly wrenching the door from its hinges. The moonlight is strong enough for me to see him clearly – and for him to see us.

Something glints in his right hand. An empty Clarke's Court bottle falls to the ground and smashes into tiny pieces.

My father steps into the room and trips on the corner of the little bed. He falls headlong towards me. The frame collapses and I scramble out of the way. He catches sight of the radio. He grabs it, raises himself off the ground and hurls it out of the window.

I'm in the corner, next to the big bed. My brothers and sisters are sitting rigid, their backs against the wall. Jeffon has clamped his hand over Jade's mouth.

To get to me, my father must launch himself across the bed. I don't like to think about what will happen if my brothers and sisters get in his way.

I run towards him, wait for him to lunge at me, then duck. I feel the swish of his arm as he grabs for me and misses. I'm where I want to be – by the door. I hardly notice the stabbing pain in my heel as I step on the broken glass.

My father stares at me and I stare at him. I turn and run, hoping he will follow. I don't know where I'm going, just that I need to be far away. If I go, maybe his anger will go too, and the rest of them will be safe.

Before I make my move, my father bends and picks up what's left of the little bed. There's a splintering sound as he pulls it from the wall. He lifts the bed above his head and hurls it out of the window as well.

I turn and run. He crashes after me, but only gets as far as the balcony before he trips and falls. I rush past the nutmeg

tree and into the bushes. There I lie down in a hollow behind
the saffron, my heart beating against my chest.

A few minutes later I hear my mother calling my name.
The sound is soft and haunting and I want so much to go
towards it. It cuts me like a knife to hear her say my name
over and over. But I stay where I am, perfectly still. I can't go
back. When I do, something bad always happens.

It's better I stay away.

It usually takes me about fifteen minutes to make the round
trip to the standpipe. Today, with the cut on my heel, it takes
a little longer. I guess it is between five-thirty and six when I
reach my gran's place.

She's sitting where she usually sits, on a large rock in front
of her house, singing to herself. When I get a little closer she
stops and smiles.

'Are you going to speak about it, then?' Her eyebrows
narrow, wrinkling her forehead.

'About what, Gran?'

'No use hidin' it. Somet'ing has happen. An' now you
goin' to speak about it.'

Maybe she heard something during the night, or maybe it's
written on my face. Somehow my gran always knows when
something is wrong. I tell her what happened. I tell her about
my bad behaviour to Hammond; I tell her about my anger
and shame at having to run from my own home. The words
nearly choke me, but I try to hold my head high and fix my
gaze on the place where the jungle meets the sky.

'I will never run away again, Gran,' I say. 'Never. Not from
anyone, or anything.'

My gran listens, her eyes closed, her face turned towards
the sun as it slowly rises above the hills. When I finish she
opens them again and stares out over the village. There's a
look on her face that is happy and sad at the same time. It's

the look she gives me whenever she has seen my grandfather. Her eyes shine.

'Is this how you want to end up?' she says. 'Fetchin' buckets of water from the pipe every day – an' doin' it for the rest of you life?'

I hesitate. I don't know what to say.

'Don't think I don't know what you do, runnin' around with them cousins an' friends, smokin' and drinkin' and wastin' all you money down at them clubs. Do you want to end up like him?' She gestures at the jumble of planks and galvanised that makes up our house.

'I don't smoke, Gran. Never have,' I tell her truthfully. Plenty of my friends do, of course, and I've seen what it does to them; I never like to lose that much control. But I've no answer for her on the drinking and she knows it.

'Me dad and me are two completely different people,' I say, staring at my feet.

My gran laughs. I look up. The sadness is still in her eyes.

'You know why he drink?' she says. 'You know what's eatin' at him?'

I say nothing. I'm not sure I want to hear what she is going to tell me.

'You father work hard all he life. An' for what?' she says. 'He see what you Gran' Uncle Hammond do for heself and know he could have achieved all them same t'ings. He angry with the way he life turn out. An' now it too late to change it. It eat an' eat away at him. Is that how you want to be?'

I'm never going to be like my dad, I tell her.

'Well, this is how it start,' she replies.

Her voice softens. 'When you was little, playin' in the roots of that tree, sometimes I look at you and I call you Michael, 'cos I forget – I t'ink it you dad, not you.

'But you an' him is different, Johnson. Every time you

make somet'ing, every time you build somet'ing wit' you hands, you make an idea in you head come real. You make it happen. You father, when he your age, he have all them same ideas, but he never act on them. He don' know how to. An that when he turn to drinkin'.'

'But why does he hate me, Gran?'

My gran sighs. 'He don' hate you. He love you, Johnson. It's heself that he can' stand the sight of.'

She turns and touches my face. 'You a good child – you smart, kind an' good. Do somet'ing with you life, Johnson. Don't throw it all away.'

I tell her I'm not sure where to begin.

No more drinking, she says. No more late nights, apologise to your grand uncle and come and live with me. 'You t'ink you can do that?'

I smile. Yes, Gran. I can do that.

I glance at the buckets I've carried from the standpipe. One of them is leaking so badly half the water has drained away. While Gran goes to make the breakfast I get up to refill it. I need the walk anyhow. It will give me time alone.

I pick up the bucket. The lid is leaning against the wall of her house. It's the lid I used as my steering wheel in the roots of the old wishing tree. I gaze up into her branches and see myself as I was then – as a seven-year-old racing driver, my head buzzing with ideas about my future.

I turn as I reach the top of the path. My gran is standing in the doorway, watching me. 'What choices do I have?' I ask her.

'People always has choices,' she says. She smiles again. 'You'll know what they are right enough when the time come.'

That night I dream I'm back in school, in Mr Narine's classroom, sitting a test. I have to write a story about my family. I can write anything I like, but I can't get the pen on to the page, no matter how hard I try.

When I look up, Roxanne and Clarice are laughing at me. Soon everybody is laughing; everybody except Mr Narine. He tries to silence the class but nobody listens to him so I get up and walk outside.

I cross the road and stand in front of the Association. The door is open, as usual, but no one is going in or coming out.

I go inside the building. Instead of crops, the warehouse is stacked to the roof with trays of eggs. I pick up a tray and look at it. A voice tells me that there are good eggs and bad eggs all mixed up together. But how do I tell the difference? I'm still trying to work out the answer when I wake up.

The peeling green paint on the galvanised above my head comes slowly into focus. I'm in the little room at the back of Gran's house. She's somewhere in the garden. I can hear her singing. I get up, stretch and walk outside.

The sun is below the hills, the village still in shadow. My gran is sitting on the steps, watching the fire she has made. A pan of rice bubbles above the flames. There's still time for me to get her water, have a shower, eat breakfast and catch the early bus to Sauteurs.

I'm rebuilding a car that got badly mash-up in a crash. If I fix it by the end of the week, Kennedy says he will pay me. I don't really believe him, but I still have a lot to do today.

I've thought long and hard about what my gran has said. It's time to get serious about work. The real money is in painting and decorating. Ali and my gran are right. I can do anything I want. When I have money in my pocket I have choices.

I tell my gran about the dream while I eat my breakfast. As I get to the part about the eggs I see her start to frown.

'Do you touch the eggs?' she asks quietly.

'I don't remember,' I say.

'Johnson, do you touch them?'

Something comes into her voice that make me go cold. I stop eating and look at her. 'What's the matter?' I ask.

'Ah'm needin' you to think – real careful,' she says slowly. 'Did you touch the bad eggs?'

'The bad eggs?'

'The bad eggs are the one that count.'

I close my eyes and think back. 'I knew it was important to separate the good eggs from the bad, but I couldn't tell them apart, so I didn't touch any of them.'

'You sure?'

'Yes,' I say. But the truth is, I'm not. The picture in my head is still fuzzy.

'What would've happen if I'd touched the eggs – the bad eggs?' I ask.

My gran spoons some rice into her mouth and chews slowly and thoughtfully.

'I don' know,' she says. 'Jus' be careful.'

She carries on eating. Twice I ask her what she is doing today, but she doesn't reply. So I kiss her and go down to the bottom of the village.

At the bus stop I meet Ali, who asks where I got to last night, and I tell him about the row I've had with my grand uncle and how I'm staying at my gran's now.

He says they're going out again tonight. Lexie is bringing his car and we can all go off to the Arena. I'm not coming, I tell him. Thanks, but no thanks.

'Johnson, my brother, what's wrong?'

Nothing, I say. I just don't feel like going out tonight.

The following morning it's raining. I lie in bed, listening to it hammer on the galvanised above my head. I wait for it to pass, but it doesn't. Soon all the lying around makes me late, so I get dressed in a hurry and go looking for my gran. There's no sign of her around the house. I look in the garden. I call and get no answer.

In the end I find her down by my grandpa's tomb. She's leaning on the top, standing with her back to the sun, staring out across the sea.

'Gran, what is it?' I ask.

'It's nothing,' she says. 'Don't pay me no min'. I's just thinkin', tha's all.'

She knows that I apologised to Hammond and that I've stopped drinking. Her mood has been strange ever since I moved in, but she tells me that's nothing to do with me. But I still feel she's hiding something.

'Gran, I got to go.' I kiss her on the cheek.

'Johnson.'

I turn.

'Don' do nothin' stupid today,' she says. 'Promise me?'

'Stupid, Gran?'

'Don' do nothin' crazy.'

'I've stopped all that,' I say, smiling. 'I've turned over a new leaf. You know that. I promised you already.'

'Come here an' hold me hand,' she says.

I put my hand in hers. There are tears in her eyes. During the night she has seen my grandpa again.

'I love you, Gran. But I've got to go.' I kiss her again, turn and run. Even if I sprint, it will take me six or seven minutes to get to the bottom of the village.

The bus is pulling away as I reach the junction. I yell for it to stop, but it doesn't. It's still raining and I'm wet through. Before I can open my mouth to cuss, a horn blares. I'm in luck: another bus is coming up fast.

I pay my fare and out of the corner of my eye I see the Association. The door is open, but no one is going in and nobody is going out. I remember my dream and a strange feeling washes over me. I realise it's the dream, not me, that's been worrying my gran.

I stand up and weave my way through the other passengers to get to the front. I want to get off, I tell the driver, but it's too late; the doors have closed and we're on our way.

The driver sees the other bus in front of us and starts to accelerate. Since Grand Uncle Bill's time, it's the one that gets to the stop first that picks up the passengers, and it's the driver that picks up the most passengers that takes home the most pay.

For a second or two it looks like we're going to overtake the other bus, but the driver in front realises what's happening and pulls away from us.

As we go into the next bend, the bus in front hits a pool of water. I watch through the windscreen as it skids, then over-corrects. A second later it veers sharply towards a bridge, either side of which there is a steep gorge.

The bus strikes the kerb and takes off. It flies through the air and slams into a telegraph pole. This stops it from going into the gorge, but flips it around in a half circle before it falls back on to the road in a shower of flying glass.

People pour out of the doors; some of them have cuts on their hands and faces; others look white like ghosts. Our driver pays them no mind. He veers around them, tooting his horn as he accelerates past.

'Why aren't we stopping?' I ask.

'Be cool,' he says. 'Everyt'ing just fine. Happen all the time on this road. There some crazy drivers aroun', drivers that shouldn't be allowed behin' the wheel of a bus at all.'

I watch the damaged bus disappear in the distance behind us, then we round a corner and it's gone.

When I get to work, Kennedy rants at me for being late, but I hardly hear him; I'm just thinking about Ali, my cousin. He wasn't on the bus with me. 'I going back to the bus station,' I tell my boss. He shouts something after me as I jog up the road. I can forget any hope of pay if I leave now. I don't care.

I spot a girl from my village. Judy-Ann is standing in a phone booth, her face wet with tears. The phone hangs limply in her hand.

'Have you heard the news?' she sobs. 'About the crash?'

'I was on the bus behind,' I tell her. 'I saw it happen.' I ask her why she's crying.

'Ali was on it. I just been trying to get through to the health centre. Someone told me he's been taken there.' She starts weeping again.

The health centre is on the other side of the town. I start running between the buses, looking at the names on the front, asking drivers if they're heading that way. Nobody takes any notice. Then I spot the driver of the bus that brought me here. It's packed with passengers. The driver has his feet up on the wheel. A flicker of surprise passes across his face as I climb on board.

'Y'a' right, man?' he says.

I tell him what Judy-Ann told me.

He stares at me, then says, 'Relax, man. You cousin get a little shook up, that's all. Happen all the time on this road, all the time . . .'

'I need to get across town,' I tell him. 'I need to know that me cousin is all right.'

'The health centre?' he says, taking his feet off the wheel and reaching for the ignition. 'Sure. Why not? No problem.'

I need to get there quickly, I tell him.

'Then me give it bus iron,' he says, flooring the accelerator.

The other passengers complain that we're heading the wrong way and the driver tells them why.

It takes just a few minutes to reach the health centre. I jump out and sprint through the main entrance. I throw open the door and enter a long, dark corridor packed with people. I hear raised voices, people demanding information. There's a lot of anger and the staff struggle to keep control.

Then, above it all, starting low but building and building, comes a wail full of such grief, such despair, that everybody stops and turns. I've heard it before. The night Ron died.

Ena.

I elbow my way through the crowd. Nesha and my sister Jill are talking to an orderly in round, silver-framed glasses and a white coat with a row of pens sticking out of his top pocket. Lexie, still with paint in his hair, is standing next to him. He looks dazed. He must have driven my family here.

A door opens and light spills into the corridor. My mum is standing there, her arm around Ena.

Ena's head is bowed, on my mother's shoulder. Broken.

Nesha and Jill are arguing with the orderly. Their faces tell me everything I need to know.

You can't see him, the orderly is saying, it's impossible. No way.

'He's me brother,' Nesha says. She is crying and shaking her head in disbelief. Jill tries to comfort her. 'You got to let us see him . . .'

Rules is rules, the orderly tells her, then turns and walks away.

I push past them and spin the orderly round. He sees the anger in my face. He puts his hands up.

'Relax, man, relax,' he says.

I've heard this said to me too many times today. I'm on the point of hitting somebody and the orderly seems to know it.

'Where is he?' I shout. 'Where is me cousin Ali?'

With a sigh, the orderly gives in. He drops his voice so nobody but me can hear him. He won't let Ena, Nesha or Jill come, only me.

I tell Jill and Lexie to take Nesha, Ena and my mum outside; get them away from this place.

The orderly leads me along the corridor and out through a back door. Suddenly we're in a courtyard, a sun-trap buzzing with flies. They're thickest above a Toyota pick-up. Its back is covered by a canvas tarpaulin, which the orderly lifts.

'Curious t'ing, you know,' he says. 'The crash only harm two people, one at the front and one at the back. Both of them killed. But nobody else have any serious injury on them – jus' cuts an' bruises.'

The two bodies lie on the flatbed.

The first is a man with what looks like a stake sticking out of his mouth. His eyes are open, staring at the sky. The stake has not cut his face at all. It looks like he's swallowing it. The point sticks out of the back of his neck. I don't want to look, but I can't help it.

The orderly tells me he was standing behind the driver when the bus hit the telegraph pole. The impact catapulted him face first into a bundle of firewood behind the driving seat.

The second body is Ali. There are no obvious injuries on him, except what looks like a fractured arm. The orderly tells me his neck snapped. Ali was the guy at the back of the bus.

'The undertaker – he come and collect you cousin later,' the orderly says, fanning the flies from his face.

'No,' I say. 'You wrap him up and take him into the hospital – now.'

The guy knows that I'm at the end of my rope. He nods and tells me it will be done.

Travelling home in Lexie's car – Nesha, Jill, my mum and Ena on the seat behind me – we pass by the boulder that hit Ron's bus. We say nothing. It's a year to the day – exactly a year – since Ron was killed.

This is what my gran saw. This is what the dream meant. My gran knew someone was going to die. But she was afraid it was going to be me.

CHAPTER FOURTEEN

Fate gives me a helping hand when Meryl Scott, my mother's cousin, and her husband, Neville, ask me to fit out their new house with built-in cupboards and then paint the place from top to bottom.

Like Hammond and Babby, Meryl and Neville have spent most of their adult lives in the UK and come back to Grenada to retire. The house they've built is not quite as big as Hammond's, but big enough. They want the work done quickly and the deal is worth a small fortune.

They've seen me work; they've spoken to my grand uncle and know that I will get the job done on time and do it well. Shannon, an old school friend, is going to help me.

Around the same time I start to date a girl called Lynthia. She lives with her family in a village down the road from Diego Piece.

I build myself a bicycle from two mash-up bikes that I buy for scrap. She's not a Porsche 911 Turbo, but she's good enough and I cycle to see Lynthia after I finish work.

I like her family very much, especially her grandad, who is full of talk about his days as a soldier during the Second World War. I've heard stories of German submarines surfacing off the coast by Point Ross, though I've never really taken them seriously. But, real or not, these kinds of stories made a lot of Grenadians focus on the war and ask themselves what they could do to help Britain fight. Lynthia's grandad was one of those who signed up.

As we sit out on the balcony and talk, I envy him his experience. He never saw action, but his army service was clearly the moment his life changed.

'Any chance you get to travel,' he tells me, 'you have to seize it. This is what the army gave me. A chance to see something of the world.'

He smiles and raises his glass – and from the far-off look in his eyes I know he's thinking of old soldiers, old friends.

'God is a Grenadian,' he says, then knocks back his drink.

'So He is,' Lynthia's mother agrees.

I say maybe I should join the army and Lynthia starts to laugh. 'With dreads that hang past you shoulders, the idea of being in anyone's army is pretty funny,' she says.

After sunset I cycle back to Diego Piece. I never much liked the dark and there are places on the journey that still scare me, even now.

The worst part is the stretch of road by the bridge, where Lou-Jean used to hang until his death a couple of years ago. Local people, including my gran, think he was killed by the Jablesse. The Jablesse lives by day as an old woman, but she can never completely disguise herself, because one of her feet is a hoof. By night she becomes a flying ball of fire that feeds on the flesh and blood of young men, which transforms her into a young, beautiful woman and ensures that she lives for ever.

A power cut has killed all the lights in the village, but the moon and the stars help me to pick out the road ahead.

As the road gets steeper I get off my bike and walk it up the hill.

A light breeze blows in off the hills. I hear a dog howl somewhere in the distance and I feel myself getting spooked.

It's close to midnight, but the air is warm. I look down at my arms; they're covered in goosebumps.

It's not just my imagination. I feel something in the air. It's like my gran says: something ain' right.

It's stupid, I know, but because no one is around, I figure it can't do any harm – so I cross myself, take off my T-shirt and turn it inside out. I put it back on again and turn my cap back to front, exactly as my gran once told me. If it's the Jablesse this will confuse the evil spirit.

As I carry on up the hill I sense somebody waiting just beyond the bridge.

I start talking to myself. Come on, Johnson, you ain' a kid no more, you nineteen, for God's sake . . .

But unlike my gran's, my eyes are perfect. The figure is still there and it's waving at me.

I pick up a rock from the side of the road, grit my teeth and walk on.

A few feet nearer and the hand that's waving at me changes into a banana leaf moving in the breeze. I'm so relieved I put my bike down, sit beside the road and laugh. I tell myself that I'm a stupid, superstitious fool, throw away the stone, peel off my shirt, turn it right side out and swivel my cap to the front.

I pick up my bike and continue on foot. I'm fifty metres beyond the bridge, when I hear a sound behind me – the sound of a shoe scraping on the road.

This time it's real.

I whip around and see someone emerging from the shadow of a house.

'Who is it? Who's there?'

'Relax, cousin.' As he moves away from the wall, the moonlight picks out Ansell's tight bleached curls.

'Been someplace nice, cousin?'

I've been someplace, I tell him.

'On that?' He points to the bike.

It works good, I tell him. I made it myself.

'Course,' he says. 'You make every'ting youself, don' you, Johnson? You doin' OK, ain' that right? I's surprise you don' have a car a'ready wit' all that money you makin'.'

'What's on you mind, Ansell? It's late, and I'm ready for me bed.'

'Me an' some of the brothers been wantin' to speak to you for a while,' he says. 'It about this work that you do . . .'

'What about it?'

'There a lot of people in Deego Pee who'd like that con-trac'. A lot of people that don't t'ink it right so much work should go to two people.'

I want to point out that Ansell has never done a day's work in his life, but I tell him instead that I got the deal fair and square.

'If you say so, cousin. But I t'ink you understand what I sayin'.'

'No, I don't,' I say.

'It would be nice – a nice gesture – if you give some of you brothers some of the money you makin'. The money go a long way to ironin' out the ill feelin' that exists wit' some of them. After all, you know that what we got we always happy to share wit' you . . .'

In the moonlight, I can see that he's holding up a bottle of Clarke's Court.

'No thanks,' I tell him. I turn and start walking up the hill.

'Johnson!'

His sharp tone makes me stop.

'I ain' done talkin' wit' you.'

'What is it you want, Ansell? You want money? Is that what you askin' from me?'

'Give it to me an' I see it get to the right people,' he says.

I see something glint low down by his waist. He has a knife in his other hand.

'You t'ink you better than we – is that right, cousin?'

'I work hard for me money, Ansell.'

'Then share a little, brother.'

'Fuck you,' I tell him, and carry on up the hill.

As I walk, the goosebumps come right back.

I strain to hear the slightest sound that Ansell is following me, but when I reach the corner and look back, he's gone.

I'm putting the finishing touches to a cupboard in Meryl and Neville's bedroom, when there's a sharp knock on the door. They are not in and Shannon is in the basement painting the kitchen. I open the front door and there is my mother. She's crying and my first thought is that this is about my father. But it's nothing to do with him. It's about what happened last night.

There are people in the village who are out to get me. She's terrified that something bad is going to happen to me.

'I so scared that somet'ing happen to you like what happen to Lou-Jean.'

Lou-Jean was discovered face down in the stream under the bridge. He'd been dead three or four days, his clothes gone and his face eaten away by crabs, and nobody ever found out how he came to be there.

My poor mum. She's shaking. I take her by the hand. 'Nothing goin' to happen. You got enough worries without having to think of me. Go home. I'm fine.' I squeeze her hand.

'I'm scared, Johnson. I ain' never hear people talk this way before.'

'They full of envy, Mummy. That all this is about.'

'If it about the money, Johnson, then give them what they want. Just give it. Hand it over. Nothing worth this pain.'

I shake my head and put a finger to my lips. 'Mummy,

quiet, don't vex yourself like this. It not about the money. This is about something else, something I feel real strong about.'

She wipes the tears from her eyes with her sleeve.

'They want money for nothing and that not right,' I say. 'What me gran always say?'

'Love, respect, honesty.'

I nod my head. 'All me life I work hard, Mummy. I never been afraid of hard work. If Ansell don't want to work, then that he business. But he ain' never going to take me money for sitting on he backside and doing nothing.'

My mother takes a deep breath and says slowly, 'God knows, I seen wha' happen to me sister when the Good Lord take she two sons from her. I seen what it do to her, Johnson. Do you want to do the same t'ing to me? Listen to me. The way they talkin', they's goin' to kill you.'

I pull her to me and wrap her in my arms. 'Go home, Mummy. Nobody going to get killed. Nobody. I promise. Go home.'

'What you goin' to do?' she says.

'I don' know. I talk to Shannon about it. He got a good head on him. Shannon and me talk it through.' I kiss her on the head. 'Go.'

I watch her walk up the hill, back to our house. I close the door behind me and set off down the road.

Everybody I expect to see is by Ena's house, either sitting on the wall or standing in the street.

The fire is going and Mack is fanning the flames with a banana leaf. Joseph has a small transistor radio to his ear. George is plucking a chicken. He has feathers all over his lap. Westy is holding a bottle of Clarke's Court up to the light, seeing how much is left before he cracks open another. Ansell is sitting next to him. There's something in his hand. At first I think it's a knife, but then I realise it's a piece of broken mirror. He's holding it up to his face and trimming his hair with a pair of scissors.

He pushes himself off the wall, the scissors in his right hand, the broken mirror in his left.

'Stay away from me and stay away from me family,' I tell him. I manage to keep myself from shouting, but he sees I'm angry.

'Easy, cousin.'

The commotion makes the limers stop what they're doing. George stands up in a cloud of feathers. Joseph puts his radio down. 'Johnson, be cool, my brother. Stop an' have some oil-down wit' us,' he says.

I keep my eyes on Ansell. 'I will never give you a cent of any money I make, is that clear?' I say to him.

'No call for that kinda talk, cousin,' Ansell says. 'No call at all.'

'If you have a problem with what I do, Ansell, you talk to me about it. If I see any fear in my mum's eyes on account of you, I'll kill you, is that clear?'

'Easy, cousin. Don' disrespec' me now.'

'How can I disrespect you?' I tell him.

Mack steps forward. He has a beer in his hand. It's a peace offering, and as I look at him I take my eyes off Ansell.

Ansell seizes the moment.

I duck and feel the swish of his arm as the scissors miss my head by a fraction of an inch.

I pull back my fist and drive it into his face with all the anger in my belly. He topples backwards over the wall, knocking down the bottle of Clarke's Court as he goes.

I turn and walk away.

'You's dead,' the voice shouts after me. 'Dead, you hear? You's a worthless piece of shit, Johnson Beharry. You never fit in this village. You don't fit on this islan'. You don't fit, you don' fit . . .'

He pauses to spit the blood from his lip on to the road.

I keep walking, my eyes on the point where the land meets the sky.

'You don't fit, you hear? You never have . . .' The words ring in my head.

'Even you own family don't want you. You own family t'ink you's a piece of shit too . . . You's dead, Johnson. Dead.'

CHAPTER FIFTEEN

That afternoon I cycle over to Lynthia's house. I need to get away. It's like my mum says: there's trouble in the air. People don't trust me. I see it in their eyes everywhere I go. I'm the guy who won't share the money he's making with people who need it. I'm the guy who lost it with Ansell. I'm the troublemaker. I'm Michael Bolah's son. I'm the guy who don't fit . . .

My mother is angry. I told her I wouldn't make trouble; I told her I would calm the situation down. Instead I've made it worse. My father is out on the porch drinking. Have I brought this on? I don't know. But I know the warning signs. It's best to stay away.

When I get to Lynthia's, two of her little cousins from St George's are playing out in the yard. Both of them are wearing Disneyland Florida T-shirts. They're just back from a holiday in the States.

These kids and their parents don't look flush with money. They don't look any different from any family you bump into in Diego Piece. But they've just been to America.

America.

'What is it?' Lynthia asks after dinner. 'You hardly said a word all evening.'

'I been thinking about you little cousins,' I say.

'What about them?'

I rub my eyes. 'I don't know. Sometimes I get this idea in my head that this island is the whole world. But it ain'.' I don't tell her about the trouble I've been having in Diego Piece. I don't want to frighten her.

I take a sip of fruit punch. 'Do you want to travel, Lynthia?'

'Sure,' she says, 'one day, when I finish school. What you drivin' at?'

I smile. 'Me gran always tells me that anything is possible. That I can do anything I set me mind to. But it never really cross me mind that I can leave Grenada. And now you two little cousins show me the way.'

She laughs. 'Two little kids with pictures of Mickey Mouse on they T-shirts?'

If they can do it, I tell her, so can I.

'You going to America?'

'Not America. England. To London. I've got an aunt and uncle over there – Raymond's my grand uncle's son and Irene is he wife. Irene says any time I want to come over, I can. My cousins Gavin and Darren too. So that's what I'm going to do. I'm going to go to England for a holiday. I'm going to go and stay with my Uncle Raymond and Auntie Irene.'

'Have you got the money for a ticket? It's August, Johnson. High season. It's going to cost you a fortune.'

I don't have the money now, but I will when I finish Meryl and Neville's house – in a week, maybe less. Then I'll fly to London.

'But you have to book the ticket. You can't just turn up at the airport.'

I know she's right. Of course I have to book a ticket.

Lynthia starts to laugh again.

'You don' believe me, do you?' I say.

'It's just that it's a bit sudden.'

'When I get an idea in me head I have to do it. It's just the way I am.'

The following day I go and see Grand Uncle Hammond. If anyone understands my wish to go to England, it's him.

I find him in the nutmeg grove above the house. He's halfway up a stepladder, pruning the branches of a big, healthy tree that will bring him a lot of fruit when it comes to the harvest next year. I can see the ladder swaying. I tell him, stop, I'll do it for you, and pull myself up into the tree. Hammond passes me the clippers and I set about trimming the upper branches. As I work, with him directing me, I tell him my plan.

'Are you sure this is what you want to do?' he asks.

'Quite sure,' I tell him.

'England isn't like Grenada.'

'I know. That's why I want to go.'

'It can be cold and lonely. The English can be cold too.'

'I'm just going for a holiday, Grand Uncle. They get a summer in England too, don't they?'

'Some call it a summer.'

When the pruning is finished Hammond says I can use his phone to call Irene and Raymond.

Irene is thrilled. 'When will you be here?'

'I've got to finish the job I'm working on. It will probably take me another week. I plan on coming for a month. Is that all right? Can I really stay?'

'Johnson, our home is yours, you know that,' she tells me. 'We've got room downstairs, if you don't mind sleeping on the settee. I can't wait to tell Darren and Gavin. They'll be so excited. There's so much to see here. They can show you all the sights.'

Two days later I catch a bus to St George's and book my ticket. I have enough money to pay the deposit, but the travel agent will need the balance before I fly. I take a deep breath. I'm cutting things fine. I've told Irene that I'm arriving on 7 August, but it will be touch-and-go whether I finish my painting job by then. But I've no problem with Shannon completing the contract – he's a good decorator and I trust him. It's how I get the money in time to pay for the ticket that's vexing me.

I see no way around it until my nan loans me the five hundred dollars I need. I arrange for Shannon to pay her back as soon as he finishes the house.

My mother is happy because she believes that my being away for four weeks will calm things down with Ansell and the others. And she knows I'll be in good hands in London.

During the rest of the week I tie up loose ends. I say goodbye to my mum, my brothers and my sisters, to Hammond and to Lynthia and her family.

On my very last night, after I finish work, I stop by Old Man Baptiste's. I find him out the front of his house with a group of workers who are about to go into his plantation for a night of harvesting by torchlight. He's older, thinner and shorter than the day he handed me a pair of shiny red and white flip-flops, but the look he gives me is the same.

Old Man Baptiste will go to his grave with one eyebrow cocked higher than the other. He still trusts nobody.

'What do you want, Beharry? You come to offer me your services?'

'I've come to buy something from you,' I tell him.

'Buy something – from me?' He's looking over my shoulder as ladders and machetes are loaded into the back of one of his pick-ups. 'Why not just take it?'

'Mr Baptiste, when was the last time I stole from you?'

He sighs. 'Probably around the same time you and those friends of yours almost piled into my pick-up in that damn boneshaker you built. What is it that you want to buy from me?'

'A coconut tree. A little one.'

'A coconut tree? What in God's name do you want with a coconut tree? Are you making one of your damn contraptions again?'

I shake my head. 'If there's somewhere you been, a place where you lived where you been happy, you plant a tree in that place. It's a kind of a . . . tradition.'

'Beharry, I don't have time for tradition. I'm a busy man, as you can see.'

'I know. So I'll take the tree now if you'll sell it to me.'

He barks orders to his foreman. Time is moving on and there's fruit to be picked. He wants to make a start before it gets dark. He doesn't trust his drivers not to put one of his precious vehicles into a ditch. By the time he gets back, he expects everything to be ready. Mush, mush, chop, chop.

The foreman relays the orders to the workers that Old Man Baptiste has bussed in from the neighbouring villages. Everybody is jumping about. Car engines turn. Tailgates slam shut.

I follow Old Man Baptiste to the back of his house. I expect him to send me with one of his servants to a field where he has hundreds of coconut trees, but we climb the steps to his terrace. Here he keeps a large number of pots with plants of all colours and sizes. It's a small piece of paradise and it surprises me.

He waves at a pot in the corner and tells me to take it. It's mine.

'But these are you own trees,' I say.

'Sure. So what? Trees are trees. Plenty more where they came from. And I don't want any of your damn money either.'

'I don't know what to say, Mr Baptiste. Thank you.'

I pick up the pot and turn to go.

'Beharry,' he says.

I look at him.

'I heard what happened down in the village.'

I say nothing.

'It took guts to do what you did. The tree is a token of . . . my appreciation.'

He sticks out his hand. 'Truce?'

I smile. 'Mr Baptiste, there been a truce between us now for a long, long time.'

'Well, just see that it stays that way,' he says.

He heads down the steps and disappears.

When I present my gran with the tree she starts to thank me but I hear the catch in her voice that she gets at moments like these and we end up, as we often do, in silence, on the steps, gazing out over the village and the mountains.

After supper we go into the garden to find a place to plant the tree.

'Here,' she says at long last. 'We plant it in the vegetable patch. I be able to see her every day when I come an' pick me veg an' fruit.'

'Gran, I'm just goin' away for a few weeks.'

She says nothing. The silence between us is so thick I'd need a machete to cut it.

'Gran, what is it?'

'I been dreamin' again,' she says. 'Dreamin' 'bout you.'

'A good dream or a bad dream?'

'I dream 'bout you a lot, Johnson. An' always it the same dream. I dream you walkin' along the road from Sauteurs to Deego Pee. I know the road, I see him, but he differen' from normal. There's all kindsa blockage – a boulder, galvanised, a dead cow, broken-down cars . . . so much blockage in the road. But you take no notice, you just climb over it or walk roun' it an' in the end you get to where you goin'.'

'That's good, then, isn't it?' I say.

'Yes,' she says, 'that's good.'

'But what does it mean?' I ask.

'It mean a lot of things,' she says. 'It mean you growin' up. It mean you won't be needin' you old gran so much as you used to need her.'

'You talk like I ain' never comin' back, Gran.'

'You ain',' she says. 'Not for a long time.'

'Gran, it's just a holiday.'

She shakes her head. You gran is right, she says; always is. She touches my face. I've never seen my gran crying before, but she's crying now. She's crying because it's almost dark and she thinks, with her bad eyes, that because she can't see me I can't see her.

'Now come along,' she says, suddenly, 'an' plan' this tree wit' me before she get so dark I trip an' break me bones.'

I get a little spade that she keeps in the house and I dig a hole two feet deep. I pull the sapling from the pot and am about to drop it into the hole, when she stops me.

'How long before you get a coconut on a coconut tree?'

Four, maybe five years, I reply.

She nods. Did I know, she says, that if you sit down while you plant a tree, it bears fruit a whole lot quicker?

I shake my head.

'Help me to sit down,' she says.

And so we sit, the two of us, side by side, up to our wrists in the damp soil, patting it down, and though I see no sign of my grandpa, I certainly feel him, and I guess that my gran does too, because she starts to hum and when she's done with humming, she begins to sing:

'*This is my story, this is my song,*
Praising my Saviour all the day long
Angels descending bring from above
Echoes of mercy, whispers of love . . .'

PART TWO

London, 1999

CHAPTER SIXTEEN

I'm sitting in a window seat, trying to get a look at England as the plane goes down, but we're in cloud. I can see nothing.

I go back to what I've been doing for the past hour, gazing at the engine that is hanging off the wing and wondering how it can develop enough power to keep us in the air.

The plane has been flying through the night, but I'm too wound up with excitement to sleep. The air conditioning is cold on my skin – I'm wearing jeans and a T-shirt with the green, yellow and orange of the Grenadian flag on it – and I'm looking forward to the moment when we land so I can warm up again.

I hope Raymond and Irene are there to meet me.

I left messages on their answering machine with details of my flight and arrival, but I never got a reply. I don't even have their address. I tell myself I'm not nervous. I met someone I know as I checked in at Point Salines – Michael, a cousin on my mother's side. Michael lives in the UK, so he knows the ropes.

He's sitting next to me, pushing his breakfast around his tray. He leans over to see where we are, but we're still in the clouds. He shakes his head and says he must be out of his mind.

'What you mean?'

'Look at it,' he says, pointing down towards the ground.

'I can't see nothing. Just cloud,' I tell him.

He shakes his head again. '*That's* what I mean,' he says.

Once we've landed, Michael points me towards a big hall filled with people and we part company. There are neon signs everywhere, pointing to 'Taxis', 'Buses' and 'Car Parks'. I'm standing staring at them, wondering which way to go, people pushing past me, when I hear someone call my name.

I turn and there's my cousin Gavin.

'Hey,' he says and we embrace. 'Did you get held up in customs?'

'Customs?' I say.

'They tend to take an interest in guys with dreadlocks hanging past their shoulders and one of those . . .'

He points to my ear.

Just before I left Grenada I got my ear pierced. My stud is a green and silver marijuana leaf. I reach up and touch it.

'There ain' no law against wearing one of these, is there?' I say.

Gavin smiles. 'Forget it, man. You're here, that's the main thing.'

A moment later Darren, Raymond and Irene rush up and greet me.

'Hammond gave us your flight details,' Irene says.

'You didn't get me messages?'

She shakes her head. 'Not your fault. Our answering machine's been playing up. Raymond called Hammond and Hammond got them from Jemilla.' She gives me a hug. 'Where are your bags?'

'I don't have no bags, except for this.' I point to the rucksack on my back.

'Oh, Johnson,' she says. 'You're going to freeze half to death.'

'They told me it was summer,' I tell her.

'Yes, Sweetie,' she says. 'But it ain' like Grenada. Not one little bit.'

It's almost midday when we finally turn into their street in Hounslow. The clouds are so low they look as if they're brushing the tops of the chimneys. It's still raining. It rains in Grenada, sure, but not like this.

I gaze up and down the road. All the houses look the same. There are so many cars that we have to circle twice before we can find somewhere to park Darren's Vauxhall Astra. When I get out of the car a plane as big as the one I've just got off screams in low over the rooftops, wheels down, wings rocking. The noise is deafening.

'I don't get it,' I say to Gavin as I watch it disappear over the next row of houses.

'Get what?' he says.

'We've been driving for almost an hour and we back at the airport.'

He smiles and tells me that this is a different airport. I landed at Gatwick. This is Heathrow, and there are two more London airports. You could fit the whole island of Grenada into the area known as Greater London, he says.

'You tired?' he asks.

I shake my head.

'Good. 'Cos as soon as you're settled in, it looks like me and Darren are going to have to give you a geography lesson.'

'A geography lesson?'

'You've got to see the sights. You know, Big Ben. Buckingham Palace. Oxford Street. Then we'll take you to some places we hang on a Saturday night. You up for that?'

Whatever they've got planned, I tell him, it sounds good.

Raymond and Irene's two-storey house has two bedrooms,

a bathroom, a lounge, a dining room and a kitchen. I'm sleeping on a blow-up bed in the lounge.

'I wish we had a bigger place,' Irene says as she helps me to unpack me things. 'But property is so expensive here. There's just no way Darren and Gavin can afford a place of their own.'

My cousins share the second bedroom. Gavin is my age; Darren a couple of years older. I say nothing, but I'm surprised. I always thought of Irene and Raymond as being rich like my grand uncle.

'Sometimes it makes me wonder why we stay,' Irene says with a sigh.

'But you're not Grenadian, are you, Auntie I?'

'No,' she says, 'I'm from Fiji originally. I've been here over thirty years. Raymond and I got married in 1973. I can't believe where all that time went.'

Raymond wanders in, drops on to the settee and turns on the television.

I sit next to him and try to concentrate on what he's watching, but I can't make head or tail of it. A girl is shouting at her boyfriend because he's just told her that he slept with her mother. He says he hates her and she tells him she's pregnant with somebody else's baby.

I ask Raymond if this is soap opera, something I heard about from Babby and Hammond. But he tells me, no, they're not acting, it's for real.

Gavin walks in. 'For real? Come on, Dad. I don't know how you can watch that stuff.'

Raymond takes a sip of his beer and says nothing.

After lunch Darren drives us the ten miles or so into Central London. I'm in the passenger seat next to Darren. Gavin sits in the back. He and Darren talk about the best route to take, while I study the concrete bridge above our heads. It's called a flyover and is at least a mile long. The only bridges I've ever seen before go across rivers, tiny rivers at that, but there is no river beneath the flyover, just another road.

There's so much to see, but everything looks grey.

We pass huge billboards beside the road, advertising airlines, cars, movies and razor blades. A little further on I see one with half a car stuck to it. I'm amazed. Somebody has sawn a car in two; what a waste.

I ask Darren about it, but he just shrugs; he doesn't know if the billboard is an advert for the car or a special kind of glue.

Five miles on, there are fewer streets and houses of the kind where Raymond and Irene live. Big buildings start to take over. Some are old and look like they could do with a good clean; others are new and shiny and made almost entirely of steel and glass.

We pass a huge one with railings outside and people milling around the front and I ask Darren and Gavin if this is Buckingham Palace and they laugh. No, it's just a museum, they say, and they don't know which one, because they're not really into museums, but somebody once told Gav there's a stuffed whale in there.

'He was probably pulling your plonker, mate,' Darren shouts, as he taps on the steering wheel to the beat of the music.

'Probably,' Gav says.

We drive on, through a park, and big drops of rain fall from the branches on to our windscreen.

Seconds later we're in a place where big old buildings rise up on all sides. Straight ahead is a place that looks a lot like the museum with the whale in it, but it turns out to be the Houses of Parliament, and right next door, something I do recognise – Big Ben. A police motorcycle shoots past us, siren on, lights flashing.

Darren turns down the music and takes a left. He points to

a tiny street with railings across it and tells me this is where the Prime Minister, Tony Blair, lives. It doesn't make much sense to me. When Hammond used to listen to the news on the BBC, Tony Blair was mentioned more times than the Queen, but he lives in a street that's smaller than the street where Raymond and Irene live.

We crawl on through traffic and crowds denser than I've ever seen to what Darren calls the West End. The plan is to park somewhere near Oxford Street, where Gav says there are shops I won't believe, and girls from all over the world who will take my breath away. Just talking about the place gets the two of them excited. Darren turns up the music again.

As we stop at a traffic light a van pulls up alongside us. I look at the driver, who's not wearing a shirt and has the window open, and I wonder why he's not cold. He's smoking a cigarette and talking to a man in the passenger seat, who's swigging from a can.

The driver glances at me and I smile. He turns to his friend and they both laugh. The driver turns back and says something to me, but I don't hear because the music is so loud and Darren and Gavin are talking about where we're going to leave the car. I wind down the window.

The man leans over and says something. He has tattoos the entire length of his arm. I lean closer so I can hear what he's trying to tell me.

'No, Johnson, don't!' I hear Gavin say.

'. . . that fuckin' jungle music down, you black piece of shit!'

These are the only words I catch, because the lights change and the van speeds away.

'Jesus!' Gavin shouts. Darren steps on the accelerator and we're off, chasing the van, but after fifty yards Gavin persuades him to stop.

We pull up at another set of lights. The van jumps them

and speeds off. I catch a final glimpse of the driver as he flicks us two fingers before the van disappears around a corner.

'Christ, man, I'm sorry,' Darren says. 'You don't need that your first day here.'

He and Gavin are more upset than I am.

What I don't understand is the hate I saw on the man's face. I've never seen him before; all we were doing was playing some music, but he looked like he wanted to kill me.

We're standing outside a club half a mile from where Gavin and Darren live. There's a long line of people ahead of us, being searched for drugs, guns and knives.

Everyone around me is black or Asian, but I don't feel at home. Darren and Gavin are wearing jeans and white singlets that show off their muscled arms. Most of the other guys around us are dressed the same. Most are wearing bracelets and chains. I see crucifixes too, with what look like diamonds in them.

Despite what Irene told me earlier, everybody seems to have money to burn.

The girls wear short skirts, heavy make-up and a lot of gold jewellery, their hair done in all kinds of different styles and shapes.

I'm wearing jeans and a T-shirt. Even my Nike trainers look tired alongside what I see here.

The rain has stopped, and I look up to the stars, but all I can see beyond the glare of the street lamps are the flashing lights of circling aircraft.

In the distance, a siren wails. I hear them all the time. The noise never ends.

I hear the dull thump of the garage sound that Gavin and Darren swear by. Every time the bouncers open the doors of the club to let someone in, the sound floods into the street and the girls behind me laugh and shriek.

We came by bus, because Darren and Gavin don't want to drink and drive, which seems strange to me because no one in Grenada gives it a second thought.

On the way Gav ran me through a list of things I should be careful about. Don't talk to any girls unless you know they're not with anyone. Be careful not to *look* at girls who are obviously with someone. If any guy tries staring you out, don't meet his stare unless you want a fight. And don't accept drugs off anyone.

They talk about a drug called ecstasy. You can get it in almost every club in the country, although it's usually white kids who are into it, according to Gav. Black guys tend to keep away from it, he says, because they don't like to lose their cool.

We make it to the door and the two bouncers frisk us. Then we go inside. It costs me twenty pounds.

At the bottom of a flight of steps we run into a group of girls who giggle as they move past us on their way to the toilets.

As we walk through some doors we're hit by a sound hurricane. The room is quite dark, with lights flashing above a dance floor. The people sitting at tables around the edge are all drinking and smoking. The heat and noise are unbelievable. The air is so thick I find it difficult to breathe.

There's a booth that's raised a couple of feet off the floor between the tables and the dance floor. Inside, behind a glass screen, is an Asian guy working the turntables and a black guy who's rapping along to the music. He rhymes so loud and fast I can't understand a word he says.

Darren nudges me. 'Come on,' he yells. 'Let's get a drink.'

We make our way to the bar. There are no guys on the dance floor, only girls. They throw their arms in the air and scream out the words of the song.

The guys are lined around the walls, watching the action. Some wear baseball caps, others wear sunglasses. I catch several of them looking at us. If someone looked at me like that in Grenada, I'd worry they'd be about to knife me.

'What do you think?' Gav asks as we reach the bar. 'A bit different from Grenada, eh?'

It certainly is, I tell him.

'What do you want to drink?'

'I'll have a Coke.'

'You don't drink?'

'Not any more.'

Darren and Gavin order themselves rum and Coke, then Darren spots some people he knows at a nearby table – four guys and six girls, most of them friends from their schooldays.

They make the introductions, but the music is so loud I can't hear a thing, so I end up watching the dance floor.

I get up to buy another round of drinks. Two of the girls are sharing a bottle of champagne; the rest are drinking rum and vodka.

The bill comes to almost sixty pounds.

I'm almost halfway way through my money after less than a day in England. When I take the drinks over to our table, everyone offers to pay, but I won't hear of it. I don't want to be seen as the outsider.

I go back to the bar and pick up my Coke. I decide I need some air and head for the door. As I move, my elbow catches something.

A second later I hear the sound of breaking glass.

I turn and find myself staring into the face of a tall, thin Asian guy. He has a gold ring in one ear and a diamond stud in the other. He has an expensive watch on his wrist, a gold ring, a bracelet studded with diamonds and a gold necklace with several gold rings hanging from it. In one hand he's holding a bottle of champagne. In the other he's holding nothing at all.

His eyes are hidden behind a pair of large mirror sunglasses, but I know they're not smiling. He looks at me, then at his empty hand, then at the floor. There's broken glass, ice and a pool of what looks like Coke by his feet. Some of it has splashed over his trainers.

I look up, see his lip curl, and the glint of a gold tooth.

'What the fuck you go and do that for?' he says.

It was an accident, I tell him. I reach for my wallet. 'Whatever it cost, I pay.'

He leans forward. 'And the shoes? What the fuck are you gonna do about *them*?' He spits out the words. I feel his breath on my cheek.

'Look, I'm sorry.'

People around us have stopped talking and are starting to stare.

'Sorry ain't good enough. What you gonna do?'

I open my wallet and pull out a note. 'That's for the drink,' I say.

He unfurls the money and looks at it over the top of his glasses. 'What's this Mickey Mouse shit?'

It's a Grenadian ten-dollar bill.

'Is this your idea of a joke?' he says, holding the note between his thumb and forefinger like it's got a bad smell.

It was a mistake, I tell him. I'm from Grenada. I just got here. I take the money back and look through my wallet for a ten-pound note.

'Where the fuck's Grenada?' he asks.

Gavin and Darren appear before I have to answer.

'What's the problem?' Gav asks.

'I spilled he drink. It was an accident. I told the guy I'm sorry and I'm offering to pay . . .'

Darren steps forward and makes me put my wallet away. No need for any money to change hands, he says, he'll take care of this.

'So what's *your* problem?' he says to the guy. Darren is powerfully built. To stay on top of his job at a security company, he works out a lot.

The guy with the gold tooth retreats into the shadows. 'Nothing, man. Easy. Easy. Everything's cool, very cool.' He looks at me and smiles. His gold tooth catches the light. 'I'm sorry, man. OK?'

The three of us watch him slink off behind the DJ booth.

'I think it's best we leave,' Darren says. 'You never know with lowlife like that. They're the kind who come after you later with a gun.'

We leave a few minutes later and walk back, dodging the puddles, eventually cutting through some side streets to reach the house. By the time I get to bed it's almost three in the morning. I fall asleep with the distant wail of a siren in my ears.

CHAPTER SEVENTEEN

Ten days after I arrive Darren and Raymond fly to Grenada to see Hammond. Gavin still has some holiday. We have been out almost every night and I've no money left. Partly because we're broke, and partly because I feel the need to do something useful, Gavin and I decide we're going to give Darren a surprise when he gets back. We're going to spend the next two weeks redecorating the second bedroom.

Then I get an idea. I'm thinking about it when I hear Irene come in through the front door. It's six a.m. I get dressed, fold away the sofa bed and walk into the kitchen. Auntie I is sitting at the table, sipping a cup of tea. It's been raining and her nurse's uniform is wet.

'Auntie I,' I say, 'I've worked out a way of giving you another room.'

She puts down her tea and rubs the tiredness from her face. 'Been a long night, Sweetie. I'm sorry. What did you say?'

'What you have here is a nice house, Auntie I, but you could really do with a third bedroom – that way Gavin and Darren would have their own rooms.'

'But there isn't the space,' she says.

'You do have the space, it's just difficult to see.'

A minute later we're standing in the middle of her bedroom. I point to the large built-in cupboard by the window.

I tell her how I can take it down and build a new set of cupboards and shelves either side of the bed. By using the original cupboard space, and by knocking the wall through and replacing it with two new stud walls – one where the cupboard is and one dividing what is now Darren and Gavin's room – I can make two perfectly good new bedrooms.

She nods slowly. 'I can see how it would work, but we'll need to get builders in. Raymond and I don't have that kind of money, Johnson.'

'It will hardly cost you anything. All I need are some tools and a few materials. These aren't supporting walls, Auntie I. Me and Gav can do it easy.'

We begin work straight away. Poor Auntie I. The next two weeks are anything but easy for her. When she gets back from her rounds – she works in the community, going from home to home – Gavin and I are already up and working, and for the rest of the day the house is filled with the sound of sawing and hammering.

We pull down the wall and put up two more. When Gav goes back to work I carry on by myself. I install the electrics and do the plastering. Then, towards the end of the two weeks, as I race to finish, Gavin helps out when he gets back from his job as a manager at a nearby supermarket. In the end the two of us have to work through the night and we're still working when Irene drives to the airport to pick up Raymond and Darren.

But it's all worth it. When they walk in through the door, they don't believe their eyes. It's now a three-bedroom house. Raymond thinks it will add another £30,000, at least, to its value. He's thrilled. Irene is thrilled. Darren and Gavin each have their own room. They're grinning like madmen.

Two days before I'm suppose to fly back to Grenada, Auntie Irene and I have a heart-to-heart. There's always a moment, around 6.30 in the morning, just as she comes in from work, and I'm up and about, when we sit around the table and talk. I tell her I've had an amazing time and that I will miss her wisdom and the warmth and love of her family. I'm sad to go.

'What are you going to do when you get back?' she asks.

I've told her about my trouble with Ansell, about refusing to give in to people who've never done a day's work in their lives. I don't have many choices, I tell her. To make money, to survive, I'll have to work as a painter and decorator. That's not a problem; I enjoy the work. The problem is Diego Piece.

How can I go back to a place where I don't feel I fit?

Irene listens patiently. 'You know,' she says after a long silence, 'I understand you a lot better than you think.'

I ask her what she means.

'I told you I came here from Fiji, didn't I? Well, when I was three, my mother and father separated. Mum had connections in England and wanted to bring me here so we could make a new life. But my dad kidnapped me and I ended up living with my aunt until I was fourteen. It was only when my mother's employer here in England threatened my father with legal action that he agreed to let me go . . .'

Her voice trails away and she takes hold of my hand.

'When I came to this country, Johnson, I could barely read or write. I was the class fool. I consistently came bottom of a class of thirty-six. They teased me, they ridiculed me, but it just made me more determined. You see, I knew what I wanted to be.

'Ever since the age of eight I wanted to be a nurse. But how could I be? I had no qualifications, no education to speak of. And yet I was lucky because one of my teachers, Mrs Isaacs, saw that passion, recognised it and knew how to channel it. She saw to it that I got the qualifications I needed. The rest – all the study, the hard work – was down to me.

Now, through my job, I'm proud to be able to say that I support this family. And I'm doing something I love.'

She gives my hand a squeeze. 'I often wonder what I'd be doing if I still lived in Fiji, Johnson.'

She pauses, then says, 'Think what you can achieve if you remain here.'

'What you saying, Auntie I?'

'What do you have to go back to, Johnson?'

'I think me gran will miss me a lot,' I tell her.

'Your gran is an amazing woman,' she says. 'But isn't she always telling you to follow your dream?' There are tears in her eyes. 'I've watched you growing up all those years at Hammond's, Johnson. I've seen the way you are. There's nothing for you in Diego Piece. If you go back you'll end up sitting on that wall outside Ena's. That wall will become your life. England may not be perfect, but it has allowed me to become something I'd never have become if I'd had that other life. It gave me a future. And it can do the same for you.'

'But what about me mum, me family?'

'Your mum is a strong woman. She can manage. And your brothers and sisters have their whole lives in front of them.'

'But what will I do here?' I ask.

'What do you *want* to do?' she says.

I hesitate. All my life I've loved cars, I tell her. When I was little I wanted to be a driver. Later, when I worked at Chris and Jane's place, until I got the chest infection, I thought maybe I could end up working in a garage – and perhaps even have my own one day. Now I don't know.

Auntie I puts down her cup of tea. When she looks at me there is a new determination in her eyes. She takes both my hands in hers.

'Let's make it happen,' she says.

'Make what happen?'

'Your dream. Let's make it come true.'

'How?' I ask.

She tells me I can become a student. All I have to do is to find a course that suits me and enrol, and then my visa can be extended.

There's all kinds of courses: electrical, mechanical, engineering . . . I can sign up to any one of them to end up where I want to go, she tells me.

'I never was much good at studying, Auntie I.'

This time it will be different, she says.

On paper it's perfect. I've signed up to do a course in motor mechanics at the local technical college. Auntie I lends me the money for the first term's tuition fees and the fact that I'm now a student means that my visa can be extended. Being on a recognised course also means I'm allowed to take on part-time work and, when I'm not studying, the theory is I can earn enough money as a painter and decorator to pay back her loan and fund the rest of the two-year course.

Although my family is sad that I'm not going back to Grenada, my mother agrees it's for the best. Ansell is still stirring up trouble, she tells me on the phone, and there are plenty of people who still think I should share any money I make with those who don't work and never intend to.

The best thing about the course is that the classes are some mornings and afternoons rather than all day, which leaves plenty of time for me to work as a painter, decorator and chippy.

The problem is, I'm still not one for studying, especially when the work seems to have nothing to do with where I want to get to.

Take today's lesson. I'm sitting in class, staring at a man who has just drawn a picture of a rectangle on the whiteboard. The rectangle is marked with symbols: a circle with a cross on it for a lamp, two parallel vertical lines and black rectangles for a battery, and a thing that looks like an open door, which is supposed to be a switch.

What I want to say to our teacher, Mr Inglis, is that I know everything I need to know about electrical circuits already – and if he needs the proof, all he has to do is come and take a look at Raymond and Irene's house, where I've just rewired the whole top floor. I know how to do these things from watching the builders back in Grenada.

Now Mr Inglis is talking about something called conductivity. Some 'mediums', like water, are good conductors of electricity, he says. Others, like air, are bad conductors. I hear the scratch of pens and the rustle of paper as my fellow students take notes.

He starts talking about negative and positive charges and how the air between them is divided between things called electrons and ions and how these collide with each other to produce lightning . . .

I look around. There are twenty-five people in the class and everybody except me seems to be hanging on Mr Inglis's every word.

I feel the four walls closing in on me. I look for some form of escape, but there is none. At the Samaritan Presbyterian my escape was the window and the view it gave of my gran's hill. Here there's nothing to look at beyond what's on Mr Inglis's whiteboard.

Later that afternoon, as I get off the bus, it starts to rain again. It's October and the days are getting shorter. It's also getting a lot colder. I pull up the hood of my anorak and dodge the puddles.

I try to imagine the warmth of the breeze that blows in off the hills above Diego Piece; the view from my gran's steps as she sits there, preparing dinner, singing her favourite hymn.

'G'night, Aaron. Mind how you go now, my brother!'

The voice makes me look up. The accent is Grenadian. A middle-aged black man wearing a narrow-brimmed leather hat closes a door behind him and glances at the low clouds. He turns up his collar, mutters something to himself, then disappears into the darkness.

I glance through the window of the pub he has just left. It's low-lit and smoky.

A guy with dreads is drying a beer glass behind the bar. There are a handful of drinkers. All of them are black.

Two men are playing cards at a table in the corner. A third is reading a paper at the bar. Another is putting some money into the jukebox.

A man is warming his hands in front of a wood-burning stove. He turns and I do a double-take because it looks like Breezy. I wipe away the rainwater with my sleeve and am a second from rapping on the window and yelling out his name. It isn't him, of course. The idea, when I think about it, makes me want to laugh.

I get back to Irene and Raymond's soaked to the bone. The lights are off; the house empty. Irene has left for work. Gavin and Darren are still at work. Raymond is God knows where.

I think about turning on the TV, but most of the programmes I've seen so far I don't understand. What I think is soap opera turns out to be real life, and real life turns out to be soap opera.

I lie down on the sofa and try to picture my gran's face, but try as I might I can't. I try to remember the words of 'Blessed Assurance', but they don't come either.

CHAPTER EIGHTEEN

Gavin and Darren know some guys who work on a building site in west London. Five months after I first set foot in the UK we meet up in a pub – me, Gavin, Darren, his friends and a couple of their builder mates. During the course of the evening Darren asks one of them whether there are any vacancies for a painter and joiner. They tell me that the firm is always looking for skilled labour and within a couple of weeks I'm employed for as much time as I can spare.

To start with I work for two days a week, but as time goes on I do more. The money is good and the work is varied and I don't need much of an excuse to dodge the classroom.

After months of jobbing around, moving wherever I'm sent, I end up working on a huge building project in north-west London and start to fall into a routine.

The days I work on the site, I get up at six, catch the tube, arrive at work by eight and stay till around four. Soon I'm pocketing close to £1500 a month.

I work with a mixed crew: Will, a stocky Irishman in his sixties, who is the main chippy; Zipi, a Bosnian who fled to England when his village was attacked and his home burned down; and Bryan, who is originally from Jamaica but dreams of relocating to Los Angeles when the film script he's writing gets bought by a big Hollywood film studio. He's so keen he keeps a notepad with him at all times and writes down ideas as we all talk together.

Every week we each put three pounds into a pot of money that goes on the National Lottery Saturday draw; and every Friday the conversation is the same – what we'll spend our money on when we win.

'So what *would* you spend it on?' Will asks me.

I don't really need to think about this too hard. I've no hankering to build a house of my own, because I don't feel settled enough to know where I want to live. I'd build a proper house for my gran, I tell them, because much as I love the place where she lives, it's small and it's old and it's not safe, what with her eyesight and her diabetes and blood pressure vexing her. I'd build a place for my family too, I say, because right now they live in a house that was built from wood saved from our old house, which got scrapped when my mum learned we didn't own the land that she was built on – and in any case, she's only got two bedrooms and there's seven people living under her roof. And there's Uncle Chris, who needs a proper facility where he can spray-paint the cars that come to him for repair. And while I'm thinking about it, Grand Uncle Hammond needs a tractor and trailer so he can get up into the nutmeg grove behind his house, instead of carting everything he picks in sacks to his Land Rover that's waiting below.

'For the love of God,' Will says, 'there'll be nothing left after that lot's got at it.'

'What *you* want, Johnson?' Zipi says, pointing his finger at me.

'For myself?' I say. 'There's only one thing I want . . .'

'What's that?' Bryan asks.

I tell him I want a car that'll get me from the capital, St George's, to my village, Diego Piece, in under nineteen minutes and twenty-five seconds.

'Why nineteen minutes and twenty-five seconds?' Will asks.

'Cos that's the record – the fastest time anyone's ever driven it – and that's the time that I got to beat,' I tell him.

Sounds mad, Bryan says, but scribbles a note on his pad all the same.

Leave him alone, Will says.

They're still talking about the Lottery – arguing about the size of tomorrow's jackpot – when I say goodnight to them. I listen to them as they disappear down the street. Will says it's five million this week, but Bryan says it's a rollover night and for once Zipi doesn't have to ask what that means.

As they all live in the same part of town, they go their way on the tube and I go mine.

On the way back, as the train rattles through South Ealing and Northfields, I wonder if anyone will be home when I get in. The odds are against it.

Irene will be on her way to work. Gavin has taken on more responsibility at the supermarket, so is rarely home before nine and Darren is doing a lot of night work to bring in extra money.

Sometimes Raymond is home and sometimes he's not, but when he is he sits in front of the TV and as I don't like the programmes he watches I might as well be somewhere else. If only I knew where.

When I come out of the tube station it feels cold enough to snow. Sure enough, in five minutes, little white flakes start to fall from the sky. I stand and watch them swirling under a street lamp. I hold out my hand and peer hard at each flake for the split second before it melts on my skin. I'm fascinated by the shape of them – every one of them so tiny and perfect. I'd love to show my gran one.

A man stands in a doorway in front of me, shaking the

snow from his collar. I think he looks a lot like Breezy, and then I think, I've been here before. I realise I'm outside the pub.

Home is still fifteen minutes from here and I've never felt so cold in my life.

Instinctively, I follow him inside.

The scene has hardly changed from the last time I looked in through the window. The guys sitting at the table in the corner are playing dominoes. There's a bloke around my age pressed up against a radiator talking into his mobile. A few others are standing around the wood-burner. The jukebox is silent and the barman with the dreads is reading a newspaper while he picks at a packet of peanuts.

Breezy's lookalike sits himself down at the dominoes table.

I ask the barman for a Coke.

'That'll be easy on the ice, yeah?' he says, pointing towards the window.

It's snowing a lot harder suddenly. I can't help it. I shiver.

The barman slides the Coke across the bar. 'You not been over long, then?'

Is it that obvious? I ask.

'No hat, no gloves, man. Either it's you firs' winter here or you's crazy.'

It's my first winter, I tell him, but I think I may be crazy too.

He tilts his head and sizes me up. 'St Vincent, right?'

Close enough, I tell him.

He holds out a clenched fist. 'Cameron, me young lion,' he says. 'From Jamaica.'

I bump my knuckles against his. 'Johnson Beharry,' I tell him. 'From Grenada.'

'Grenada?' He picks a peanut out of the packet and throws it across the room. It hits the back of the head of the guy with the phone pressed to his ear.

'Hey, Keely, man, one o' yours in tonight.'

Keely rubs his head exaggeratedly and snaps his phone shut. He swaggers over to the bar.

'This is Keely,' Cameron says. 'Keely, meet Johnson. You both from the same neck of the woods.'

Keely is dressed entirely in black. He's wearing black jeans, a black sweatshirt and has a black leather jacket to ward off the cold. He's also wearing a lot of gold: a necklace, rings and a bracelet all catch the light. His watch looks expensive and his mobile is top of the range.

Compared with the other Caribbeans in the pub, Keely stands out a mile. He looks me up and down. We couldn't be more different. My jeans, sweatshirt and Nikes are flecked with paint.

'What you drinkin', man?' he says. The accent is hard and, to my ears, very English.

Thanks, I tell him, but I've already got a Coke.

'And you just got in?'

I've been here a few months, I say.

'Then we gotta celebrate.' He claps a hand on Cameron's shoulder. 'Cameron, my man, I need to fire one. An' so does my brother Johnson. You got any Clarke's Court back there?'

Only the best – Appleton – Cameron tells him, and he gives me a wink – from Jamaica.

'Then, tha's goin' to have to do,' Keely says.

He slides a fiver across the bar and gets two large shots of rum. He passes one to me, raises the other and clinks my glass.

'To Grenada,' he says, and tips it back down his throat.

To Grenada, I say, and do the same.

'Cameron . . .' Keely points to our empty glasses. 'Fire us two more.'

'I'll get these,' I tell him.

'No,' Keely insists, 'they're on me, man.'

I tell him my story and he tells me his. It turns out his

parents are from Gouyave, but they have been here eighteen years and he has lived most of his life in the UK. Grenada is a place he knows only from visits to grandparents, aunts, uncles and cousins. He's no more Grenadian than Darren and Gavin are. As it's a small island, though, there are people he knows that I know – mainly in the Victoria area. Just talking about the place and the people brings it a whole lot closer.

We talk well into the night, drinking shot after shot of rum. Suddenly I notice the time. It's almost midnight. I have to be getting on back.

I slide off the bar stool and one of my legs gives way.

Keely laughs. 'Not used to the real thing, eh?' he says.

It's been a while, I tell him; quite a while, in fact.

I throw up in a pile of snow that's collected between a 5 Series BMW and a Mercedes S-Class parked at the top of Raymond and Irene's street.

The house is empty when I walk in through the door. I'm too tired and drunk to bother with the sofa bed. I pull the cushions and bedclothes on to the floor and fall across them fully clothed.

It's not long before I drop out of college completely and work full-time instead. Irene is disappointed, of course. But when we sit down and talk about it she agrees there's no point in throwing good money at something I really can't stand.

The work is good and so, for the moment at least, I plan on staying. I'm earning a small fortune by Grenadian standards, but after paying back my tuition fees and giving something every week to Irene and Raymond for my board and lodging, my money goes as fast as I earn it.

What Irene, Raymond, Darren and Gavin don't know is that I'm spending most of my spare time and money with Keely and another mate, Abs. They know I enjoy the odd drink, but they think I'm hanging with Will, Zipi and Bryan. Only I know how badly my life is spiralling out of control; and this time I don't know how to stop it.

One evening Keely invites me around to a friend's place. It's not far. The idea is to grab a takeaway pizza, have a few drinks, then go out clubbing. I get home after work, change and call him on my mobile to find out where they all are. He gives me an address that turns out to be within walking distance and ten minutes later I'm ringing the bell.

The door is opened by an Asian guy dripping with jewellery, topped off by a short fringe that's plastered on to his forehead with buckets of gel.

I'm still trying to work out where I know him from when he smiles and I catch a flash of a gold tooth. 'The man from Grenada,' he says.

He throws an arm around me and ushers me into the lounge. The air is thick with smoke. The smell takes me straight back to Diego Piece. If I were to close my eyes I would see Ansell, Mack, Joseph, Westy and George. Instead, through the haze, I see Keely and Abs. They wave to me. There are four unopened pizza boxes on the table. Among the glasses I also spot a bottle of Clarke's Court.

An expensive-looking sound system fills the room with a low, pulsing beat.

'Hey, Johnson, my brother,' Keely says.

The guy with the gold tooth still has his arm around my shoulders. 'Mr Grenada Man,' he says, 'we got off to a wrong start.'

'You know each other?' Keely asks him.

'Sure,' he says, turning to me and holding out his arm. 'The name's Aziz.'

I look at his hand.

'Hey, it ain' gonna bite ya.' He sniggers. Keely and Abs laugh too.

'Keely, Absy and me is old friends,' Aziz says. 'Come on, it was my mistake down at the club.' He's still holding his hand out. 'Any friend of Keely an' Absy is a friend of mine. How about a drink? I got us a bottle of Clarke's Court special. Keely's Grenadian, you know . . .'

He puts his hand in mine and we shake, hands clasped, brother-style, like we're about to arm-wrestle.

'That's more like it. You live pretty close, I hear.'

'Yeah, not far,' I say. I'm careful not to tell him more.

'Who were the two heavies you were with that night?'

I tell him they're my cousins. Good guys.

'Yeah, well, like I say, we all got off to a wrong start.' He reaches for the bottle. 'How do you like your rum?'

Straight, I tell him, with a glass of water to chase.

'The only way,' he says approvingly.

He pours out four shots and hands them around.

'To new friends,' he says.

We chink glasses and wash down the drinks in one. Aziz is quick to pour me another.

By the time I've had three I start to relax.

The joint comes around the table and everyone is taking hits. Even when I was partying back in Diego Piece I never smoked. Here it seems to go with the territory. I take a pull, sucking the smoke down. For a second I think my head is going to explode, then I let fly and hack the smoke back into the room.

'Whoa,' Aziz says, patting me on the back, 'someone's out of practice here.'

The next time the joint comes round, I know everyone is looking at me. I've watched the limers enough to know the routine.

This time the smoke goes down and it stays down. I pass the joint along.

The rest of that night is not too clear.

We try to get into some pubs where Aziz says he knows the owners and where, on a Friday night, they do a lock-out, keeping the pub open just for a group of regulars. But each pub we try is already closed, so we go back to Keely's place and smoke and drink some more.

By six in the morning everyone is on the point of passing out. Keely says I can stay, but I tell him I'm only just down the road and I might as well go home. Aziz staggers to his feet as I get to mine.

'Hey, Bro,' he says, 'we must do this again sometime. Now I know where you hang, I'll catch you down the pub.' He gives me a rabbit punch on the upper arm. 'Till next time, yeah?'

I step out into the dawn. Spring is supposed to be here, but the air is still freezing.

For once I'm thankful for the rain. It feels cool on my face. I need to sober up.

I suck in a great lungful of air. When I reach the end of the street I turn to check I'm not being followed, then quicken my pace.

I look up as the first flight of the morning – a BA jumbo – drops down through the cloud.

Ten minutes later I reach the house. I fumble with the keys and step into the hallway. I walk through to the kitchen, where I pour myself a glass of water and sit down at the table in the darkness.

As I drink, I think of my gran. I think back to the last time I saw her, how we planted the coconut tree together, and I remember what she told me. I thought I was coming to England for a holiday; I told her I'd be coming back.

But my gran knew. You won't be coming back for a long time, she said. She was right.

Is this what she saw?

I'm never going to be like my dad, I told her. Yet, here I

am, hanging out with Keely, Abs and Aziz; drinking and smoking myself senseless.

This is how it starts, she said, this is how it all starts . . .

I drink another glass of water and go into the sitting room. I want to be in bed before Irene gets back. I don't want to look into her eyes when she walks through the door. And I don't want her to look into mine.

When I turn on the light I see there's a handwritten note on the sofa bed. The writing is Irene's. I unfold it and hold it up to the light.

She says I got a telephone call last night. From Lynthia. She's finished school and is flying over to see me. She and Irene had a long chat.

Auntie I says she can stay here.

'That's good news, isn't it, Sweetie?' her note says.

I switch off the light and close my eyes, but I can't sleep.

CHAPTER NINETEEN

At the end of her four-week trip Lynthia says there is nothing for her to go back to in Grenada and that she wants to stay in England. Irene, as ever, is brilliant and takes it all in her stride. As soon as the new term starts, she enrols Lynthia into college.

A couple of days later I get back in the evening and hear a rap on the door. Irene is already out on her rounds. Raymond is watching TV. Darren and Gavin are still at work. I open the door, expecting to see Lynthia, who doesn't have a key, but Keely, Abs and Aziz are on the doorstep.

'Hey, JB, how's things?' Aziz says. 'I hope you don't mind us dropping by?'

'I . . . no,' I stammer.

'We ain't seen you down the pub in a while,' Keely says.

'Wondered what had happened to you,' Abs adds.

'You look surprised, man,' Aziz says.

'I didn't realise you knew where I lived,' I say.

'Got your address from Cameron, didn't we?' Keely says.

'Cameron?'

Aziz sniggers. 'You were legless one night. Cameron ordered you a taxi. You gave him your address. Ring any bells?'

Inside, a part of me is dying. I do now remember staggering out of a taxi after a heavy night at the pub. I must have given the barman my address when he called the cab company.

Aziz rolls up his sleeves. 'You going to ask us in, mate? It's getting cold out here.'

I have to think on my feet. I tell him I'd like to, but I can't – it's my aunt and uncle's place and they're expecting guests. It's a family occasion. I roll my eyes. You know how it is. Gotta be on my best behaviour . . .

As I watch them go, Raymond calls out from the sitting room. He wants to know who was at the front door.

Nobody much, I tell him. If Raymond saw Aziz, Keely and Abs, he'd have a heart attack.

Lynthia asks me what's wrong several times that evening, but I can't tell her. I can't tell anyone. How am I going to deal with this?

A couple of days slip by.

I go to work.

Lynthia goes to college.

Another day passes.

I start to hear the tick of a clock. Any moment now Aziz, Keely and Abs are going to come looking for me.

God, what am I going to do?

On the last day of the working week I'm on the tube, on my way to work, reading a newspaper someone's left on the seat next to me, when I spot something – a recruiting ad for the British Army. I read it and flick on to the next page. But something about it pulls me back.

Recruits don't have to be British to apply; Foreign and Commonwealth applicants will be considered on their merits.

Once the idea gets a hold inside my head, I can't shake it. Grenada is a former British colony, so I'm eligible. If I joined the army it would solve my problems at a stroke. I can remain in the UK. I might even get a British passport.

I'll also get a reasonable wage, but best of all, I'll break completely with the past.

As I walk on to the building site I feel like I'm on a

mission. It's like a light's gone on. Joining the army. It's the solution to all my problems.

I wait till lunchtime, when we're sitting down with our sandwiches and mugs of tea, before telling Will, Zipi and Bryan.

I have to tell someone. I can't keep this to myself.

'I, um, I'm joining the army,' I tell them.

Will stares at me. A strand of long white hair falls across his face. 'Is that a fact?' he says.

I nod. Yes, I say. My mind's made up.

Bryan reaches for his notepad. 'You're takin' the piss, right?'

No, I say, I'm not.

Zipi shakes his head slowly from side to side. 'My friend,' he says, 'think about this. Life in army very tough. I know. I spend three years of my life in army, fighting Serbs. There is discipline. There is boredom. But worst of all, there is times . . .' His voice trails away.

'Yeah?' Bryan says.

'I saw many, many things. I don't like to think about what I saw. But you, Johnson, my friend, you do not have to fight. Britain is not your country.'

'Hang on a second,' Will says to Zipi, 'who's talking about fighting? When the British Army went to your neck of the woods a couple of years back, they never fired a shot. It was the RAF that did all the work. I had a couple of brothers who joined the army after the war. They always said it was the making of them. Never fired a shot, but they loved it. And they're no great friends of the English either.' He turns to me. 'Is your mind really made up, laddie?'

I nod.

'Not sure it's all a bit sudden?'

When I know something's right, I go for it. And this is what I want to do, I tell him.

'Well, good on ya,' he says.

I call in at the pub on the way home. Keely and Abs are there, and Aziz turns up after Keely calls him on the mobile. I tell them I've made a big decision and I want them to be the first to know.

At first they think I'm kidding. The mood only turns serious when they see I'm not going along with their backslapping and high-fiving.

'The army is seriously racist,' Aziz says. 'You won't last a minute. What fuckin' planet is you on, man?'

'Yeah, the army is the same as the cops, they treats black people real bad,' Keely says. 'Don't do it. You're in a good job, earning good money. Why blow it, Bro?'

'And we'd never see you again!' Aziz flashes his gold-tooth smile. 'Ol' Aziz is always right. You'll be stuck in some shit-hole on the far side of the world, dishin' out parking tickets to Arabs. Don't do it, man. Stay here.'

He doesn't realise it, but this is the best reason I've heard yet for giving it a go.

The person who nearly derails me is Irene. She knows nothing of the people I've been hanging with, the crap I've been smoking and how much I hate myself for doing it.

For a year and a half she and Raymond have made me as much a part of their lives as their own children.

In return I've betrayed their trust, and the trust of everyone I love in Grenada.

Just distancing myself from Aziz, Abs, Keely and Co. is not going to work. It's not just them; it's everything. In Grenada I was just messing about. Here I can feel myself sinking.

I think of my dad. I have to start again. I have to make something of my life.

To break the silence, I ask Irene whether she'll help me find the nearest recruiting office. I've lost the ad in the paper. Is it something you can find in the Thomson Local?

Irene just sits there, shaking her head.

'It will break your mother's heart,' she says. 'All that danger. So much fighting in the world. Why do you have to be a part of it? Why put yourself in the firing line?'

We agree it's best, for the moment, to say nothing of this to any of my family in Grenada.

CHAPTER TWENTY

The next day I leave work early and head over to Wembley, not a million miles from the stadium.

The recruiting centre looks more like a shop than an office and I wonder how its plate-glass window is still there – the newsagent and off licence on either side are protected by serious amounts of heavy wire mesh.

A life-size cardboard cut-out of a black guy greets me as I walk in. He's wearing a T-shirt with a Union Jack and 'BE THE BEST' written in big letters underneath. His good looks and perfect white teeth make me wonder if he really is in the army or some guy they've pulled in from a modelling agency.

Perhaps I should forget all this and go home.

'Can I help, mate?'

Before I can turn for the door, a thick-set guy with a severe haircut gets up and walks around from behind his desk.

'Can I help?' he asks again. I notice the three stripes on his arm.

'You're a sergeant, right?'

'Right,' he says. 'What can I do for you, son?'

'I'm thinking about joining the army,' I tell him. 'I need . . . some information.'

He nods and walks over to a rack containing a load of brochures, but stops before he gets there. He hesitates, then smiles. 'A word to the wise, son. Do you smoke?'

Now that I think about it, a haircut might have been a good idea. My dreads have become matted with dust and paint. I'm a world away from the guy in the cut-out.

'I don't make a habit of it . . .' I look him squarely in the eye. 'But, yeah, I have.'

'Recently?'

I pause. My residency in the UK is perfectly legal, but I guess the Home Office doesn't need much of an excuse to deport me. I look at him warily.

'Listen,' the sergeant says. 'We get a lot of kids come in here. You've been unusually straight with me, so I'm going to be straight with you. If you're not clean, we can't use you. But if you still think you want to give it a try, get yourself sorted out, stop smoking that shit – it fucks you up anyway – and get yourself fit, then come back and see us in six months. Maybe then we can use you.'

'Six *months*?'

'Takes about that long to get the toxins out of the body.' He thrusts a box into my hand. Four guys and a girl wearing black shorts and T-shirts stare back at me from the lid. The video is called *Fit for the Best*.

He's back behind the desk before I reach the door. He doesn't give me a second glance. I know he's banking on never seeing me again.

'How were you so sure?' I ask. 'About the smoking?'

He looks up and touches his earlobe. 'The stud you've got there? The mari-ju-ah-nah leaf? Bit of a giveaway . . .'

My hand reaches up. I'd completely forgotten about it.

When I get home Irene has good news. Her sister, who owns a flat in Kidbrooke, south of the river, is going travelling for a year. It's clean, well-decorated and has two bedrooms. Lynthia and I can move in straight away.

For the next four weeks I get up and run – five miles building in a fortnight to ten – every morning before I go to work. I do press-ups and pull-ups. Like the army training video says, I 'push myself to the limit'. It feels good. Slowly I leave my old life behind.

I go back to the recruiting office. This time I take out the earring and sweep my dreads back. I manage to look half-respectable.

The same sergeant is on duty. He's talking to a couple of white kids. Their hair is cut short and one of them is wearing jeans with creases down the front. They look the part.

The sergeant glances my way. He doesn't recognise me.

'Hi,' I say, 'I'm interested in joining the army.'

He reaches for a form.

The next time I go there the sergeant asks if it would be helpful to talk to another Grenadian who's been in the army a while and who can tell me about army life.

He leads me into the next room and I'm amazed to see someone I already know. I met Jeremy Forrester, another Grenadian, on a building site in London around a year ago. Then I moved on to other jobs and lost touch. I had no idea he'd joined the army.

'How does it work from here?' I ask him.

'OK. We get you to come back and do a theory test. It's pretty basic – they're not looking for people with university degrees. You just have to demonstrate you can read and write and do a bit of multiplication. You can do the BARB test as early as next week.'

'What's that?'

'The British Army Recruit Battery test. It's a psychometric test. Common sense, basically. Pass that and you'll go down to Pirbright, where they'll put you through two days of leadership and teamwork exercises, plus they'll see if you're up to it physically.

'At the end of the two days, provided you're still with the

programme, they'll interview you. Don't tell them you want to join the army because you want to kill people. Do tell them the kind of unit you want to be in and how joining up is something you've given a lot of thought to.'

'What kind of unit *do* I want to join?' I ask.

'Well, in terms of the front line, there's the cavalry and the infantry. In the cavalry – we're talking tanks, basically – there are eleven armoured regiments and one mounted ceremonial regiment . . .' He starts to go through a list of names.

'What regiment are you?' I ask.

'I'm infantry. The Princess of Wales's Royal Regiment; the PWRR.'

'Then that's what I want to be in.'

'You don't want to think about it? I mean, I can give you a bit of background . . . how the regiment was formed in 1992 from the amalgamation of the Queen's Regiment and the Royal Hampshire . . .'

'I've thought about it,' I say. 'If it's good enough for you it's good enough for me.'

The 1st Battalion PWRR, the one Jeremy's in, is set to deploy to Kosovo in March of next year, roughly a month after my training ends. 'Not everyone likes foreign deployments. It's tough on wives and girlfriends.'

Lynthia will be OK, I tell myself. She's settled in Kidbrooke, likes the course she's doing at college and is working part-time in a bank.

'Let's do it,' I tell Jeremy.

A week later I return to the recruiting centre for two formal interviews and the BARB test. I sit down at a computer terminal and get fed a series of questions designed to assess my reasoning, my use of English and my mental arithmetic.

The questions are easy: 'High is to low, as full is to what?' You have to pick one of three choices. Or, 'Which number comes next in the following sequence: one, two, four, eight . . .?'

I pass the test easily and they give me a pamphlet about the infantry and the PWRR, which I'm to read before I head down to Pirbright, near Aldershot, for two days of assessment. I arrive a week later, undergo a full medical, pass that, get a series of briefs about army life, march around a parade ground and eat my first meal at a NAAFI.

Throughout this time, recruiting personnel watch your every move – assessing your character as well as your ability to get on with others.

The next morning we are sent on a mile-and-a-half run. You're supposed to complete this in no more than ten minutes and thirty seconds. I do it in less than eight.

After some strength tests – lifting a few weights in a gym – we're divided into groups and set a series of initiative tests designed to see whether we can solve specific challenges while working in teams.

This is the bit I like best of all, as you're given a plank, an oil drum, a couple of poles, a rope and a pulley, and have to use them to get you and your team across an imaginary stream.

Finally I'm interviewed by an officer, a major. He's sitting behind a desk and barely looks up as I enter the room. I haven't been nervous before, but I am now. This is it. When I leave this room I will know whether I've passed or failed.

He starts by asking whether I've encountered any particular problems during the selection process and I tell him, no, none.

'So you want to join the infantry?' He glances up at me.

'Yes, sir.'

'Do you know the role of the infantry?'

I tell him that the infantry has peacekeeping and humanitarian roles, in addition to a war-fighting responsibility, and that it can be sent almost anywhere in the world, often at very short notice.

I don't know whether this is strictly accurate, but it is as much as I can remember from the pamphlet I was given at the recruiting centre.

The major scribbles something down, then asks me whether I know where I'm heading if I'm selected for enlistment.

'I'll be going to the Infantry Training Centre in Catterick for twenty-four weeks of drill, fieldcraft, weapons training, fitness, individual and team skills instruction, endurance training, live firing and battle camp, sir.'

The major looks up. 'Very good,' he says. 'There's nothing wrong with your memory, Beharry. Now, why don't you tell me why you're really here?'

'Because this is what I want to do, sir. More than anything.'

'Enough to chop off those?' He points at my hair.

'Me dreads, sir?'

'Whatever they're called.'

'Yes, sir.'

The major gets to his feet. I get to mine.

'Well, that's probably a good thing,' he says.

'Excuse me, sir?'

'A good thing that you're ready to chop them off.' He holds out his hand. 'Out of the fifty potential recruits that came here, twenty have passed – and you're one of them. Well done.'

There are still one or two formalities to go through. I return to the Wembley recruiting centre and swear an oath of allegiance to the Queen, then a date is set for my training. I'm to report to the ITC at Catterick, North Yorkshire, at the end of August – four weeks from now.

Irene and Raymond hold a dinner for me the night before I leave. I know it's going to be an emotional evening. I see Irene the moment Lynthia and I walk in through the door.

Her eyes are red-rimmed and her voice is close to breaking. I give her a hug and she hugs me back.

'I can't believe this is actually happening,' she says as we sit down to dinner. 'Do you really have to go?'

'Anybody would think he's going off to a war,' Darren says. 'He's only going to Yorkshire, for God's sake!'

'Have *you* ever been to Yorkshire?' Irene says.

'My God,' Gav says, 'I think Mum just cracked a joke.'

Irene throws a serviette at him and everybody laughs.

After we finish eating, Raymond gets to his feet and taps his knife against his wine glass.

He draws himself up to his full height and takes a deep breath. He looks at me. 'When did you get here, Johnson? Was it September 1999?'

'August,' I say.

He shakes his head. 'My God. Two whole years. And look at you now, about to join the British Army. It's hard to believe.'

'Get on with it, Dad,' Gav says.

Irene nudges him. 'Let him have his say.'

'I don't want to say much, just a couple of things,' Raymond begins. 'My father, your Grand Uncle Hammond, always told me you liked to work with your hands, Johnson, but thanks to your skill, all your hard work . . . and my own layabout son's' – at this moment Gavin throws *his* serviette at him – 'you have transformed this house. How do we ever repay you for what you have done?'

'Blimey,' Gav says, 'it's like *Changing Rooms*. It's all that TV he watches.'

'Shhh!' Irene says.

Raymond looks down at his wine. 'Irene and me, we want you to know that there will always be a home here for you for as long as you need it.'

Irene reaches for the nearest napkin and dabs at the corners of her eyes. Gavin and Darren say nothing. Suddenly the whole of London seems to go quiet. I hear no planes, no police sirens, no traffic.

Raymond looks me in the eye. 'I know that these next twenty-four weeks are going to be tough, Johnson, but one thing you don't have to worry about is Lynthia. We'll make sure she's well looked after. You just concentrate on . . .'

'Being the best,' Darren says with a grin.

'Exactly.' Raymond raises his glass. 'Just, be the best, OK? We're all very proud of you.'

Everybody drinks, then they look at me. I know I should say something. But I know the words will come out wrong, so I thank Raymond and ask if I can be excused from the table for a moment.

I go upstairs into the bathroom and close the door behind me. I open the cupboard, take out the scissors from the first-aid box and stare at myself in the mirror.

I look into my eyes, take hold of a dreadlock and cut it off close to the roots. I tell myself, whatever happens I'm not going to go back to my old life. This is it now.

I move to the next dreadlock, and the next, cutting as I go, until every single one lies in the bin.

A minute later I go back downstairs. For a second or two everybody just stares at me. I rub my head self-consciously. It feels weird without them.

'Now I *know* you're joining the fuckin' army,' Gav says.

'Gavin!' Irene scolds.

'Sorry, Mum. But, I mean, look at him.'

It breaks the ice. Lynthia starts to giggle and everybody starts talking again. We talk about Grenada, my gran, Hammond and Babby, my mum, my brothers and sisters, and Ena and her family . . .

The good, happy memories.

Then, as the time approaches to leave, we agree that, for the moment, it really is best that we continue to keep my decision to join the army a secret – until I know whether I'm in or out. Forty per cent of recruits fall by the wayside between signing on and passing out.

After a couple of months I'll know whether I can hack it. Only then will I tell my family back home.

Just before I get up from the table, Irene says she has something she wants me to have. She hands me a little leather box. Inside is a silver cross on a chain. I pick it up and hold it in my fingers. It catches the light.

'I want you to promise me something.'

'Of course.'

'If ever you find yourself in danger, you must hold this little crucifix close and pray to God and all His angels for help. Do you understand me?'

Irene takes my hands in hers and closes my fingers around the cross and chain.

'Is that clear, Johnson. Promise me.'

'I promise, Auntie I.'

The train pulls out of King's Cross and heads north. Soon after I settle into my seat, a guy sits down opposite me and starts reading a book with a picture of a soldier on the front, *The British Army, A Pocket Guide – 2001–2002.*

I hold out my hand. 'Hi,' I say. 'Johnson Beharry. Looks like we're going to the same place.'

'Jimmy Bryant,' he replies. 'Pleased to meet you, mate.'

It turns out that joining the army is all he ever wanted to do. His father was a soldier and his father's father before that. A Bryant has fought in every major war waged by Britain in the twentieth century.

The Light Infantry operates as part of the Light Division, which consists of two battalions of LI and two battalions of Royal Green Jackets. The PWRR's two battalions, two battalions of the Royal Regiment of Fusiliers and two battalions of the Royal Anglian Regiment make up the Queen's Division. Forty battalions made up of approximately thirty regiments make up the infantry of the British Army. Each battalion comprises around six hundred soldiers.

The bitter rivalry between regiments starts in training. Jimmy has already made it plain that the LI is superior in every way to the PWRR. And for a reason I can't explain, I find myself starting to get annoyed.

Jimmy also tells me exactly what we can expect over the next twenty-four weeks.

In the first six weeks we'll be taught individual skills, drill, weapons training, fitness and fieldcraft. In the second phase, weeks seven to twenty-one, we'll learn team skills, endurance training and patrolling skills. The final two weeks are live firing and battle camp.

At Darlington we pile out of the train on to a grimy platform. As I fall into line behind Jimmy, I notice that he's already swinging his arms.

We aren't the only ones bound for Catterick. Around fifty recruits scramble out of the train with us. Some, with their regulation haircuts and smartly pressed shirts and slacks, already look the part. Others, their hair still long, look a little less certain.

A soldier at the ticket barrier booms at everyone to 'fuckin' hurry up' and we break into a run to where a civilian bus and two army lorries are waiting.

We throw our bags into the lorries and jump aboard the bus.

The following morning we're woken at 0600. After washing we make sure our rooms are spotless.

We eat breakfast between 0700 and 0730, then go into our first lessons of the day – basic disciplines like PT, drill, first aid and weapons instruction.

There are sixty-four of us on the ITC course. I'm in A Company, 3 Platoon, Section 4, led by Corporal Mitchell. I've already run into some of the instructors in camp, so I know I'm lucky. Mitchell is from Jimmy Bryant's regiment, the Light Infantry, but I try not to hold this against him.

'Work with me and I'll cut you some slack,' he says.

Two weeks after we kick off our training, Al-Qaeda terrorists fly airliners into the World Trade Center and the Pentagon. Our instructors remind us daily that the world is now a very different place, that what we learn here won't just be the difference between pass and fail – it may also be the difference between life and death when we go to war with these bastards.

Our goal is to pass a set of written and practical tests in weapons handling, PT and basic nuclear, biological and chemical (NBC) drills by the end of week six.

By mid-December I'm well into the second phase of my training. We have learned everything from the basics of soldiering to advanced tactical techniques, such as how to mount section and platoon attacks.

We're also put through a relentless series of fitness tests – long marches and runs – to prepare us for life on the ground as infantrymen.

As 2002 begins I set my sights on the day that I'll get passed off the square for good.

Lynthia and I also decide to get married.

'Johnson,' Irene says, 'I really want you to think about this.'

'I've thought about it, Auntie I,' I say. 'We've talked about it and now we're going to go through with it.'

'Go *through* with it? Listen to what you're saying. This isn't something you go through. This is the person you're supposed to spend the rest of your life with.'

Irene is one of the wisest people I know, but after Catterick I will be heading for the Balkans. What will Lynthia do then?

'Me being away six months will be tough on Lynthia, Auntie I. But if we get married, she can move into married quarters at Tidworth. The army will look after her there. I owe that to her.'

'You don't owe anybody anything,' Irene says. 'This is your life too. You're both still so young. Don't rush this. That's all I'm saying.'

But I've made up my mind. We'll be married the day I finish at Catterick.

CHAPTER TWENTY-ONE

On the day we graduate as soldiers we put on a demonstration in front of family and friends – a section attack in the square – and then the recruit that has demonstrated the best fitness, improvement and all-round performance is given an award. I'm somewhere in the middle – neither the best nor the worst – but my sense of achievement is huge. Of the sixty-four recruits that turned up in late August, only twenty-three have passed.

Raymond, Irene, Gavin, Darren and I pile into a mini-bus with a small group of friends. We eat lunch at a pub, then Lynthia goes off to change into her wedding dress. After the service we pose for a few photographs in the icy wind, then travel back to London.

We spend the next week preparing for our move. Everything we own fits into a few suitcases.

The 1st Battalion PWRR has only just been assigned its armoured infantry role. In its previous, light infantry role, it was transported in the Saxon, a wheeled armoured personnel carrier or APC. Not much more than a battlefield taxi, this could protect its occupants from shell splinters and machine-gun fire, but little else. The Saxon was OK in Northern Ireland and Kosovo, but it can't hack the high-intensity ops of the modern battlefield.

Now 1PWRR is kitted out with the Warrior, an Armoured Infantry Fighting Vehicle (AIFV) with a 30mm cannon. The battalion is made up of around six hundred men divided into three rifle companies – A, B and C – and Y, a fire-support company. I've been assigned to 7 Platoon, C Company. Each company is divided into three thirty-man platoons – 7, 8 and 9 Platoons in the case of C Company – each with four Warriors. Personnel are either vehicle crews or dismounts, the infantrymen who will engage the enemy on the ground once they have been delivered to the heart of the action by the Warrior. I know that 1PWRR has a lot more training to do before it will be ready for front-line combat duties.

It's a miserable, late-February day when we leave London. The cloud is so low it brushes the tops of the buildings. As we approach Tidworth it's even worse; the red-brick buildings of the garrison are almost invisible in the drizzly fog that hangs in curtains over Salisbury Plain.

I report to the guardhouse and then battalion HQ. A corporal escorts us to our married quarters, a two-bedroom apartment in a drab accommodation block.

The place is like a ghost town: the only activity I've seen is a mash-up Warrior being driven through the town on a low-loader.

'You picked a good time to show up,' the corporal explains. 'Half the fuckin' battalion has fucked off on fuckin' exercise and the other fuckin' half has gone down with fuckin' flu.'

I must pick up my first set of orders, so I leave Lynthia to unpack.

After taking several wrong turnings in the fog I eventually arrive at Sergeant Major Falconer's office around fifteen minutes late.

I knock on the door, hear a booming 'yes', turn the handle and step inside.

There I see a desk strewn with paperwork and a man with tattoos on his forearms. Falconer looks up, a cigarette clamped between his lips. His eyes are ice-blue and don't seem to move.

'Well?' He rubs a hand through his bristle-length fair hair.

'Private Beharry reporting for duty, Sarn't Major, sir!' I snap him a sharp salute.

'I know who you fuckin' are, Beharry, because it says so in large letters on your tunic. What I really want to know is why you're fifteen fuckin' minutes late.'

'I took a wrong turn in the fog, Sarn't Major.'

'Not a brilliant start, is it, son?'

'No, Sarn't Major. Sorry, Sarn't Major.'

Falconer stubs out his cigarette and lights another. 'Well, as it happens,' he says, 'it's your lucky bloody day.'

He watches me through the cloud of smoke he has just exhaled. 'What sort of day is it, Beharry?'

'My lucky bloody day, Sarn't Major.'

'You want to know why?'

'Yes please, Sarn't Major.'

'I'm going to offer you a chance to redeem your bloody self, Beharry.'

He pauses. 'Do you know why?'

'I think I can guess, Sarn't Major.'

'Can you now, Einstein?'

'Yes, Sarn't Major.' I look him straight in the eye. 'Half the battalion has fucked off on exercise, Sarn't Major. And the other half has fuckin' flu.'

'Good to see you're catchin' on, son.' Falconer rolls his cigarette between thumb and forefinger. 'Why the fuck are you grinnin' like an idiot?'

'I don't mean not'ing by it, Sarn't Major,' I say. 'Sometimes I just can't help myself.'

'Sometimes you just can't help what?' he bellows.

'Smilin', Sarn't Major.'

When he stubs out his cigarette this time, he keeps his eyes on me.

'I want you here at 0700 tomorrow to assist in the transportation and distribution of rations,' he says. 'Some stupid bastard forgot that soldiers on exercise need to bloody well eat occasionally. You'll get the details when you show up. Have you got that?'

'Yes, Sarn't Major.'

'You're still bloody smilin', Beharry.'

'I'm happy, Sarn't Major.'

'Where are you bloody from, Beharry?'

'Grenada, Sarn't Major.'

'Is everybody so bloody happy in Grenada?'

'Yes, Sarn't Major. Some people are even happier.'

Falconer shakes his head and tells me I need to report back here again at 1100 hours.

'There'll be transportation waitin' here to take you to Andover train station.'

'Andover train station?'

'There's no need to repeat every bloody thing I say, Private bloody Behappy. In case it has escaped your attention, we're an armoured infantry unit. We need vehicles to drive us to war and vehicles need bloody drivers. Leconfield is home to the Defence School of Transport. I see from your file that you picked up a drivin' theory package while you were at Catterick. You're off to Leconfield to put all that new-found knowledge into practice. Lucky you, Behappy. Some of the lads have to wait years for this. You won the lottery on day one.'

I need a UK driving licence and the army is going to see that I get one. I have no idea where Leconfield is, but anything that gets me behind a wheel can't be bad.

'How long will I be gone, Sarn't Major?'

'You could be away days, weeks or months, so my advice is, take a good book.'

I salute and dismiss myself.

The next morning the alarm goes off at 0600 and I lie in bed for a few moments and think about my orders. Sergeant Major Falconer must have got it wrong. He can't mean for me to help shift rations around Salisbury Plain *and* be ready by 1100 to go to the station. The more I think about it, the more I convince myself that there's been a mistake. I'm meant to do one or the other, but not both.

On the train I run into a PWRR private called Scott, who tells me where Leconfield is: somewhere near Hull. I'm fairly sure that Hull is in Yorkshire. I'm almost back where I started.

When I tell Scott my name, his eyes widen.

'Christ!' he says. '*You're* Beharry.'

I realise my decision to bunk off this morning was not a good one. Scott tells me that Falconer went ballistic. He has given Scott a message for me.

'What is it?' I ask.

'When you get back from Leconfield, prepare yourself for God.'

It takes the Defence School of Transport two months and three weeks to set a date for my driving test. By the time I get back to Tidworth, fully licensed to drive a Land Rover, the bank Lynthia worked for in London has found her a job in Andover. The other bit of good news is that I've been away so long Sergeant Major Falconer seems to have forgotten all about me.

My first day back at barracks we're called out on parade. As I answer my name I hear laughing. I wonder what the hell's going on.

After we're dismissed a black guy comes up to me and

prods me in the chest. He's grinning from ear to ear. 'I'm finding out if you're for real, man,' he says. He gives me another prod with his finger. 'Beharry, right?'

'Right,' I say. 'Johnson Beharry. From Grenada.'

'Grenada! Man, you guys are taking over the place.' He laughs – a big, infectious laugh – and holds out his hand. 'Troy Samuels,' he says. 'From Jamaica.' We shake and he jabs a thumb at two other black guys at the edge of the square. 'We've been takin' bets about you. For damn near three months we've been hearin' this name . . . Beharry, Beharry. Every bloody parade. And nobody ever owns up to it. In the end I bet them that you're never goin' to show up. I thought this was some kind of army piss-take.'

'How much did you lose?' I ask.

'It's not the money, man, it's my reputation. I'm the king of skivers around here. If anyone's doin' any skivin' in this company, it's me.' He's laughing again.

'I wasn't skivin',' I say. 'I was taking me drivin' test.'

'A skiver *and* a jammy bastard,' Samuels says. 'There are people around here who've been waitin' half their lives to get on that course.'

'Includin' you?'

'Includin' me.'

'So you're a dismount,' I say. 'What about them?' I nod towards the other two.

'Beggsy's a dismount too, and Eddie's a driver.' He claps me on the back. 'Come on. I'll introduce you.'

There's forty-five minutes before I have to be in my next class – PT. The rest of the day is taken up with weapons handling and an introduction to the sheds where the vehicles are housed and serviced.

We head back to the C Company accommodation block, where Eddie and Beggsy have rooms. Samuels – Sammy – is married, so, like me, he lives in quarters a few minutes' drive from the camp. He's a couple of years older than me and came to the UK from Jamaica in 1999, the same year I arrived from Grenada. He stayed with his sister in Croydon for a year before deciding to join up. He has been with the battalion since September 2001.

Eddie fixes us coffee. He and Beggsy are both from the eastern side of Grenada, near Grenville.

Sammy, Eddie and Beggsy give me a crash course in how to survive Tidworth. Some tips are obvious, like: never volunteer. Others only come with experience. For example, because Eddie is a Warrior driver he is allowed to form work posses to help him maintain his vehicle. The trick is to time the maintenance to coincide with a ten-mile run, or with shooting on the ranges.

'Once you're in the sheds you get into the back of a Warrior, get a brew on and play some cards or take a nap,' Eddie says. 'There's a checklist for all the things you're supposed to do, like toppin' up the oil and fuel and checkin' the tracks, but a lot of the time the guys don't bother. You just tick the boxes and get the vehicle signed off. If it breaks down because it hasn't had enough oil or it's thrown a link, you can always hide behind the maintenance sheet.'

They try to make this and their other dodges sound like a walk in the park, but the way I look at it, Sammy, Eddie and Beggsy waste more energy skiving than they would working.

The biggest skive of all for a private in an armoured infantry regiment is driving, and we're all jealous that Eddie has made the grade. As a dismount I have to get used to watching him and the other drivers of 7 Platoon sitting in their hatches while we freeze our arses off during the countless exercises they put us through on Salisbury Plain.

And there is no shortage of training. Proficiency level CP1 means you can fire a rifle and eat out of a mess tin. CP2 – where we are in March 2002 – means being able to function tactically at platoon level; CP3 at company level and CP4 within a battle group. The aim is to get us up to CP5: the highest you can achieve. We're being trained for war as part of an armoured brigade.

In Kosovo our mission is to support the Police Service, the KPS, while they rebuild what was destroyed in the 1999 war.

We're based in a barracks in Pristina, the capital, and most of our duties as dismounts are extremely dull. For the first three months we spend a lot of our time guarding a Serb church that the Muslims keep threatening to burn down. Occasionally we go out on patrol in our Land Rover snatches.

Before Kosovo I hadn't thought of Zipi the Bosnian in a long time, but every time I drive through the streets of Pristina I see him – the day I told him, Will and Bryan I was joining the army – shaking his head and saying, 'I seen many things. Things I don't like to think about. But you, Johnson, my friend, you don't have to fight. Britain is not your country . . .'

We're told that there isn't as much battle damage in Pristina as there is elsewhere, but when I do see a house with its roof blown off, or scorch marks around blown-out windows, I wonder how it came to this. Most of the damage was done by the Serb militia, who shelled the town when they were forced to retreat from it.

Pristina used to have a Serb population of forty thousand out of a total of half a million, and almost all of them have fled.

A few hang on, like the people who attend the church we guard. I see children with no legs, hobbling on crutches, and old women with blankets over their shoulders. The men stare at us as they file in through the doors. At first I think they look on us as saviours. Later, when my patrol route takes me past the main post office – a tall, abandoned block, its windows blown out by NATO bombs – I realise that they see us as no different from the people we're protecting them against.

I can't get my head around it. Everybody hates everybody. The place is a mess.

The only time we come close to any action is during elections in neighbouring Macedonia, when the factions competing for power start shooting at one another. The NATO bosses decide that the civilians monitoring the elections are in danger of being kidnapped, so for two weeks we train in the mountains along the border for a hostage-rescue operation.

In the end the elections pass off smoothly, no one is taken hostage, the locals stop shooting at one another and we go back to our regular duties.

One day, in between foot patrols, Sammy collapses on the floor. It's such a good performance that we all start to clap.

'The Oscars were last month, man,' Beggsy says.

'It ain' fuckin' funny, man,' Sammy says, clutching his sides. 'It feels like someone's stuck a knife in me guts.'

'Yeah, right,' Eddie says. 'Anyone got the number for Holby City A&E?' He and Beggsy high-five each other.

'I'm not jokin', man,' Sammy says. 'This is for real.' He starts groaning again.

I look at his eyes and realise that something really is wrong.

'Hey, guys,' I say. 'Sammy's hurt. We need to get a medic in here.'

'You in on this too?' Eddie says.

'No,' I tell him. 'This *is* for real. Look at his face.'

A couple of days later I go and see Sammy in the field hospital, where he is recovering from an emergency operation to remove gallstones.

'Hey, Bee, I owe you,' he says. 'If it wasn't for you I'd

probably still be rollin' around in agony with that lot handin'
out points for me actin'.'

'Forget it,' I say. 'You'd do the same for me, wouldn't you?'

'Yeah, I would, mate, an' that's the truth.'

'Whatever?'

'Yeah, whatever.'

He looks at me. 'Hang on. What is this?'

'I just heard. Yesterday . . .'

'Heard what?'

'I've been selected to go on the Warrior drivin' course,
startin' immediately.'

Sammy stares at me, then starts beating the crap out of the
bedclothes with his fists.

'Shit,' he says. 'Shit, shit, shit . . .'

'Sammy, you goin' to do yourself an injury.'

'You're such a jammy sod, Beharry. Right from the word
go. Were you always this lucky, man?'

I smile. 'Yeah,' I say. 'I guess I always was.'

CHAPTER TWENTY-TWO

Eddie has been chosen to go on the 'NCO cadre', a course designed to promote you from private to lance corporal, so we're both heading for a camp outside Pristina.

Sammy, when he gets out of hospital, is still vex and mutters endlessly about the injustices of army life. All he can see ahead is another winter as a dismount, freezing his balls off on Salisbury Plain.

Eddie and I tell him he was just raised on the wrong island: God is a Grenadian, not a Jamaican.

I can't wait to get behind the wheel of a Warrior. In my spare time I've been learning all I can about its performance.

The Warrior is an armed and armoured taxi that weighs more than twenty-five tonnes. It's fitted with an immensely powerful Perkins Rolls-Royce diesel engine. The CV8 produces 550 brake horsepower, giving the Warrior a top speed, according to the manual, of almost fifty miles per hour, and Eddie tells me that he's got his running close to seventy. It's not as quick as a Porsche 911, but I don't care.

Eddie says the track and suspension are so good that you can hammer over rough terrain and still feel like you're gliding, although the boys in the back don't always agree. When you hit the brakes on a twenty-five tonner that's pushing close to seventy, it tilts right on to its nose, so you're in trouble if you're not strapped in.

'Hear them dismounts squeal!' Eddie says, chuckling to himself.

Technically the Warrior is supposed to be capable of ferrying seven fully equipped soldiers around the battlefield, but normally it's no more than three or four. There really isn't a lot of room in the back: a bench seat to the right and left of the door, and the wall space behind them stuffed so full of equipment that it looks like a quartermaster's store.

The commander and gunner sit in an electrically operated turret, behind a Rarden cannon, which can fire 30mm high-explosive and armour-piercing rounds for over a mile.

Mounted next to the Rarden is a Hughes 7.62mm chain gun, a belt-fed weapon capable of high firepower and great accuracy. But it can be temperamental; it was originally developed as a helicopter weapon and the electric feed system that draws the ammunition from where it's stored beneath the gun sometimes jams.

After a week of theory I'm taken out to the sheds. Warrior maintenance has to be done by the book and I have to learn strange names for pieces of kit that look no different from the spanners, wrenches and screwdrivers I used at Chris and Jane's repair shop.

I learn how to take readings from the torque meters on the nuts that fasten the bolts between each of the eighty-two pieces of track link on either side of the vehicle. I'm taught how to check the levels of the cooling oil in the road wheels and rear rollers that stops the bearings from going into meltdown when the Warrior is on the move.

Next I learn how to change a track, and finally how to change an engine. It's normally done under the supervision of the REME, the army's Royal Electrical and Mechanical Engineers, but should take two men less than an hour once they're up to speed.

After a week of theory and three weeks of maintenance instruction I'm allowed to take my first driving lesson.

I stroll across the parade ground under a cloudless Balkan sky and climb on to the Warrior's hull. The aluminium armour is lightweight compared with the steel hull of a main battle tank, but it's designed to provide protection against 14.5mm armour-piercing rounds, 155mm air-burst shell fragments and nine-kilogram anti-tank mines.

The driver's position is at the front of the vehicle, to the left of the power pack as you look down from the turret. Standard operating procedure is to drive with the hatch open, your head partly exposed – heads-up. The front of the vehicle slopes downwards at thirty degrees, so the driver has a good field of view.

When you have to close the hatch under high threat or combat conditions, things get complicated. You're protected from small-arms fire but can only see out through a periscope – known as a day sight – no bigger than a letterbox. For night missions, or when the vehicle is enveloped in battle smoke, the day sight can be switched to a passive night-vision system.

The noise inside a Warrior on the move is so bad that you can't even make yourself heard by shouting, so you communicate via an internal radio net.

I lower myself into the seat and plug in my headset, which is built into the inner layer of my helmet.

'Are we sitting comfortably?' Corporal O'Neill's voice crackles in my ears. He's sitting in the commander's position.

The harness is similar to those used by Formula 1 drivers. I pull it over my shoulders and plug the catch into the buckle, then pull the straps in hard. If we have to stop in a hurry, they are all that will prevent me from losing my front teeth on the rim of the hatchway.

Before starting the engine I familiarise myself with my

surroundings. The driver is separated from the rest of the crew by a two-metre-long tunnel. I like the feeling of independence this gives, but some drivers hate the isolation. The tunnel is the driver's only means of escape if the vehicle turns over or the hatch jams shut in an emergency. It leads to a cage that surrounds the base of the turret mechanism.

As well as holding ammunition and a maintenance kit, the cage is designed to prevent the gunner and commander from losing their hands and feet as the turret traverses. However, as it doesn't provide all-round protection, it isn't fail-safe. 'Tankies' are full of stories of people who have lost fingers, hands and even feet in the turret mechanisms of tanks and APCs. If there is an emergency and I need to use the tunnel, I must first wriggle past the cage, into the base of the turret, and from there make my way into the dismounts' section.

You can activate the electrically powered door from the back of the vehicle by hitting a button or, if the power is down, crank it open with a T-shaped handle known as a 'ram' that sits under one of the seats.

A panel to the left of the U-shaped steering wheel tells me that the vehicle is in neutral. The transmission system, which is fully automatic, has four forward speeds and one reverse.

I clasp the lever that releases the footbrake with my right hand, find the spring-loaded toggle on the side and push it with my thumb. It disengages with a thud. I push the starter button on the control panel above it. Beyond the bulkhead against my right shoulder I feel a surge and then the steady pulse of the power pack as the Warrior roars into life.

A ground instructor stands a few feet away, his eyes locked on mine. His arms are held out in front of him, fists together, knuckles forward. He makes a jab to his right and I turn the steering wheel hard over in a full lock. I then touch the accelerator and the Warrior lurches to the left. If I keep pressing the pedal the vehicle will spin around a full 360 degrees.

I smile. As soon as there are no instructors around I'll give it a go. I follow the instructor's directions, revving more gently, building up the power, and the Warrior glides to the left, as if on a cushion of air. I've carried out my first 'neutral turn'. My second attempt is even better.

'Nice one, Beharry,' O'Neill says. 'Shall we head for the open road?'

Five minutes later we're thundering along an empty Kosovan highway, heading for the foothills outside Pristina. Although I'm only doing twenty miles per hour, the breeze in my face and the growl of the Perkins diesel make it feel faster.

'Right a bit,' O'Neill says, reminding me which side of the road I'm supposed to be on. 'Watch for the bend – and the pedestrian two hundred metres ahead on your left.'

A running commentary on the route ahead is part of the commander's job. I crank up the power a fraction.

The tension falls away and I ease back into my seat. The steering is surprisingly light and even the smallest adjustments produce an immediate response.

Half an hour out of camp, I feel as if I've been driving the Warrior my whole life. I feel so good about it that I don't hear O'Neill's warning. I take a bend slightly too wide. For an instant I'm convinced that I'll hit the horse and cart coming towards us. Judging by the look of horror on the face of the Kosovan at the reins, he thinks so too. I yank the steering wheel to the right and the Warrior responds. I catch a fleeting glimpse of the cart in the mirror as it veers off the road, bounces over a ditch and vanishes in a cloud of dust.

'Steady, Beharry,' O'Neill says. 'You're not Michael Schumacher, and this isn't a fucking Ferrari.'

'Is he OK?' I ask anxiously.

'He'll live. Which is more than I can say for you, mate, if you pull another stunt like that.'

Despite this, and flattening a signpost during a neutral turn at a T-junction a few minutes later, my first outing in a Warrior seems to have been a success.

I park up and jog down to the gym, where I'll work off some of the adrenalin. An NCO is screaming at some poor bastard in the middle of the square as I pass the parade ground.

When I get closer I realise that the guy on the receiving end is Eddie. The NCO's face is right up against his; he's purple with rage and calling Eddie every name under the sun.

I've never understood this side of army life. Some NCOs and officers think the only way they will get private soldiers to respond is by screaming at them. Anybody who screams at me is going to get nothing back. There are plenty of NCOs and officers I respect, but they haven't got it by hurling abuse around.

Poor Eddie. If this is what he has to go through to make corporal, I wonder if he'll stick it. He's been talking about quitting. Maybe this will be the final straw.

After I've punished my body for an hour in the gym, I jog back to my quarters for a shower. My mind is somewhere else when I turn a corner and almost collide with the sergeant who was giving Eddie so much grief. I take a step back. He has hair like a scrubbing brush and a nose that looks like it's been broken in at least two places. His jaw is set like a bull-dog's and he pushes out his chin and twists his neck around like he's looking for a fight.

'What the fuck are you staring at?' he says.

'Not'ing,' I say. 'Not'ing at all.'

'Nothing at all, *Sergeant*.'

'Yes, Sergeant.'

'What's your name?'

'Beharry, Sergeant.'

'*Beharry*? What kind of a name is that?'

'It's Grenadian, Sergeant. Indian originally. Some people believe that a long time ago my family came from the state of Bihar in north-east India. Bi-har. Be-harry.' I say the name slowly. 'Interestin', don't you think?'

He takes a step back, the wind completely knocked from his sails.

'Well, Harry Hoojamaflip, wherever the bloody hell you're from, you should watch where you're going. Otherwise, mate, I'm going to sort you out with Lennie and Ronnie.'

'Who, Sergeant?'

He brings his face close to mine. 'Not who. What, mate.' He raises his left fist, then his right. 'Meet Lennie and Ronnie. My two best pals. You don't want to get on the wrong side of 'em, believe me.'

'I'm sure I don't, Sergeant.'

'You're a cheeky sod, ain't you, Harry?'

'If you say so, Sergeant.'

'I bloody well do, mate. I don't like cheeky sods, Harry. Is that clear?'

'Clear as crystal, Sergeant.'

He narrows his eyes. 'Gleaming,' he says. 'Abso-fucking-lutely gleaming.' Then, with a last piercing stare, he disappears around the corner of the building.

Later, when I'm talking to Eddie, I find out who he is: Sergeant Chris Broome. Although with 1PWRR, he is, thank God, in a different company.

As I suspected, Eddie is going through a bit of a crisis. Although he looks set to make the grade, he is struggling with the whole idea of the army.

'How can I skive if I make it to corporal?' he says, shaking his head.

Two weeks later Eddie gets his stripes and I pass my Warrior test, despite racking up a couple of 'minor infringements' – one for speeding, the other for overtaking.

It's the best thing that has happened to me in a long time.

The day before we fly out of Pristina I dream I'm six again, playing in the roots of my gran's wishing tree.

'Look, Gran,' I shout as I spin the bucket lid in my hands. 'Look at me! Look at me!'

When she doesn't answer I glance over my shoulder, sensing that something's not right. I play in the tree when she is sitting on the steps, humming to herself as she prepares our dinner. But today the steps are empty and the only noise I hear is the sound of the wind through the branches and dried leaves scraping across the porch.

When I turn back again I'm sitting in a driver's hatch. The roots no longer have the smooth, clean lines of a racing car, as they used to when I was a child, but the squat, angular profile of a Warrior. The next thing I know I'm in the driver's tunnel, trying to get to the turret. But my shoulders are stuck; no matter how hard I push I'm wedged tight.

A feeling of panic starts to overwhelm me, but suddenly, miraculously, the tunnel loosens its grip on my body and I kick my way past the cage and into the turret. But the feeling of relief doesn't last. There's some unseen danger waiting for me – I can feel it. I don't know whether it's inside or outside the Warrior. But it's close. I have to get out. Yet when I try to open the gunner's hatch it doesn't budge. The same with the commander's. I push against them with all my might, but they're stuck fast.

The only other way out is through the door at the back of the vehicle. Following procedure, I rotate the turret, flip a catch and kick open a hinged section of the cage, but before I can wriggle through into the dismounts' section I hear the deep boom of a gun and a shell whistles past. I hear a second boom, followed by a loud bang at the front of the Warrior.

After settling into the gunner's seat I take a look through the sights. A tank is advancing towards us, its main gun levelled straight at me. It's preparing to fire again. This time I know it will destroy us.

I reach down and pull out a box of ammunition, but when I open the lid, instead of neat clips of ammo for the Rarden, I see rows of eggs with serial numbers on them. Never mind that they are eggs, a voice tells me, I have to load them in the Rarden and fire at the tank. When I look up I see that the voice belongs to Sammy.

'I can't,' I tell him. 'I can't touch them.'

'Why the fuck not?' he pleads. 'We goin' to die if you don't.'

'Trust me,' I tell him. 'I touch the wrong ammo, *I* goin' to die.'

'What the fuck are you talkin' about, man?' Sammy lunges and grabs the box with both hands.

I no longer know if the box contains ammunition or eggs. It doesn't make any difference. Whatever's in there, some of the objects are good and some of them are bad. If I touch the wrong ones they'll kill me.

'Fuck this,' Sammy says, and puts his hand into the box . . .

I come up gasping for air, my hands outstretched in the darkness, my whole body drenched in sweat. I lie there for a moment, trying to shake it off, but I can't. It was just too real.

I get up and shower, hoping that the heat and the water will go to work on me, but they don't. The dream sticks to me like the smell of smoke.

CHAPTER TWENTY-THREE

Sammy, Eddie, Beggsy and Campbell talk excitedly throughout the two-and-a-half-hour flight, pausing only to ask me what's wrong. There's no use trying to explain it – they'll think I'm mad – so I tell them I'm tired and try to get some sleep. But when I close my eyes I'm back inside the Warrior.

Soon after we touch down at RAF Brize Norton I feel my mobile vibrate. There's a message from Irene, asking me to call her as soon as I get the chance.

In just under a week's time the battalion is set to go on three weeks' leave and on the coach that takes us on to Tidworth everybody is in party mode. Everybody except for me.

'Auntie I,' I yell over a rugby song that's sprung up from the rear of the coach, 'it's me.'

Her voice is faint and there's a lot of distortion on the line, but I know something is wrong.

'Oh, Johnson,' she says. I hear the catch in her voice. 'I'm afraid I have some terrible news.'

'It's me gran, isn't it?' I say.

She doesn't answer, but her silence and the emptiness I feel inside tell me I'm right.

The dream has prepared me for this moment. I know now what it means.

I take a deep breath and move to the front of the coach, as far as I can get from the singing. I press the mobile to my ear and cup my hand around it.

'What happened? It's all right, Auntie I. I'm OK. You can tell me.'

'Your mother called a few hours ago. Your gran got sick. They took her to hospital, but there was nothing they could do. She's been fighting for so long, Johnson, and in the end she couldn't fight any more. Her heart gave out. I'm so sorry.'

I feel numb. All I can think about is the promise that I made her. She wanted to see me before she died. She wanted me to go back to Grenada one last time. But I never did. She'd been there for me my whole life and I thought she'd carry on for ever.

'Johnson?'

I swallow hard and ask Irene about the funeral. It's the day after tomorrow. There's enough time for me to buy a ticket and catch a flight.

The moment I get off the coach I go to see the company sergeant major. He has been back in camp a few days, with the advance party. I walk into his office, salute and start talking. The CSM listens, but I can see where this is heading. The battalion has just got back from a major deployment and there is a whole heap of admin to sort before our leave starts.

'Listen, son,' he says, 'I'm sorry about your gran, I really am. But rules is rules. You're not going to get any compassionate. She's not immediate next of kin – your mother and your father are.' He goes back to stamping some papers on his desk.

'She brought me up, Sarn't Major,' I say. 'All I need is two or three days.'

He looks up, irritated now that I'm still here. 'Let me put this on the line for you,' he says. 'We're all tired and we're all looking forward to a spot of leave. I'd like nothing better than to sod off to a Caribbean beach for a nice spot of R and R with a pina bloody colada in my hand, but as you can see, there's a whole lot of shit I've got to get through here. Book your ticket, catch a plane, but not before everything you're meant to do is squared away and your leave kicks in. You and your mates may think you've got the system down pat, Beharry, but me and *my* mates weren't born yesterday. Do I make myself clear?'

'Perfectly, Sarn't Major.'

I spend the next two hours talking things through with my mum. We manage to delay the funeral by a week.

It's September, the height of the rainy season, and a huge tower of grey and white cloud boils up over the Grand Etang, the volcanic lake that nestles in a bowl of jagged hills between St George's and Grenville.

White houses dot the lush green slopes on either side of the road as I follow its twists and turns through the nutmeg and cocoa plantations. I can see the main street in Victoria, where I used to drink and play pool, and the shops and the restaurants along the beach. Fishing boats bob in the surf and, further out, where the turquoise shallows meet the deep ocean currents, I can make out yachts and tankers en route to St Vincent.

I try to pick out the road that winds up from the coast to Diego Piece, but the plane makes a sudden turn as it descends towards Point Salines and I miss my chance to get a glimpse of the hill and the world that my gran and I used to look out on from the porch of her little house.

Fifteen minutes later I'm walking down the aircraft steps and passing through customs and immigration. I hear somebody call my name and I search the faces beyond the barrier.

Shannon still has paint in his hair – probably the same paint that was there when I last saw him, the day I left for England.

'It's good to see you, my brother,' he says.

He explains that my family are busy making the final arrangements for the funeral and that he will drive me to Diego Piece. For the three days I'm on the island I'll be staying in my own house. It's what my family want – for us to be together again. I haven't stayed there since the day my father threw the little bed out of the window.

As we reach the junction at the bottom of the village I'm greeted by a sea of white shirts. We have hit Diego Piece's rush hour, when the school bell goes and three hundred children spill into the playground and out on to the road. The shouting and screaming are deafening, even above Shannon's rattling exhaust and the soca music that blares from his stereo. He honks the horn, but few kids take any notice. Footballs continue to bounce and the girls carry on skipping. No one moves until Shannon threatens them with his bumper.

Mr Mark, the principal, has retired, and so has my old teacher, Emrol Narine. Drugs and alcohol, which were never much of a problem when we were kids, are now, Shannon says, even among kids of twelve and thirteen.

As we press on up the road the sky suddenly darkens and the heavens open. We park at the top of the hill and wait for the rain to blow over, then make our way down the path to the house. The scents of oranges and wet earth fill the air. As the dogs begin to bark I feel a knot in the pit of my stomach.

The village is full of people I've missed and some I haven't. Who will I see? Who will be at the house?

I spot Jemilla on the porch. She sees me in the same moment and waves.

My brothers and sisters come running out. Kellon is there too. Everyone is talking to me at once. I hug and kiss them and follow them inside.

My mother has her back to me, her hands in a basin of water. Around her women from the village prepare food for tomorrow's wake. She stops what she is doing, turns and slowly dries her hands. As she raises her eyes they begin to fill with tears. I walk over and hold her. Her body has become thin while I've been away. I can scarcely feel her in my arms.

She holds my face in her hands. 'I'm so sad and so happy in this moment,' she says.

'Me too, Mummy. I've missed you so much.'

She smiles through her tears. 'Thank God you're still the same.'

'What did you expect?'

'I thought the army, married life, you know . . . So much has happened while you been gone.'

The next morning I wake up when it's still quite dark and tiptoe from the room where my brothers are still sleeping.

If my father returned during the night, I didn't hear him. According to my sisters, he has managed to cut down his drinking, but the death of his mother has hit him hard and there are any number of places where he may have dossed down for the night.

As I climb the path to my gran's house the sunlight starts to spill over the hills above Red Mud. It's the time I like best, before the air fills with the smell of wood smoke and cooking and the sound of Old Man Baptiste's pick-ups grinding up the road.

I reach the top of the hill and see a solitary palm tree. A cluster of coconuts is just visible beneath its leaves. There are fruit, exactly as my gran said there would be. She was absolutely right: 'If you sit down while you plant a tree, she bear fruit a whole lot of time quicker . . .'

I sit down beside the tree and weep.

When I'm done crying I pick my way quietly past the house. One of my gran's brothers has already moved in and I don't want to disturb him. I just want to spend a few moments up here on my own, because soon the little hill top will be swarming with mourners.

I would have preferred a small service, but my gran knew a lot of people and funerals on the island follow a tradition. There will be a service at the church, then her body will be brought here for burial. Along with my cousins – Ainsley, Gary, Timmy, Jason and Keith – I'll carry the coffin up the hill from the road.

Afterwards 150 people will gather at our house for the wake.

I edge down the slope below the house, picking my way through the roots and creepers that have grown up in the time I've been away. I know exactly where I'll find my gran's tomb. She left precise instructions with the family. She wanted to be buried right next to my grandpa: she wanted her tomb to touch his.

On reaching the spot where you can see the sky in one direction and the village in the other, I give my eyes a moment to adjust to the light. The two tombs – seven feet long, five feet wide and four feet high – are separated by a gap of several feet. I move closer and smell paint. The end of my gran's tomb is open, ready to accept her coffin. A slab of granite rests on the ground nearby.

I run my finger across the paintwork, first on the inside, then on the outside. It's still wet. When I brush my hands along the sides, expecting to find them plastered smooth, I discover rough brickwork instead.

The tomb is in the wrong place and it isn't even finished.

I walk back up to the house and stand in front of the wishing tree. I look down at her roots. In the semi-darkness, and through half-closed eyes, I'm able to pick out the clean lines of my imaginary racing car. I lower myself into the seat and stare up into the branches.

As the sun begins to fill the tree with light, my old guilt is replaced by anger. I pick myself up and run to Kellon's house. He's already up and dressed. I tell him how I've just been up to my gran's tomb and what I found there. My old friend can't believe it. He's almost as angry as I am.

'What we goin' to do?' he says.

'Have you got some plaster and some whitewash?' I ask.

'Sure. They all here. An' the tools.'

I tell Kellon we can't move my gran's tomb, of course, but we're going to plaster it, wait for it to dry, then paint it as best we can – all before the funeral. He doesn't bat an eyelid. He grabs the things we need and comes up the hill with me. We roll up our sleeves and get to work, finishing the job twenty minutes before the service begins. There's no time to shower or wash the paint from my hands. I throw on a shirt and tie, button up my suit and race down to the bottom of the village.

My cousins are waiting for me. We pick up the coffin, carry it inside and set it down in front of the altar. I manage to hold myself together until the upright piano strikes up the first few bars of 'Blessed Assurance'. I lower my head; I don't want anyone to see me cry.

When the service is over we follow the horse-drawn hearse up the hill. When it can go no further we carry the coffin the rest of the way. The path is still wet and several times I feel like I'm going to slip. But I don't and nor do my cousins, though my suit ends up spattered with mud.

We reach the little plateau between the cedar and the mango tree and we slide the coffin into the tomb. Everybody crowds around as the priest starts to read the final prayers. The moment he puts down his book, my father, Tan Jane, Abigail and my other aunts and uncles kneel down and place flowers inside the tomb. I have none to give, so I take off my regimental tie and drape it over the coffin.

Two of my cousins pick up the granite slab and set it against the opening. They jiggle it a little and look at each other. Then I hear one of them say, 'It doesn't fit.'

I can't believe it. When it's set against the edge of the tomb it overlaps by two inches.

Somebody calls for a hammer and a chisel, but this is the final straw for me. I take a step forward and push my cousins out of the way. 'All my gran wanted,' I say, unable to hold back my anger any longer, 'all she asked, was to be buried next to her husband. Was that such a difficult thing?'

Nobody answers. Some can't bring themselves to look at me. Others stare at me as if I've gone mad. I couldn't care less what people think. Isabella Bolah was my grandmother. She was my rescue camp. She loved me and I loved her.

The service fizzles to a halt and the crowd shuffles away. In a couple of minutes the only people who are left are me, Kellon and my brother Jeffrey.

While everybody else is at the wake the three of us carry a load of bricks and cement up the hill. They offer to help me with the brickwork, but if it's all the same, I tell them, I'd like to do it on my own.

It takes me two hours to get the job done, but I'm not in a hurry. I don't want to join the wake, and this way I get to say goodbye on my own. A moment before I set the final brick in place I speak the words I've been meaning to say all day.

'Gran,' I tell her, 'I get me wish. Me dream come true.'

I listen to the wind. I listen to the leaves. I watch the birds and the insects for some sign that she has heard me.

'I did it, Gran. I get to be a driver.'

CHAPTER TWENTY-FOUR

I'm driving a Warrior in an army simulator complex in Warminster, just down the road from Tidworth. My task is to carry out a 'tactical bound', leapfrogging two other Warriors that have just shot past us towards the enemy. As I glance to the right I can just see the other vehicles out of the corner of my eye. I wait to receive the order to move.

'Can you see the bridge?' Randsy asks me.

'Bridge, Boss?'

'That brown thing – that splodge – half a klick up the road.'

'What's a splodge, Boss?'

He swears under his breath. 'Don't they teach you anything in Grenada?'

'Didn't do a whole lot of school, Boss.'

'Bloody hell,' he says.

I blink and stare through the day sight again and focus on the splodge. If I squint and try very hard I can just about turn it into a bridge.

'Got it, Boss. What you want me to do now?'

'Wait for the signal, then floor it – go as fast as you can. When we're on the bridge, we'll go static to let the other multiple leapfrog us. Understood?'

'A' right, Boss.'

'No, not "a' right, Boss". Is that *understood*?'

'Yes, Boss.'

'And try not to fuck up this time.'

I ease myself back into my seat and wait.

The Warrior I'm driving doesn't feel much like a Warrior. The instructors swear that it's just like the real thing, but it isn't. When I drive for real I sense the motion of the tracks and the health of the engine and the transmission system from the vibrations that come up through the steering wheel and the pedals. I *feel* a real Warrior the same way I used to feel Breezy's Datsun and the Seddon Atkinson in Chris and Jane's repair yard. But I don't get any of these signals from a simulator. Randsy can do all the shouting he likes. It's just not the same.

I first came across Lieutenant James Rands after I got back from my gran's funeral, when we were sent to Northern Ireland to man the British Army's Green Goddesses: Bedford fire engines from 1955 rolled out by the army whenever Britain's firefighters go on strike. I loved those Green Goddesses, because each one had her own character and reminded me of Indian's pride and joy.

In Northern Ireland Randsy seemed permanently vex – running around with his chest puffed up and yelling at people. Just my luck, then, at the beginning of the year, to get transferred from 7 Platoon to 8 Platoon, with him as my new platoon leader.

I've had enough of all the yelling and so have a lot of my friends, so today I've decided I'm going to even the score. In the past hour I've managed to disqualify us twice – once by deliberately driving over a civilian vehicle coming towards us; the second time by taking a short cut through a mine-field.

Randsy is still muttering about it. 'This is embarrassing – I mean, really fucking embarrassing,' he says.

'If you say so, Boss.'

'I do fucking say so,' he says. 'You're next to sodding useless. They told me you could drive. That you were a natural. Jesus wept!'

'I do what comes natural, Boss, and this don't come natural.'

As if to prove the point, a helicopter flies overhead, a hundred feet above the road, heading for the town.

'I mean, Boss,' I say, 'that don't look much like a helicopter to me. He looks more like . . . I dunno, an insect or somet'ing.'

'It's supposed to be a test of our tactics – never mind the bloody helicopter. In any case . . .'

Randsy is interrupted by a sudden burst of radio traffic.

I slip the vehicle into drive. Here we go again.

'OK, go, go, go!' he yells.

I hit the accelerator and the Warrior leaps forward.

'There's the minefield on your left,' Randsy says, excitement in his voice. 'Do not, I repeat, do not, drive through it this time. Is that clear?'

'Yes, Boss.' I keep the vehicle nice and straight.

My task is to take Whisky Two Zero to the bridge, stop just short of it, then wait for the other multiple to leapfrog us on its way to the town. I accelerate, easing our speed to forty miles per hour.

'Shit!' Randsy says. 'Mines!'

I slam on the brakes and the Warrior slews to a halt. I peer through the day sight. Strung out across the middle of the bridge, thirty metres in front of us, I can make out several black dots.

'Those are mines?' I ask.

'Those are mines.'

'Why can't I just drive straight over them?'

I hear Randsy swear under his breath. 'Because they'll blow us to kingdom come,' he says. 'Why do you think?'

'But they ain' real.'

'None of this is real. If you drove over a mine for real, one of two things would happen – we'd lose a track or, if the mine was big enough, it would rip a hole in the belly of the vehicle. Serious shit.'

'But it's not.'

'It's not what?'

'Real.'

'Oh, for Christ's sake, I don't want to talk about this any more. Turn to the right, where the ground slopes into the wadi. If you edge up on to the far bank, we can still provide covering fire for the other multiple. Think you can manage that?'

I turn to the left and gun the engine and run us straight into the minefield.

Before Randsy even has time to swear, there's a bang in my headset and the screen freezes.

A minute later I'm standing outside the tin box we've just been holed up in for the past hour. Randsy has his hands on his hips. I've never seen anyone so cross since Mr Narine blew his top at me for bunking school.

'What *is* wrong with you?' he yells. 'I said, turn to the right.'

'I thought you said left, Boss.'

'How can you mistake right for left, you idiot?'

'It's your accent, Boss.'

'*My* accent!' he shouts.

'The way you speak to me.'

Randsy looks at me. 'The way *I* speak to *you*?'

'Yes, Boss.'

'You're a bloody private.'

'I's also a good driver, Boss.'

His face goes a deep shade of red. 'Good?' he says. 'You're one of the worst drivers I've ever had the misfortune to get into a vehicle with. And you have the temerity, the gall, to blame your appalling skills on the way I speak to you. Jesus!'

I stand there, taking it, while he shakes his head. Then he's off again. 'I mean, whenever I say right, you turn left and when I say forwards you go backwards. What is wrong with you, Beharry? Three times we got endexed [ordered to end our part in the exercise] this morning. Three times! That's worse than useless. It's laughable. Anybody would think you were doing it deliberately.'

He looks up and his lips go so tight that for a moment they turn white. 'Oh, my God,' he says, 'you *are* doing it deliberately.'

I say nothing.

'OK,' he says, his voice trembling with anger. 'I'm getting Rushforth back. You're sacked. Fired. Do you understand that? I never want to see you anywhere near my vehicle – any vehicle in my platoon, for that matter. When I joined C Company your name came up as one of the shirkers. The people that count in this battalion know you're a skiver, Beharry. My mistake was believing them when they said you could drive.'

Two days later I'm in the driver's compartment of the boss's vehicle, Whisky Two Zero, strapping myself in and plugging my helmet into the radio console, when Randsy jumps up on to the hull. He does a double take. 'Beharry, what the hell are you doing here?' he says. 'I thought I sacked you.'

'Rushy didn't want the job, Boss. I'm afraid you're stuck with me.'

He shakes his head. 'Christ, anybody else who gets sacked from the boss's wagon would think all his Christmases had come at once. But not you.'

'I got no beef drivin' for you, Mr Rands. I take pride in me work.'

'Then what was with the bolshie behaviour in the simulator?'

'I don't like the way you talk to me.'

He laughs. 'You don't like the way I talk to you? That's rich. Do you want me to say, "Pretty please" every time I give you an order?'

I remember Aziz, sitting there in the pub, flashing his gold tooth and telling me about the shit life I could expect in the army. And then I remember Forrester, my fellow Grenadian from the recruiting office, telling me there would be times when I would want to quit. Don't question your orders, just do it, is what he told me.

'In case you hadn't heard, Beharry, this is the army and I'm not paid to be nice to you. I'm here to get the best out of you – and, God knows, if we go to war I might just need your pitiful best. Have you read a paper lately?'

'Yes, Boss.'

'Then you'll know that there's quite a strong possibility we may invade Iraq any day now. So now you've got that little lot off your chest, how about showing me if you can drive one of these things for real?'

It's six o'clock in the morning and there is still a lot of mist about when we head out on to the Plain. I have to leave my anger behind and concentrate on what's ahead. We're due to take part in a 'company integrated attack' – a manoeuvre that will see twenty Warriors giving it all they've got across the ranges.

In a real battle, moving fast is the best protection we have, because however good our armour, the best idea is not to get hit in the first place.

The company integrated attack is part of a schedule that is

designed to prepare us for our 'operational year', now just six months away. We have progressed from CP2 (platoon-level) attacks and our tactics are now being assessed at CP3 or company level. The next stage, CP4, will assess our ability to perform as a 'battle group'. These BG exercises will take place later in the year at BATUS – the British Army Training Unit Suffield – in Canada. Whatever happens, we're not going to be combat-ready until the beginning of January. And by then Randsy's war will long be over.

In the back today we have half a section – three Fijian dismounts led by Corporal Adam Llewellyn. Lewy, as he is known, is one of 8 Platoon's three section commanders. Lewy can hear what's happening through a headset that's plugged into a wall socket behind him.

He will have told the men to strap in tight. Being in the back of a Warrior during a company formation attack can throw you about worse than a bus trip between Diego Piece and Sauteurs.

As Major Coote, the OC, takes evasive action, Randsy issues a stream of instructions to the other vehicles to maintain station. My job is to stick to Major Coote's vehicle like glue. This I do, right up to the last second, when I bring Whisky Two Zero to a halt several hundred metres from a network of enemy slit trenches.

I hit my mark. Whisky Two Zero shudders to a halt and the back end rears up, then crashes back down. Ahead I see muzzle flashes from the enemy – another unit brought in for the task – and I hear Randsy's directions to Lewy in the back: where the enemy is and which way the section should break as they come out from the back.

I see Lewy and the other dismounts disappear into the battle smoke. We're under mortar attack and some of the detonations from the flash-bangs are close. Our gunner, Aitken, responds with some covering fire from our chain gun. But in

less than three minutes it's over. Our dismounts have stormed
the position. The attack is a success.

There's a crackle in my headset. 'Beharry?'

'Yes, Boss.'

There's a pause.

'Nice work.'

We're in a column of vehicles heading back to camp. The
mist has burned off and the heat is rising. Salisbury Plain
seems to be a place of extremes – freezing in winter or scorch-
ing in summer.

My battledress is soaked. Sweat trickles down from under
my helmet, giving the dust kicked up by the Warrior in front
something to stick to. My eyes sting, but it's my hearing I'm
wondering about. Did Randsy just pay me a compliment? I
twist my head around. He's commanding the vehicle with the
hatch open – a handkerchief tied around his nose and mouth.
He sees me and gives me a thumbs-up.

I turn back to the front. My headphones crackle again.

'There's clearly nothing wrong with your driving, Beharry,'
Randsy says.

'Thanks,' I tell him.

'So let's clear this up. What is it that's pissing you off?'

I don't know where the boss is taking this, so I say nothing.

'Come on,' he says. 'I want you to get this off your chest.
What is it? What's wrong?'

I take a deep breath. 'Last year, Boss, me gran died. I know
that don't sound like much, but she meant a lot to me. She
brought me up. Me gran really was like a mother to me. She
was everyt'ing . . .'

I tell Randsy I'm pissed off because the army showed me
no compassion over the death of my gran. And I realise I
didn't even know this was what was on my mind till he asked
me.

For almost a minute all I get in my headset is the sound of static. Then Randsy says, 'Listen, I can understand how you feel, but it would be a pity to throw away a promising career simply because you're hacked off with a few people.'

'It's about respect,' I tell him. 'Discipline ain't got not'ing to do with it. I'll follow an officer or an NCO to the ends of the earth if I respect him.'

'Respect is a big thing for you Caribbeans, isn't it?' he says.

I tell him there should be more of it around.

Through the dust I catch sight of a series of little hills beside the track. People have told me that these are the burial mounds of ancient kings and maybe this is why I get a strange feeling every time I pass them by. I get a strange feeling now – the same as I used to get in Grenada when I walked up the hill in Diego Piece at night.

Maybe because we've just been talking about her, I also think of my gran. I picture her sprinkling rice and salt about the place to ward off the Jablesse. I smile at the memory and I hear her voice. She is scolding me. 'It's no laughin' matter, the feelin's you get inside from places like this. You take care now, Johnson, an' you remember the t'ings I tell you.'

I see a main road and a set of white posts up ahead. We're approaching Crossing Point Charlie-Charlie.

There's a set procedure for crossing a main road, designed to prevent civilian drivers from ploughing into Warriors. The idea is for the front vehicle to stop and for somebody to get out, marshalling the civvie traffic until all the vehicles are safely across. The column goes at once, following the lead vehicle till all of them are safely on the other side.

There's so much dust in the air today it's difficult to see the road at all. Then, through the haze, I see a van with a big ice-cream cone on its roof trundling lazily up the road in the direction of Stonehenge.

As it passes us by I catch the sound of its bell.

'Anyone for a choc ice?' Randsy says.

'Make mine a 99,' Aitken says.

'And four more in the back,' I hear Lewy say.

The ice-cream van disappears into the haze.

I switch my gaze back to the Warrior in front of us and as the column comes to a halt I bring Whisky Two Zero to a gentle stop a decent interval from its brake lights. I reach down for the water bottle I keep next to my seat and unscrew the top. I'm raising it to my lips when Randsy yells, '*Shit, brace!*'

A second later there is a bang and a terrible shriek of metal. Something slams into the back of us with such force that my seat shears from its mounting and the rim of the hatch accelerates towards me at lightning speed.

There's no time to raise my hands. My chest hits the steering column and my face slams into the hatch. Lights explode behind my eyes. I feel a terrible pain in my head.

Then nothing.

When I come to, I have difficulty opening my eyes. Randsy is kneeling beside me. He is pressing his handkerchief to my cheek.

I can't feel a thing.

I'm lying on my back. I can see the outline of Whisky Two Zero's hull against the sky. The sunlight is blinding, the pain inside my head like someone hammering the inside of my skull.

Behind Randsy, shadows move. The boss is talking to someone. He looks like he's seen a ghost. Randsy turns and shouts something. I see the concern on his face and wonder what the problem is.

Forget it, I tell myself. It can't be important. The problem will sort itself out . . .

I close my eyes and feel myself float free.

When I open them again, Randsy and Whisky Two Zero are gone. Huge white clouds tower above me with splashes of blue in between.

I'm back in Grenada.

Then I feel myself sinking. It's as if the ground beneath me has turned to quicksand and is sucking me in. A voice tells me to give in to it, and as the numbness takes hold I let myself slide. I go deeper and it feels good. It's a feeling I've had before. I try to place when and where, but I can't. The voice tells me that it's important, that I must give it another go, so I concentrate with all my might and a picture forms. I see my father. He's standing on the porch of our house, holding a bottle of Clarke's Court.

We sit down at the table in the kitchen. There's nobody else around. My father takes the top off the bottle, raises it to his lips and takes a long swig. He smiles and offers the bottle to me. I grasp it by the neck, tip it back and drink.

Now I know the feeling. This is it. I let go and the numbness spreads.

Then my eyes snap open and I come to, gulping down air. '*Daddy!*'

'Take it easy, Beharry.' The voice is calm and reassuring. 'Help's on its way. Just hang in there, OK?'

Randsy is back. He's kneeling beside me. He dabs at my cheek with the handkerchief. The pain in my head and chest is terrible.

A helicopter is hovering somewhere nearby, and as the rotors whirl nearer and nearer, the volume increases. The whine of its engine and the beat of the blades combine with the hammering inside my head. The noise is killing me.

I try to move my arms so I can put my hands to my ears, but Randsy won't let me.

'Easy there, Beharry. Try to keep still. We're going to get you out of here, OK?'

Dust and grass swirl in the air. I taste grit in the back of my throat.

Somebody gives me some water. I try to drink, but end up almost coughing my guts out.

Then I'm surrounded by people and hands lift me on to a stretcher. I pass beneath the rotors of the helicopter and am hoisted into the cabin.

I feel straps being tied across my legs and chest and a man holding a syringe says, 'Where does it hurt, son?'

I want to tell him it hurts everywhere, but the pain is worst in my head and this is what I manage to shout in his ear.

As we lift into the air I see him stab at me with the needle. Then I feel myself falling again. This time I don't fight it. I let go and slide into the blackness.

When I wake up in hospital Aitken is on my right. I can see a strand of his ginger hair through the bandage that's wrapped around his head.

Lying on the bed opposite, his leg in a sling, is Harris, a guy I recognise from another platoon. Randsy is in the bed next to him.

When the doctor comes he tells me that I've had a bad concussion but I'll live.

Aitken and Harris fill me in on what happened. Harris was the driver of the vehicle behind. As he came through the dust cloud he saw Whisky Two Zero far too late to do anything about it.

One of the faults of the Warrior is that the steering locks up when you slam on the brakes. You can't emergency-brake and steer at the same time. Harris's Warrior rammed into ours with such force that it shunted us into a tree and drove us thirty feet up a bank.

The driver's seat is mounted on bolts above the Warrior's main battery. To get to the battery during servicing you have to remove the seat. The trouble is, every time you do this you weaken the bolts. The four holding my seat sheared clean, propelling me into the rim of the hatch. By the time Randsy got to me I was having trouble breathing. He and a couple of the Fijians pulled me from the hatch and laid me out on the grass in front of the vehicle.

Randsy gets out of bed, picks up a crutch and hobbles from the room.

'Christ, talk about a close shave,' Aitken says. 'You went fuckin' blue in the face, mate.'

'We thought you were a goner,' Harris says. 'Jesus, Beharry. I'm sorry. I feel bloody terrible about it. We just never saw you till it was too late.'

I tell him I'm fine and not to worry about it.

But my head hurts and I'm not thinking too straight. I have trouble following the story.

'What do you mean, I was a goner?' I don't know what Harris means.

'You were dead, mate. At least, that's the way it looked to the rest of us,' Aitken says. 'Randsy was on the radio, directin' the chopper, when one of the Fijians says you've stopped breathin'. Randsy jumps down and grabs you and literally shakes the life back into you.'

'When you started breathin' again so did we,' Harris says. 'Clinically, mate, you were with the ghosts of your forefathers for a moment or two back there.'

Randsy hobbles back into the room. He glances at me and smiles. 'It's good to have you back,' he says.

'Thanks,' I tell him. I don't know what else to say.

CHAPTER TWENTY-FIVE

I'm standing in a giant tent in the searing heat of the Canadian summer, watching grown men trying to get organised.

BATUS, which covers one thousand square miles, is a giant test and exercising range that the British Army shares with the Canadian military. We're here in brigade strength, our first proper showing as 1st Armoured Brigade, and this is part of the problem. BATUS's permanent buildings were designed to house a battalion of around six hundred, but we're five or six times that and somehow everybody has to squeeze in. It's quite something to see the officers and men of C Company – from Major Coote downwards – all crammed into one tent.

The place looks like a refugee camp. The whole battalion is accommodated under a sea of canvas. Tents like ours stretch into the distance, merging with the heat haze.

Flies get into almost everything, and what they don't is covered in a fine layer of dust.

Eddie has organised transport to take me, Sammy, Beggsy and Campbell to Medicine Hat, the nearest town, which is around forty minutes away. Even if the camp is a shit-hole, Eddie says, at least we have a night on the town to look forward to.

Tonight we really do have something to celebrate. Sammy

has just qualified as a gunner and is gunning for Corporal Geordie Davison, 8 Platoon's Warrior sergeant.

'Why do *we* get left the tents?' Sammy says, as we make our way to the edge of the camp, where Eddie's taxi is waiting.

''Cos rich fuckin' officers from the tank regiments grabbed all the real buildings,' Beggsy says. 'Typical fuckin' tankies.'

This isn't exactly true. Our brigade has only one tank regiment, as far as I know: the Queen's Royal Lancers. They are equipped with the Challenger 2 main battle tank – Charlie 2s, we call them – a monstrous machine powered by a twelve-cylinder diesel engine that weighs in, fully loaded, at almost seventy tonnes, more than twice the combat weight of a Warrior.

The brigade's armoured infantry battalion is 1PWRR, while the 1st Battalion the Cheshire Regiment and the 1st Battalion the Royal Welch Fusiliers make up our two mechanised battalions. Mechanised battalions are equipped with the Saxon.

The war in Iraq has come and gone. President George W. Bush has declared combat operations in Iraq 'over'. There's still some fighting, but in military terms there's little to get excited about.

Our training in Canada is designed to make us combat-ready for our operational year, which is due to start in four months. We're due to deploy to Northern Ireland.

'Complete fuckin' waste of time, this,' Sammy says, as we overtake yet another convoy of combine harvesters.

I can see his point. When I was there during the fire strike I didn't see a single wheat prairie. 'Relax,' I tell him. 'You're vehicle crew now.'

'Yeah, easy, man, easy,' Kevin Campbell says. He's Jamaican and another driver in the platoon.

We pull up outside a dingy-looking bar near the centre of the town.

'Here we are.' Eddie steps out on to the pavement. 'This place is famous throughout the British Army for some of the most gorgeous women on this continent.' He points to a fizzing neon sign above the door.

We dig into our pockets and hand over a small fortune in Canadian dollars to Eddie, who pays the driver.

There are four people inside and one of them is the barman. He's the only one who is not wearing a large cowboy hat.

There are no windows. The room is very dark, but I can just make out a stage and a pole at one end.

The cowboys are all turned our way.

Eddie wanders up to the bar, rubbing his hands. The cowboys stay right where they are.

'Good evening,' Eddie says. 'Looks like we're the first in today.'

He gives a mock salute to a cowboy on a barstool, who continues to stare at us over the top of his glass.

Eddie asks what time the floor show starts.

The barman doesn't bat an eyelid; he just tells him straight. The floor show's over and it's not due to start up again any time soon. There's a new lady mayor in town and part of the ticket that got her elected was a promise to clean up the town. Strippers are banned.

'Banned?' Eddie says.

'No girls at all,' the barman says. He sticks out his hand and demands forty dollars.

Beggsy laughs and Campbell almost spits his drink on the floor.

'Thanks, man,' Sammy says, clapping Eddie on the back. 'Great place. Really.'

Our training builds from platoon-sized trench-clearing exercises to repeats of our company integrated attacks and finally to exercises in which 1PWRR has to mesh with the other battalions of the brigade in massed tank and Warrior attacks across the Canadian plains.

I start to feel 8 Platoon is beginning to mesh as a team. There's the Boss, of course, and Chris Adkins, the platoon sergeant, who spends much of the time in the back of Whisky Two Zero.

Also in the back is the platoon signaller, Ervin, known as 'Big Erv' or 'Fingers', because he lost one as a kid while playing Knock Down Ginger – the game where you shout through someone's letterbox, then run like hell before they can get to the door. Too bad for him that someone happened to be standing right by the door and pulled it back so quickly that Erv's finger stayed in the letterbox.

Then there is Corporal Joe Tagica, 'Big Joe', a six-foot-five Fijian who commands Whisky Two Three. Joe joined the British Army after serving eighteen years with his own. He is a quiet man, built like an oak tree, and a committed Christian.

A month into BATUS, Geordie Davison, 8 Platoon's Warrior sergeant and commander of Whisky Two Two, sticks his foot out of the turret cage while Sammy is traversing. He gets sent home with a badly smashed foot, but we all know that he is lucky: he could have ended up losing it altogether.

Corporal Lewy Llewellyn, one of the section dismount commanders, is forced to take over, even though he has no day-to-day experience of the Warrior, and Sammy gets transferred to Whisky Two Zero. Sammy has taken to calling me 'Paki' because of the colour of my skin.

We're queuing in a long line of Warriors, Charlie 2s and Saxons for spaces in the sheds where each vehicle has to be washed down, then serviced. After the buzz of a mock battle, this is the part we hate. There are hundreds of vehicles in the brigade and only a limited number of bays where they can be washed and inspected. It's like being stuck in a traffic jam on a blazing-hot summer's day. Nothing happens for ages; we just sit in the heat and sweat it out. Then we fire up our engines and shunt forward again. It can take hours to get to the front of the queue.

We're still stuck a long way back when Randsy starts talking about the Common Equipment Schedule. The CES is an inventory of every tool and item of kit that makes up an army vehicle, from the weapons and radios down to spares, cables, connectors, nuts, bolts, washers, screws and grommets. When BATUS is finished everything has to be accounted for. If it isn't, and we don't have a good excuse for why bits of kit from the CES are missing, the cost of replacing them could end up getting docked from our pay.

Randsy knows we're missing a set of jump leads, a load of spanners and an oil gun. I don't know where they went. The one thing you never, ever do is thieve from another vehicle in the platoon to get the kit you need. Just about anywhere else is fair game, though – unless you get caught.

It's almost sundown and the vehicles of B Company are next up to enter the inspection shed. A handful of Charlie 2s belonging to the Queen's Royal Lancers and some Saxons from the Cheshires stand in our way. It will be some hours yet before we're able to crawl back into our tent.

I notice that one of the six bay doors of the inspection shed is closed. As the queue shows no sign of moving I decide to investigate. Bay 5 is completely empty. When I ask why, one of the inspectors tells me that the door is jammed. This is crazy. Because a door won't open, a whole bay isn't being used.

The rest of the shed is buzzing with activity as crews try to satisfy the inspectors that their tanks and AIFVs are cleaned and ready for tomorrow's action – our last big exercise before we go home.

I go back to Whisky Two Zero and start up the engine.

Randsy's voice comes over the intercom. 'Beharry, what are you doing?'

'I'm getting us out of this mess, Boss. I just need you to get the rest of the company to follow.'

I pull Whisky Two Zero out of the line and start hammering towards the head of the column, past the Charlie 2s and Saxons and past B Company's Warriors as they start to move – the right way – into the inspection shed.

Randsy has done his stuff: the rest of C Company is following.

I drive to the back of the building, make straight for Bay 5 and reverse us in. The other Warriors of 8 Platoon do the same. In the general chaos none of the inspectors notices that we have jumped to the head of the queue.

I figure we have a couple of minutes before the QRL and Cheshire boys realise what has happened. We have to move fast.

There's a low growl. A Charlie 2 has followed our example. And another, then another. In a couple of minutes the area behind the sheds is filled with revving tanks and APCs. In next to no time the whole area is gridlocked.

'While I'm sweet-talkin' the inspectors, you go and do whatever it is you have to do,' I tell Sammy.

'What are you talkin' about?' he says.

'The CES,' I say, nodding towards the B Company vehicles. 'You always tellin' me you can scrounge anyt'ing.' I hand him a list of the equipment we're missing. 'Here's your chance to prove it.'

When we set out the next day I'm able to tell Randsy that we have a complete CES. The boss doesn't ask me how this has come about, but if he were to, I would be able to tell him – truthfully – that I don't know. I last saw Sammy disappear into a group of B Company Warriors in the inspection bay next to ours. When I checked Whisky Two Zero again in the early hours of this morning, the inventory was complete.

The upside of this is that Randsy knows that Sammy and I work well as a team. Sammy has proved himself not only a good gunner, but someone who can help me maintain the vehicle. When I ask Randsy if Sammy can become a permanent member of Whisky Two Zero, he promises to put in a good word with Major Coote.

Sammy and I continue to discuss who is available to replace Geordie in the role of Warrior sergeant the following afternoon, after we have been knocked out of the TESEX (Tactical Engagement Simulation Exercise) by a Spartan reconnaissance vehicle. In this exercise all the tanks and AIFVs have lasers positioned alongside their guns. They also have sensors on their hulls that tell the judges who has been hit and whether the hit is bad enough to take them out of the battle.

The Spartan is lighter and more agile than the Warrior, and took us completely by surprise. Our sensors tell us that we have been totally disabled. As the driver I must play dead for the remainder of the exercise by staying with the vehicle. Sammy is dead too, because he has removed the batteries from his TESEX vest. Randsy, Adkins and Big Erv, whose sensors show that they are all very much alive, have to go on fighting on foot. We watch them disappear into the heat haze, then set about making ourselves comfortable for the rest of the afternoon.

I get up into the turret and scan the surrounding area. From the dust on the horizon I know the battle is being fought a long way off and that we'll be left in peace.

Except for a couple of parked-up Charlie 2s and a Warrior that was disabled by a missile shortly after we were hit by the Spartan, there's nobody else around. The Charlie 2s are lying up a couple of hundred metres away and the other Warrior about fifty metres in front of them.

By a stroke of luck the driver of the Warrior turns out to be a friend from 7 Platoon, a fellow Grenadian called Maxian Lewis. Lying in the shade of his wagon, he has his head propped on his day sack and a partially disassembled Minimi machine-gun spread out on a groundsheet beside him.

Sammy and I agree it will be more fun chilling with Maxian than hanging out on our own, so I drive over and set up next to his Warrior. While Sammy and Maxian stretch out in the shade, I open up our engine hatch.

'Johnson, my brother,' Maxian says, 'what you doin'?'

I tell him I'm about to inspect our engine, which has been running a little rough. The timing is out. I plan on fixing it.

'Why?' he asks.

''Cos she need fixin', Maxian. You cleanin' you Minimi, ain' you?'

Maxian laughs. 'The Minimi's just for show. In case anybody come.'

'He can't stay still for a bloody minute,' Sammy tells him. 'He's always gotta be doin' somet'ing. It drive me nuts.'

'An' you call youself a Grenadian,' Maxian says, shaking his head.

'If I not busy,' I tell him, 'I just end up in trouble.'

'Then do somet'ing useful,' Maxian says, 'an' make us a cup of tea.'

He and Sammy high-five each other and start to laugh.

Still listening to their banter, I go around to the back of our vehicle. I open up the rear door, get out the gas stove and set it up on the ground. I pour some water into a bivvy can and put it on the gas ring. Then I sit on the lip of the door and stare at the cloud of dust on the horizon.

A slight breeze blows across the prairie and cools the sweat on my cheeks. I close my eyes and pretend I'm on my gran's little hill, my face turned to the sun as she rises over the village. If I concentrate I can smell wood smoke, spices, cooking . . .

The rev of engines brings me back to the present. The throaty roar of big CV12 diesels: tank engines.

The Charlie 2s are preparing to move.

I look down at the stove. The water is boiling. I pick up the can and pour water into the cups. Then I hear the revs pick up and the squeaking, clanking noise of tracks. As I squeeze out the tea bags the sound gets closer and closer.

Far too close . . .

I jump up as one of the Charlie 2s roars past us and I'm spattered with mud kicked up by its tracks.

'Hey,' I shout, shaking my fist at the driver, 'what you t'ink you doin'?'

The tank is driving in reverse, its turret facing forward. It has missed us by a foot, two at the outside. At first I think they have done this deliberately to scare us. But the commander is head down, reading a map. The driver, who seems to be concentrating on his wing mirror, shows no sign he even knows we're here.

As I watch the tank disappear into the heat haze, I feel a burning sensation on my left leg. I've spilled tea on my thigh. Before I have time to curse I hear more revving, more squeaking and clanking. The ground rumbles. I feel the vibration through the soles of my feet. The second Charlie 2 is on the move. And this time, amid all the noise, I hear cries of alarm from Sammy and Maxian.

I poke my head around the door in time to see the back end of the second Charlie 2 heading straight for the front of our Warrior.

My first thought is that it's going to run over Sammy and Maxian. But suddenly it changes course. I don't know whether it has done enough to miss us. If it has, it will follow the same route taken by the first tank; if not, seventy tonnes of Challenger will strike our front left-hand side.

I'm frozen to the spot. If I run clear and the tank does miss us, I'll move straight into its path. If I stay where I am and it hits us, the impact will drive the Warrior straight through me.

I throw myself backwards and am still in the air when there is an ear-shattering crash. I hit the ground and roll, bracing my body for a collision as our Warrior shoots backwards. But as I come to a stop with my arms around my head, there is no pain, no blackness – only silence.

Opening my eyes, I get to my feet. The Warrior is no longer where I parked it. It has been driven back twenty feet. The Charlie 2 has taken its place. There are two giant gouges in the ground from the force of the collision.

I bend down and look under the vehicle at the point where I've been standing. By a miracle, the stove is untouched. Steam rises from the water that's still bubbling in the bivvy can.

Then I hear a shout. Sammy is standing by the front of the Warrior, staring at me, his eyes wide.

'Jesus, Paki, y'all right?'

'I think so,' I tell him. 'Maxian?'

Sammy says Maxian is just fine. Alerted by the first tank, they managed to scurry out of the way of the second at the very last moment. Maxian's Minimi wasn't so lucky. He's now running around trying to pick up the pieces.

Seconds later a tall, thin tankie lieutenant appears. As he slips down from his turret one of his legs almost gives way. He is trying to maintain his composure, but his face is very white. 'Good God,' he says, 'you people could have been killed.' He says it as if what has just happened is nothing at all to do with him.

Sammy and I glance at each other.

The lieutenant walks towards us a little shakily. He's staring down his nose at us. He has two big front teeth and looks a little like a rabbit.

'Are you all right, old man?' he asks.

I nod.

'Are you sure?'

'Yes, sir, I'm fine,' I tell him.

'Seem to have made a bit of a hash of your Warrior,' he says. 'What on earth were you doing here?'

'I'm sorry?' Sammy says.

'I'm just wondering what on earth possessed you to park where you did,' the officer says.

'Are you sayin' this is our fault?' Sammy says.

I can see his blood beginning to boil.

'Sammy,' I say. 'Easy . . .'

'They had the whole fuckin' prairie to drive around us,' Sammy says. 'They weren't lookin' where they was going. This is their fault, not ours.'

'Steady, old man,' the officer says.

Sammy storms off, leaving me and the officer to assess the damage.

For some reason the commanders of both Charlie 2s decided to reverse out of their positions. The driver of the vehicle that hit us only changed course when he saw Sammy and Maxian scrabbling to their feet in his rear-view mirror.

While we wait for the recovery vehicles to arrive and our nerves to settle, I see that our Warrior has just got a minor dent at the point of impact and a busted track link.

The Charlie 2, on the other hand, will be off the road for weeks.

When our vehicle is towed clear of the impact point, something catches the light in one of the gouges made by our tracks. I bend down and pick up the end of a tiny chain. I tug gently and a little silver cross lifts from the dirt.

A shadow falls across me.

'What's that?' Sammy asks.

'Somet'ing me auntie gave me,' I say, holding up the chain and the cross.

I've had two close shaves in as many months. Both have involved the Warrior and both, in their different ways, almost ended up killing me.

Auntie I's words fill my thoughts: 'If ever you find yourself in danger, you must hold this little crucifix close and pray to God and all His angels for help.' I hold the cross tight in the palm of my hand.

CHAPTER TWENTY-SIX

Soon after our return to Tidworth we lose Randsy. He is being promoted to captain and made battalion intelligence officer. Sergeant Adkins assumes temporary command of 8 Platoon. After the intensity of BATUS we feel that we have been cast adrift. We don't have a platoon boss, we're minus a proper Warrior sergeant, the CO of the battalion is leaving, we don't know anything about his replacement and we still don't know where we're set to deploy in our operational year, now just six weeks away.

Northern Ireland still seems to be the hot favourite, but there are also rumours that we're going to Iraq.

Today I have to change a track link on Whisky Two Zero. I've chosen Sammy, Beggsy and Campbell to help me. I don't hear them complaining; it's sleeting outside and the sheds are kept warm by blow heaters.

I want Whisky Two Zero to be as perfect as she can possibly be every time she leaves the sheds. This is what Chris taught me when I worked for him in Woodlands. Be thorough, Johnson, my brother. If you don't do it properly first time, you're only going to have to do it all over again.

'Can't we just change the oil and wipe the windows?' Beggsy says.

'No,' I tell him. 'There's supposed to be a five-millimetre gap between each track link. I'm readin' a gap of five to ten mills between some of the links. We have to replace a link to get the tension back.'

'Five mills? Ten mills? Who cares?' Beggsy says.

'You'll care,' I say, 'if we're out there and we lose a track.'

We have a special tool for measuring track tension, but I can now see whether there's a problem just by looking at the sag between the top rollers.

Each track system is made up of six road wheels, a sprocket, an idler and the three top rollers. The sprocket is a giant cog with teeth that meshes with the links to drive the track forward. The track is looped between the sprocket and the idler.

Before I do anything else I check that each wheel is topped up with lubricant. Then I check the tracks themselves. You can usually maintain track pressure simply by increasing tension on the hydraulic rams that support each of the rear rollers. But if that doesn't work you need to take out a link.

Removing one of the eighty-two links in a track restores the tension, and although it's a simple procedure it takes at least four people to do it. We always carry two spare links on a Warrior and each piece requires two men to lift it.

As Campbell is also a driver I put him into the driver's seat of Whisky Two Zero so I can direct things. When you're in camp a vehicle is always supervised from the ground, not the turret.

The first thing I do is drain the grease that maintains the pressure in the ram, then I ask Campbell to turn the vehicle to the right. This collapses the ram and makes the track go slack. We can now get to work on removing one of the links.

Each link has a male and a female edge which slot together and are held in place by a locking pin. I knock the locking pin out with a sledgehammer and a guide pin, then give the track a tap and the two halves come apart.

We go through the same procedure again with the link that we want to remove. When it's clear, Sammy and Beggsy manhandle it to the ground.

'Hey, Paki, let's take a break, eh?' Sammy says. 'This is killin' me, man.'

'We break when we finished,' I tell him. 'Not long now.'

I move around to the front of the vehicle and whistle to get Campbell's attention. I gesture to the right with my clenched fist. Campbell puts the Warrior into a neutral right turn, spinning the track we've been working on.

As soon as the tension starts to come back, I signal for Campbell to stop and apply the handbrake, then switch off the engine. The gap is now positioned between the sprocket and the first road wheel and we can start to link it together again.

I get a clamp from the back of the vehicle and use it to bridge the gap, then crank the two links together with a spanner. When the male and female edges are locked I get Sammy to hit the top of the track with a crowbar. This nudges the two links into alignment. I bang the guide pin back in with a sledgehammer and remove the clamp.

Sammy, Beggsy and I have worked up quite a sweat, but we aren't done yet. I knock the guide pin out with the locking pin and secure it with two large nuts. I check that there is an equal amount of thread at each end of the locking pin, as any mismatch can be a sign of wear and tear. A 360 torque reading on each nut tells me that it's correctly adjusted.

I pump grease back into the ram and watch the tension come back into the track. I use a measuring tool to show me when I've got the correct level of tension. Too much and you get wear on the links. Too little and the track could fly apart.

'Tea,' Sammy says. 'About time.'

We're all sitting in the back of the vehicle enjoying a brew when the shed doors rumble open and I feel a blast of icy wind. As I pull our door shut I hear a commotion just outside Whisky Two Zero. Someone is getting a bollocking.

'Who's doin' the yellin'?' Sammy asks, looking up from his mug of tea. 'That don't sound like Lewy.'

I poke my head around the door. I pull back so quickly that I hit the back of my head on the rim. 'Oh no . . . It's him. It's *him*.' I rub my head.

'Who?' Beggsy asks.

'Whatsisname,' I stammer. 'That guy, that sergeant . . .'

'For God's sake, Paki,' Sammy says. 'You concussed or somet'ing? You not makin' any sense.'

'We were in Kosovo. I saw him bollockin' Eddie. I mean *really* bollockin' him. Like that.' I gesture outside the Warrior. 'Then I ran into him. The way he looked at me, I thought he was goin' to kill me.'

'What's his name, man?' Sammy says.

'Broome,' I say finally. 'Sergeant Chris Broome.'

'Broomstick?' Sammy says. 'What's he doin' here?'

'You know him?'

'Know of him. He's C Company. An instructor. Always on courses. Never around. Not since I been with the battalion anyway.'

'Well, he's out there now,' I say. 'Large as life.'

The door opens. Broome stands there, hands on hips. I look at his knuckles and wince.

Lennie and Ronnie are back in town.

'Well, well, well,' Broome says. 'If it ain't the four bloody stooges, caught in the act. Out, you lot. Come on, out. Now!'

We jump out of the back of the vehicle and do our best to look sharp.

Broome asks for our names. Sammy and Beggsy spit theirs out. Then he gets to me. 'Let me see if I can get this right,' he says. 'Beharry. Grenadian name. Originally from somewhere near the Taj bloody Mahal.'

I say nothing. He pushes out his jaw and moves closer. 'The great thing about me, Harry, is I've got a terrific memory for names and faces. Who's your mate?' He gestures to Campbell. 'No, let me guess. Private Kevin bloody Campbell. Right?'

Campbell nods.

'Well, I know all about you lot,' he says, 'because your reputation precedes you and I've done my homework. You're the artful bleedin' dodgers. The guys who think they've got it all sorted.'

He pauses. 'Well, I'm here to tell you that you ain't, 'cos there's a new sheriff in town. Me.'

Over the next couple of weeks Sammy, Beggsy, Campbell and I end up spending a lot of time on guard duty. Beggsy, Campbell and I do what we have to to get by. Sammy takes a different approach. The more Broome yells at us, the more he digs in his heels.

I should have seen this coming. The problem is that we four have stuck together. As a group we look like trouble.

I realise the best thing I can do is spend as much time as I can in the sheds, get to know the vehicle inside and out and keep my head down. There's always something new to learn. Today's lesson is attaching the armoured skirts which protect the tracks – if we're lucky – from an RPG attack.

The wing mirror, the stowage bins and the four towing eyes all have to be taken off, then refitted. There's a set procedure for this, but with thirty Warriors jostling for space and kit all over the floor, a lot of nuts, bolts, spanners and screwdrivers end up getting lost or stolen.

I'm back in Chris's yard, but without the chalk. I buy some plastic bags and write the name of the part type on the bag along with Whisky Two Zero's call sign and registration number. Each part goes straight into its bag as I remove it from the vehicle. The idea soon spreads. Next to nothing gets lost or stolen any more, and we're no longer in the shit.

Broomstick walks into the sheds a few days later, strides over to Whisky Two Zero and asks me if he can have a word.

'Sure,' I say. Broomstick has never asked me for anything before. 'What's up?'

'You know that system you developed? The bags and that? Well, I've got a confession to make.'

'A confession?' I know I look like he's hit me over the back of the head with a sandbag. 'What you mean?'

'I got called in this morning by the OC. Old Cootesy is chuffed to bits with the way things have been going in the sheds. He congratulated me on running a tight, well-organised ship. Then he makes a special mention of the system you came up with. Told me it was a brilliant yet simple idea and that I should take great credit for it. Yeah, I know. He thought it was me. And you know something, Harry, for a minute I didn't say a thing. I just stood there, puffed out me chest and soaked it all up. Then I left.'

He looks me in the eye.

'I may be a lot of things, Harry, but takin' credit for another man's work ain't part of my bag of tricks, mate. So I went back to Major Coote and told him the truth.' He holds his hand out. 'I'm here to apologise.'

As Warrior sergeant for the platoon, 'Uncle Stick' holds the keys to the stores – a section of the sheds that holds the spares for 8 Platoon's four vehicles. He cuts another key for me, so that when he's not around I can take responsibility for their maintenance. Part of this understanding is that I can choose who I work with.

The other part of the deal is that my three friends have to accept that they are in the sheds for a reason. It's a fine balance, but it works. For Sammy, Beggsy and Campbell, being in the sheds is better than being out on the Plain. And Broomstick can count on things getting done. I even get to talk to him about his life.

'I'm from Dover,' he tells me. 'The bit of Dover that makes the docks look like a holiday camp. My dad was in the army, but he wasn't ever around much, and him and my mum split when I was a kid. I was running around with a crowd of losers, always in and out of trouble. Smashing up a bus shelter was the absolute highlight of my day.'

'But why the army?'

'I needed a job, mate. Easiest thing to do if you live in Dover is work on the ferries. I had a shitload of interviews, but got turned down for every job I applied for. Being colour-blind meant I couldn't be a deckhand, for some bloody reason, and they weren't exactly queuin' around the block to employ me at the captain's table.'

He takes a sip of coffee.

'So I walked into a recruitin' centre and signed up. I was seventeen. First thing we did was get sent to Northern Ireland. To me, then, the army was a job; a way to put a bit of money in my pocket and keep me off the streets. But try tellin' that to the twelve-year-old kids chuckin' fridges at us from a block of flats on some God-forsaken estate in West Belfast.

'The first time I'm back home on leave, I go and see my mates, who are either down the pub, on the dole or kiddin' themselves that they're Arthur bloody Daley – plastic Londoners, the lot of them. When I start tellin' them about my day in South Armagh I might as well be talkin' Polish. That's when I decided, no more pissin' around. Make the time that I'm here the real deal.'

When I hear him speak this way I realise that Broomstick's story is not a million miles from my own. We're all running from something. The army has given us a place to hide.

He drains the rest of his brew, gets to his feet and asks whether I've heard the news. I shake my head.

'The new CO's arrived. He's goin' to address the whole battalion at 1400 hours.'

'What you think he goin' to say?'

'Put it this way. If it's Northern Ireland again, I might just go and blow my bloody brains out.'

There are six hundred of us in the gym, waiting for the new CO. There's a buzz in the air. It's the first time I've seen the whole battalion gathered in one place. Major Coote, the OC, is standing a few feet away, fiddling with his mobile phone. Next to him is Randsy, looking a bit heavier in the face since he's taken up his new desk job. I turn and spot Broomstick, Lewy and the CSM, Sergeant Major Falconer, standing in a huddle with some of the other NCOs a few feet behind me. Everybody is doing his best to look relaxed, but most of us aren't making a very good job of it.

We all want to know what happens next.

The door opens and a small group of officers walks into the room. Everybody comes smartly to attention.

The man who takes the podium is tall and well built. His brown hair is cropped short and he wears glasses.

'My name is Lieutenant Colonel Matt Maer,' he says. 'I'm your new commanding officer. In twenty weeks' time we deploy on operations in Southern Iraq. It will be a tour like no other. You will all be in contact. You may remove your berets and sit easy.'

Iraq.

We're all excited, but as we walk back to the sheds most of us think it will be very different from the way Colonel Maer has described it. The war is over. The Americans may still be getting a hard time, but the papers are all full of pictures of British soldiers strolling around Basra in their berets, talking to the locals and handing out sweets to children.

'It's goin' to be like Kosovo,' Sammy says. 'Except a hell of a lot hotter, and with ten times as many flies.'

Our new platoon leader, Second Lieutenant Richard Deane, arrives in Tidworth at the beginning of February. He watches us closely as the OC calls us together. Mr Deane has transferred to 1PWRR from the Royal Irish. Before that he worked in a bank in Northern Ireland.

Pre-Iraq training begins twenty-four hours later with a thirty-kilometre route march across the Plain. The bad news for me is that everyone gets to do this, including drivers. And soon after we set off it starts to snow.

We get dropped off in two multiples, one led by Mr Deane, the other by Corporal Llewellyn, now an acting sergeant.

In peacetime a platoon is organised differently from the way it is for combat ops. For our peacetime role in Iraq we're broken out of our normal structure − three sections of eight men − and grouped in two multiples of twelve instead. Each multiple is broken down into three teams of four men. I'm in a team with Sammy, Campbell and Mr Deane.

The exercise contains a number of different situations that we might encounter in Iraq − a road traffic accident involving civilian casualties; a Land Rover stuck in a ditch that we have to pull out − but I can't really get my head around any of it, mainly because I haven't been this cold since training.

Soon after dawn we're in a ditch, sheltering from the wind and the snow. Sammy is using our ten-minute rest period to take a nap, I don't know how. Mr Deane drops down next to me.

'Where I come from, this is considered half-decent weather,' he says, as another bank of grey cloud approaches from the north. 'What's your name, Private?'

'Beharry, Boss.'

Mr Deane takes a swig from his water bottle. 'The driver, right?'

'You know about me drivin', Boss?'

'I know about all your foibles, Beharry.'

'Me foibles, Boss?'

'They told me you're the best bloody driver in the battalion. They also told me not to tell you, because it'll swell your head.'

He casts a glance at Sammy, who's lying on his back, hands behind his head, snoring gently.

'And this, I take it, is your mate, Samuels. I hear that you two are as thick as thieves.'

'Thick as what, Boss?'

'That you're inseparable.'

'We good friends. Yes, Boss.'

'They also told me that if there's any skulduggery going down in the battalion you two are either in the middle of it, or know all about it.'

'Skul-what, Boss?'

'Bejesus, Beharry, am I going to have to repeat myself every time I open my mouth?'

'I'm sorry, Boss. I . . . it's . . .'

'Yes?'

'It's your accent, Boss.'

'Well, you'd better take a crash course in Irish, because you're driving for me and your mate Samuels is going to be my gunner.'

I think about waking Sammy with this piece of news. He'll be pissed off, because it means that Mr Deane will be keeping an eye on us. Maybe this is why we've been put in his vehicle. Either way I'm not going to let it bother me. Although our Warriors are coming with us to Iraq, chances are we're never going to have to use them.

'We won't let you down,' I tell Mr Deane.

'You'd better not. I sat in a Warrior yesterday and it scared the hell out of me.'

When I ask him why he tells me, 'Because I'm an infantry-man – a proper one, not like you taxi-driven softies – and I rely on my hearing and my vision to get me through a situation when it arises. I don't see how you can do that battened down in an iron coffin.'

'She's a real nice piece of engineerin',' I tell him.

He looks unconvinced.

'And she'll save you from havin' to carry a whole load of kit on your back.'

Mr Deane sits up and tightens the straps of his Bergen. We're carrying three days' rations on our backs.

'Yeah, well, I'll take my chances in a Land Rover any day,' he says.

A couple of weeks later we're down on the ranges at Lydd and Hythe on the Kent coast for some more operation-specific training. We spend some of our time in the Warrior, but mostly we stick to practice-deploying in the snatches.

Lewy gets completely worked up about our casevac – casu-alty evacuation – and emergency procedures; he runs around shouting, 'What if . . . what if?' the whole time.

On one of our training packages our platoon has been ambushed and several of us have sustained life-threatening injuries. Those that aren't hit have to pick up those that are under realistic combat conditions.

We practise a lot of different scenarios, including what hap-pens when a soldier is injured in a killing zone. If a member of a four-man team goes down, one of his colleagues provides covering fire while the other two drag him to a place of safety, then provide suppressing fire while the fourth member of the team rejoins them.

What happens next gets Lewy totally vex. The 'casualties' keep getting to their feet and jumping on to their rescuers' backs.

'No, no, *no!*' Lewy shouts as Sammy throws an arm around my neck and hobbles on one foot while I try to get him into a good lifting position. 'What if he's so badly injured he can't stand? Then what are you going to do?'

'What if, what if?' Sammy says under his breath. 'It's never goin' to bloody happen, Lewy.'

'You're supposed to be half-dead,' Lewy tells him. 'Shut up.'

Sammy starts to laugh.

I can see Lewy getting more and more annoyed. He looks around and spots Joe Tagica, the Fijian man-mountain, lying on the ground.

'Joe,' he shouts, 'over here, mate. I need you to demo something for me.'

Big Joe springs to his feet. For all his height, he moves with speed and agility. He jogs over to us. 'What's up?' he asks.

They are both corporals, although Lewy, as acting platoon sergeant, technically has seniority in the field.

'Beharry, lie down,' Lewy says. 'And act like you're dead. Unlike your mate Sammy, I don't want to see you move a muscle. Clear?'

I do as he says. Sammy stands back and watches. Everyone else has stopped what they're doing and gathered around to watch as well.

'Try and get him on to your shoulders, just as he is,' Lewy says, talking to Joe and pointing at me.

Joe bends down and tries to pull me on to him in a fire-man's lift. I'm carrying a Bergen that weighs almost as much as I do and Joe makes three attempts to lift me, but he can't do it. Eventually Lewy tells him to stop. 'OK,' he says, and turns to address the platoon. 'Big Joe, as we all know, is the biggest bloke in the platoon and Beharry is one of the lightest.

Without Beharry's help, and without sticking to procedure, Big Joe simply can't lift him. And this is how it's going to be on the battlefield.'

'Now,' he tells Joe, 'show us how it's supposed to be done.'

Joe rolls me on to my side and removes my Bergen. He then rolls me back, pulls up my knees, so my feet are in contact with the ground, my legs bent, and stands on the tips of my toes. Next he bends down, grabs my webbing and pulls me to him. I come up easily and drop into position on his shoulders.

Lewy tells us to go away and practise till we get it right. Practise, practise, practise . . .

By the beginning of April we're as ready as we'll ever be. On the morning of the 4th I slip out of the apartment and make my way to a marshalling point where a bus is waiting to take us to Brize Norton.

Ahead of us is a six-hour flight to Kuwait, then two weeks of acclimatisation in Shaiba, close to the Iraqi border, before we head for Abu Naji, the camp where we'll be based for the next six months.

PART THREE

Al Amarah, 2004

CHAPTER TWENTY-SEVEN

The gate is set into a long, high wall and flanked by a pair of reinforced watch towers covered with camouflage netting. As we present our papers the sentry glances over his shoulder at the dark area of scrubland opposite the camp. He waves us through and we park up close to the headquarters building.

I climb out of the low-loader. Two hundred metres off, a Chinook beats its way into the night sky from a floodlit landing pad. I shield my eyes, nose and mouth from the sandstorm it whips up as it roars over us and disappears into the night. I can make out a vehicle park to the left of the headquarters building, crammed with Warriors and Land Rovers.

As we retrieve our kitbags from the back of the vehicles, the Regimental Quartermaster sergeant shows up. Dave Ashton was with the advance party that has been here for the past week preparing for our arrival. He motions for us to follow him.

'Man,' Sammy says, 'I had no idea Abu Naji was goin' to be this big.'

I nod. We've had the briefs and been told what to expect, but this is something else. Vehicles come and go the whole time. Another helicopter comes into land. There's dust everywhere even though it's the middle of the night.

Abu Naji used to be an Iraqi Army corps headquarters.

They never got round to finishing the place. It's littered with half-finished bunkers and buildings, and dotted with the stumps of dead palm trees. This is now the main military base for 1PWRR battle group, led by Colonel Maer.

While we were getting the hang of things in Basra we got fed a whole lot of situation briefs from Randsy, the battalion intelligence officer. The BG is made up of a squadron of Challenger 2 tanks from the Queen's Royal Lancers, a company of Royal Welch Fusiliers and our own C Company and HQ Company. Y Company, 1PWRR's recce and mortar unit, is five and a half klicks up the road in a place called Al Amarah. Their job is to protect the Coalition Provision Authority (CPA), based in CIMIC House, a secure compound in the centre of the town.

Our job is to police Maysan province, of which Al Amarah is the capital, for the next six months and assist the ICDC maintain law and order. Everyone has told us that our Kosovo tour will serve as the model: a combination of foot patrols, Land Rover patrols and vehicle checkpoints, or VCPs.

The area is heavily populated with rival tribes, many of which have been enemies for centuries. Up until now the Light Infantry have mostly got caught up in their crossfire. Since there seems to be at least one AK47 assault rifle for every household around here, these incidents could get ugly – but not as ugly as the stuff the Americans have had to put up with further north.

Sergeant Major Ashton points out some of the facilities: a pair of shipping containers, known as Caramecs, filled with tables and computer terminals – our local internet cafe; more Caramecs, converted into shower blocks; the NAAFI, the laundry and, way in the distance, the cookhouse.

Finally we reach a row of tents. We chuck our bags on to our beds. This is where I, Sammy, Campbell, Rushy, Big Erv and the rest of 8 Platoon will be sleeping for our first couple of nights. We can only move into our Caramecs when the LI move out in another couple of days.

Sergeant Chris Adkins – now part of the intelligence section in the Ops Room – sticks his head into our tent. 'At 0700 hours tomorrow you're to report to the Warrior park. The OC is going to brief you.'

I'm getting undressed in the darkness when I hear what sounds like a vehicle backfiring in the distance. Moments later there is a high-pitched whistle followed by a bang.

From the back of the tent Charlie Malloy, another 8 Platoon driver, says, 'I think that was a fuckin' mortar going off.'

If it was, I'm too tired to care. I check that my helmet and body armour are within reach under the bed, then roll over and fall asleep.

In the cookhouse the next morning I run into Broomstick and Mr Deane.

'How're you doing, Bee?' the boss asks as we line up for breakfast.

'Good, sir.' I feel myself smiling. 'Now we can do the job we trained for.'

'It beats working in a bank, I'll tell ya,' he says.

'I'll bet it does.'

'Did you hear that mortar go off last night?'

'I heard somet'ing. Was it close?'

'Close enough,' he replies cheerfully. 'But all it managed to do was blow a big hole in the desert.'

'Inside the perimeter?'

'Just inside.'

'Well, maybe that was our bit of excitement for the tour, sir.'

'Maybe. But I doubt it.'

I ask Mr Deane what he means.

'The last couple of days before you lot arrived have been . . . interesting . . .'

Broomstick is complaining loudly to the cooks about our breakfast – a cheese roll, an apple, a can of Fanta, a packet of crisps and a Kit-Kat in a bag. Back home in camp we call them 'horror bags'.

'Look at this,' Broomstick says, holding up his crisps. 'It's hot enough to boil a monkey's arse, so what do they go and give us? Salt and fucking vinegar. Gleaming. Abso-fucking-lutely gleaming.'

Mr Deane shakes his head, picks up his breakfast and moves outside.

I follow him. Our briefing from the OC is due to start in ten minutes.

On the way to the vehicle park I ask Mr Deane what he meant about the last couple of days being interesting.

'You married, Bee?' he says.

I nod.

'Any kids?'

I shake my head.

'I've got a little girl. She's just three years old. It's funny what you think about when you're being shot at.'

'You been shot at, Boss?'

He opens up the bread roll, sniffs at the curled-up slice of cheese inside and takes a bite. He washes it down with a gulp of Fanta, turns to me and says, 'Yeah, a few days back.'

'What happened?'

'There's this place called Majar al-Kabir – Mak for short. It's where those RMPs got killed last year. You remember?'

It made all the papers. Two of the RMPs were killed on the spot. The other four surrendered to the mob and were shot with their own weapons.

'Me and the OC went there two days ago as part of an LI patrol. The LI have been fantastic about showing us around and handing over the ropes. They thought it'd be a good idea to get some of us over to Mak as part of the hand-over process. So we took three snatches, and on the way in, just outside the town, we got stoned by a bunch of kids.'

'Our low-loaders got stoned by kids on the drive up from Shaiba last night,' I tell him. 'Didn't think too much about it to be honest, Boss.'

'Yeah? Well, nor did I,' he says. 'But then some bastard fired an RPG at us. We're driving out of the town and I see a flash on our left-hand side, then a blur as the grenade passes between our snatch and the one in front. I'm standing up, trying to get a bearing on the launch point, when there's another almighty whoosh and a second RPG passes right over my head. We skedaddle out of there as fast as we can after that, I tell you.'

He takes another bite of his roll. 'I'm rather hoping that's going to be *our* little excitement for the tour.'

I hear what he's saying, but the look in his eyes says something different. Whatever happened in Mak, I can see he's excited by it.

If I'm going to be shot at I want it to happen quickly, so I'm not forever wondering where it's going to come from or what it will be like. I want to get it over with. 'Blooded' is what the white guys call it.

Part of me wants to find a deep hole to hide in; the other part envies the boss his experience.

As we line up in front of the Warriors, Major Coote is already waiting. He's a bit like the boss: not too tall, but built like a rugby player and full of energy. When everyone is present he waits for a helicopter to land, then starts by welcoming us to Abu Naji.

'Two weeks ago a number of things happened that may have contributed to a destabilisation of the situation here in

Maysan province,' he says. 'It's too early to be certain – we're still monitoring the situation, but here is what we know.

'As we were leaving the UK the Americans decided to shut down a newspaper belonging to Muqtadar Al-Sadr; it was reporting anti-Coalition Force propaganda as fact and winding everybody up. They also arrested one of Al-Sadr's sidekicks – a joker called Yacubi.

'As some of you are already aware' – the major looks at Mr Deane as he says this – 'these two incidents have kicked off a backlash here in Al Amarah and the surrounding area, where Al-Sadr is a bit of a folk hero. As the advance party of the 1PWRR BG, we have already experienced some of that backlash at first hand.'

Major Coote was also in the snatch convoy that was ambushed in Mak.

The backlash he is talking about didn't stop there. Three thousand people rioted in Al Amarah on 3 April, a few days before the 1PWRR advance party set foot in Abu Naji. I think about last night's mortar attack.

'We're still trying to assess what this all means,' the OC says. 'We know that there are at least three hundred members of the Mahdi Army within Al Amarah. The Mahdi Army is loyal to Muqtadar Al-Sadr, and Al-Sadr is an angry man right now. The next few days are going to be critical. With any luck the excitement will all die down and we can get into our routine – the job we came here to do.

'We know very little about how the Mahdi Army is organised, but we do know that they are well armed and we have to assume they are capable of causing us trouble if they want to. Over the next few days, as the LI hand over the ropes, we'll need to keep our eyes peeled and our ears open.'

I still can't get my head around this place. I don't understand why we've allowed the Iraqis to keep their weapons, and

I don't understand why the Mahdi Army is left free to roam the streets.

'The whole world is fucked up, Paki,' Sammy says. 'Why should Iraq be any different?'

'Yeah, but do they want us here, or not?'

'The Iraqis? Damn' if I know, man. I don't think anybody knows.'

I've heard a lot of officers describe our mission out here as 'Smile, shoot, smile'. If we run into trouble we must deal with it then restore order as quickly and quietly as possible.

Smile, shoot, smile . . .

If that isn't a crazy way of running things, I don't know what is.

'Christ, Beharry, this really is a pile of old junk. I can't even get the hatch to shut properly,' Jimmy Bryant says through my headset.

It's been more than two years since I last saw Jimmy. Our reunion isn't getting off to a good start. We're less than a minute out of the gates of the camp and already he's dissing Whisky Two Zero. We're deployed as a mixed-crew vehicle – part LI, part PWRR – on my first patrol into Al Amarah.

'She shuts fine,' I tell him. 'You just need to put some muscle into it.'

'I am,' he says. 'I'm telling you, mate, the damn thing's stuck.'

'Then try asking her nicely,' I say. 'She always manage to shut for our gunner.'

'She?' Bryant grunts. 'It's a tank, mate, not a bloody woman.'

'Careful,' I tell him. 'She might hear you.'

His boss – the LI platoon leader, sitting in our turret in place of Mr Deane – tells us both to shut up.

All the main routes into and out of Al Amarah have been

colour-coded for ease of recognition, but they still don't make a lot of sense to me. Red Route – Route 6 from Basrah – lies ahead. It's a long, straight stretch of highway that leads from Abu Naji camp into the centre of the town, running along the west bank of a tributary of the Tigris. Blue Route runs north–south along the opposite bank.

From the map it looks like Al Amarah's two rivers link up at its northern edge to form a 'T'. Purple Route branches off Red Route and loops back towards the town centre from the west, cutting Red Route in half by a tall water tower at the north-west corner of a large housing quarter, at a junction known as Red Eleven. When you see the water tower you know you're in the centre of the city.

Jimmy tells me the OMS is on the opposite side of the river, next to a junction at a road bridge called Yellow Three.

'What's the OMS?' I ask.

'The Office of the Martyr Sadr – the local HQ of the Mahdi Army.'

Major Coote has been talking about the Mahdi Army, but I still don't really get what they do or why they are here.

'Think of the OMS as being a little like Sinn Fein and the Mahdi Army as being the IRA,' Jimmy says.

This still doesn't help me much. 'What's so special about it?' I ask.

'The OMS? It's supposed to be stuffed with weapons – RPGs, 120mm mortars, 107mm rockets – or that's what we're told. Enough bloody hardware to start a war.'

'If there's weapons in there, why don't we do somet'ing about it?' I ask.

'For the same reason they let anybody in a dish–dash carry an AK47, I guess.'

'And what's that?'

'Nobody wants to stir up trouble,' he says. 'Anyhow, as of tomorrow, it's not my fucking problem. It's yours.'

Most of the town's other major landmarks – the police HQ, the telecoms building, the TV station, the bus station and CIMIC House, the CPA's administrative centre – are bordered by Red and Blue Routes north of Red Eleven and Blue Nine.

It's forty degrees plus now. I've never felt anything like it, even at home. As we continue along Red Route, moving north, I feel like I've got my face in an oven. To my left, Sparrowhawk, the coalition airbase to the north-west of Abu Naji, shimmers in the heat.

A little further on, just after Purple Route splits off from Red Route, we pass what used to be a prison, codenamed Broadmoor.

The air is thick with the smell of shit and chemicals that burn the back of my throat. The chemical smell comes from the brick factories on the outer limits of the town; the shit smell from the slow-moving river alongside us. There's no sewerage system to speak of in Al Amarah. It all empties into the waterways and only washes down into the Tigris when the rain comes. We're now into the hot season and it will stay like this well into October. We're just going to have to get used to the stink.

'Watch for civilians, right, on the edge of the road, two hundred metres ahead,' I hear the LI commander say. I don't know his name and make no special effort to learn it, because Mr Deane will be back in the turret of Whisky Two Zero tomorrow. He and Sammy are now on their own orientation tour of the city, in other mixed-crew vehicles.

I squint through my goggles and make out a group of people digging up the ground with pickaxes and home-made shovels. Bryant tells me that they're excavating a street lamp that got blown up by an IED during the riots.

I'm about to ask Jimmy what it was like during the riots when the intercom crackles and I hear Zero come on the net.

Zero is the Ops Room at Abu Naji, staffed by a couple of senior officers, a 'watch-keeper' who keeps tabs on each unit, and several signallers who are responsible for comms.

All I hear is the word 'contact' and then the name of a place.

'Sorry, Beharry' – it's the commander's voice in my head-set – 'your downtown tour is going to have to wait.'

'Sir?'

'Spin her around,' he says.

I check my mirrors and wrench the steering column hard over, putting Whisky Two Zero into a neutral turn . . .

CHAPTER TWENTY-EIGHT

. . . I'm still smiling as I think of that kid unscrewing Whisky Two Zero's light clusters while his mates were helping themselves to my chewing gum. But, following the battle at the OMS and the extraction of the dismounts, I've got work to do.

I start to clean the tracks. I need the vehicle to cool before I can get a proper reading from the gauges that monitor the oil pressures of the systems and sub-systems that make up the power pack, the transmission and the drive system.

First I chip all the mud off the links, road wheels, top rollers and the rear roller and sprocket, left and right. Chipping the mud off the tracks, wheels and rollers allows me to take readings from the torque meters on the nuts that fasten the bolts between each of the eighty-two links. I don't have the time to check every nut, so I start by taking a reading every five or ten. If the readings are good – I'm looking for 360 on the gauge – I carry on.

If I get a bad one I go back and check every single nut.

I'm also looking for any tell-tale cracks or oil leaks in the track. If I see a gap of more than five mills between the links I know there's a problem. The last thing I want to do in this place is to throw a track.

The track pressures on both sides are OK and I breathe a sigh of relief. I don't much want to change a track in this heat.

I undo the hatch that opens on to the power pack, next to

the driver's compartment, throw the lid back and stick my head inside.

We use OMD90 oil in the Rolls-Royce Perkins CV8 diesel. When it leaves the can this is very thick, but if the engine gets particularly hot the oil thins out. There's a 'hot' and a 'cold' reading on the dipstick, but I don't really trust what the manual says. If the oil is thin you can top up the system too much and then you get back pressure, an unacceptable level of strain on the power pack and a loss of power.

There's nothing wrong with the oil, so I know where the problem lies. I go around to the back of the vehicle and dig out the tools I need. In among the spanners, wrenches and screwdrivers are a long piece of clear plastic tube, a wire brush and a sealable plastic box. I take the tube in my hand and walk around the vehicle to the fuel compartment. I open up the cap, stick the tube inside and suck on the end till I get the bitter taste of diesel in my mouth. Then I tip the end of the tube into the plastic box.

When I've got enough diesel I spread out an old cloth on the front of the vehicle, next to the open hatch. Then I remove the cylinder head, the rocker cover and the rocker shaft and hold each part up to the light.

Sure enough, the ports of the cylinder head have become blocked with gunge. I chip it away with the point of the screwdriver. Then I wash the cylinder head with diesel and scrub at it with the brush. It takes me longer than usual, because my mind isn't really on it. As I work on the ports – scrubbing, washing and scrubbing again – I hear Chris, Coxy, Indian and Edmund laughing, and I hear myself laughing too. And as I laugh I feel the tension slipping away from my body; and as the tension goes I find it harder and harder to see the expression on the face of the man with the jeans and the T-shirt and the cloth on his head . . .

'Paki?'

I turn.

'What you doin'?' Sammy asks.

'Just fixin' the engine.'

'I hear it was pretty bad downtown.'

'Yeah. Pretty bad.'

'You want to talk about it, man?'

I make absolutely sure the cylinder head is not only free of gunge and grease but, most importantly, sand as well, then I carry it over to the engine compartment. I start to reattach it to the engine block.

'Will you do somet'ing for me, Sammy?' I reply.

'Sure,' he says. 'Anyt'ing.'

'We need two new light clusters. You think you can get them for me?'

Sammy smiles. 'No problem. You need 'em now?'

'Yeah,' I say. 'And Sammy?'

'Yeah?' he says.

'Don't t'ief 'em, eh? Get 'em from stores.'

He smiles. 'I don't never t'ief, man, you know that. I get 'em official.'

'I mean it.'

'I know. So do I.'

He turns to go.

'Sammy?'

He stops. 'Yeah, Paki, what is it?'

I look into his eyes. 'They hate us, Sammy. I seen the look on they faces, man. They really hate us.'

''Course they do,' he says, shaking his head. 'It's why we're here.'

'It ain't goin' to be like Kosovo.'

'I know,' he says. 'But we manage. We're soldiers. We always do.'

★

After watching him go I turn back to the engine. I tighten nuts with the spanner and wipe away the excess grease till she looks almost like new.

I'm closing up the hatch, when I hear a pop. It's very distant, but as I listen I hear it again. It's like a car backfiring and it's followed by a whistle that grows louder and louder until there are two thumps, both close by.

Turning to the south-west, I see clouds of smoke and dust rising just beyond the perimeter of the camp. I reach up and touch the little silver cross at my neck.

The rockets and mortars keep coming, and we just sit in camp and take it. None of us understands why.

'The way I see it, Boss, these people just don't respect us at all,' Sammy says as we cut across an area of wasteland to the east of Abu Naji. 'They see us as weak, 'cos we sit in camp and do not'ing.'

'The BG isn't here to kick seven bells out of the place,' Mr Deane replies. 'We're here to help rebuild it.'

Mr Deane, Sammy and I are on our way to a junction on Blue Route where we're due to set up a VCP.

After the contact at the OMS building the snatch is not quite as popular for our vehicle patrols. Either foot patrols are mounted from CIMIC House or we go out in the Warrior. It's too dangerous to do much else.

'But, Mr Deane,' Sammy says, 'Saddam Hussein was a tough guy, right? He controlled this country for years an' nobody much argued with him, 'cos if they did, he just turned around and killed 'em.'

'Your point being?' Mr Deane says.

'The Mahdi Army is hammerin' us every day and we letting 'em do it. We need to show 'em who's boss.'

'It's more complicated than that,' Mr Deane says.

'The people want law and order, don't they?' Sammy says.

'Most of them,' Mr Deane says. 'Most of them hate what Al-Sadr and his thugs are doing.'

'The bloke that's stirrin' up the trouble?'

'Right.'

'So why don't we go get him – and the rest?'

'Because Al-Sadr and his family were fierce opponents of Saddam. Saddam murdered Al-Sadr's father and his brother, and Al-Sadr has a lot of sympathy here. If we go in and thump the Mahdi Army, we don't just risk alienating the vast major-ity of the population; we could actually turn a lot more of them against us.'

'Say what you like, Mr Deane,' Sammy says. 'But in they eyes we just look plain scared.'

I'm only half-listening. Thirty metres in front of us is a stream. This place is criss-crossed by waterways and the going can get sticky.

'Why are you slowing, Bee?' the boss says.

'I don't like the look of the ground,' I tell him. 'I'm worried if we go any further, we goin' to get bogged in. I think we should go round it.'

'But I can almost see the VCP from here.'

'Jimmy Bryant said a lot of Warriors got stuck on this patch of land, Boss.'

'Ah, bollocks,' Mr Deane replies. 'That's just the LI for you.'

'I'm tellin' you, Boss, if we go any further we're goin' to get bogged.'

'Well, I'm telling you to carry on.'

'Can't do that, Boss.'

'Beharry, are you disobeying an order?'

'I know me vehicle, Boss, and I'm tellin' you, if we go on, we get stuck.'

'For crying out loud,' Mr Deane says. 'Brian, are you catch-ing any of this?'

He's talking to Lance Corporal Brian Wood, the leader of our dismount section, at the back.

'Guys,' Woody says, 'whatever you decide, just do it quick. We're burning up back here.'

It's forty-five degrees outside and sixty-five in the back of the wagon.

'Yeah, Paki, let's just cross, eh?' Sammy says.

It doesn't make any difference how many people ask or tell me. I'm not doing it. I'm not doing anything that will endanger the vehicle, and that's that. And since I'm in charge of vehicle safety, my word is final.

Mr Deane orders me to look for a place where we can cross the stream and I turn left. Several minutes later we reassess the situation. If anything, the water looks even deeper here, and both banks are dangerously steep.

'Let's cross here, for Christ's sake!' Mr Deane says.

'Sorry, Boss, can't do that. I don't know how deep the water is and we could topple over on that bank.'

'Beharry,' Mr Deane says through gritted teeth, 'we need to be on station at that VCP in ten minutes.'

'Boss, if you want to do this, you drive. Or you dig us out if we get stuck.'

'Stubborn son of a bitch, ain' he, eh?' Sammy says.

'I could kill him,' Mr Deane says.

'Some of us have to put up with this shit the whole time,' Sammy tells him.

'Get a fuckin' move on!' Woody yells.

There's a bridge marked on the map and we make our way towards it, but when we get there we discover that it's little more than a strip of reinforced concrete – something to allow goats and camels to cross from one side of the wadi to the other.

'I t'ink it take our weight,' I say, 'but . . .'

'But *what*, in the name of Heaven?' Mr Deane says.

A Charlie 2 makes its presence felt on a street corner during Operation Waterloo – the battle group's surge operation to defeat the enemy in Al Amarah and bring stability to a city that was sliding out of control.

Sadr militiamen engaging British troops from a rooftop during Operation Waterloo.

A Warrior patrol getting ready to roll from Abu Naji camp. The heat was unbelievable. Some days the temperature in the back of a Warrior could reach 70°C.

A Warrior, complete with armoured skirts, churning up dust as it returns from patrol to Abu Naji. Most days we left camp we knew we were going to be targeted by rocket-propelled grenades.

The helmet I was wearing during the contact on 1st May. The gash at the top is where an AK-47 round penetrated the Kevlar and grazed my scalp. Afterwards, I got it signed by every member of the platoon.

This is the helmet I was wearing when the RPG exploded six inches from my face in the early hours of 11th June, the night, by rights, I should have died.

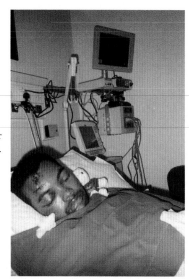

In Kuwait, shortly after I emerged from coma.

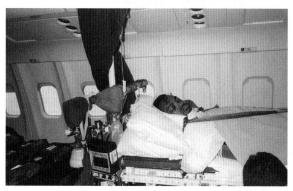

Being flown by RAF TriStar back to the UK.

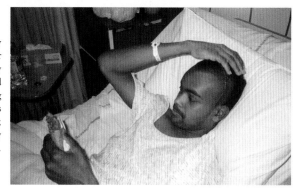

Admiring my operation scar sometime after my head returned to something approaching its normal size; Birmingham, July 2004.

Standing in the driver's seat of a Warrior in Germany, the day of the VC announcement.

Me, Sammy and a Warrior. We're happy, as you can see, but inside we're both still reeling from the news of our respective awards.

(left to right) Sgt Broome; the CO, Lt Col Maer; me; Sgt Perfect; and the CSM, Sgt Maj Falconer.

The guys who accompanied me in Whiskey Two Zero on 1st May and 11th June 2004: (from left to right) Cooper, Big Erv, me, Sammy and Woody. Only Mister Deane is missing.

Receiving the VC from Her Majesty at Buckingham Palace.

Proud and happy to be the first living recipient of the VC for nearly forty years.

Me, in Germany, the day of the announcement, ready for whatever life decides to throw at me.

'I t'ink it's too narrow, Boss.'

'Beharry,' Mr Deane says slowly, 'find a way of getting us across this bridge, right here, right now, or else . . .'

'I won't do it, Boss.'

'You won't?'

'No, Boss.'

There's a pause, then he says, 'Do you know? I reckon you're chicken. Ain't that right, boys?'

Sammy and Woody start making chicken noises.

'I'm not chicken.'

'Says who?' Mr Deane says.

'Me. I say,' I tell him. 'I'm *not* chicken.'

Cluck, cluck, cluck . . .

It sounds like I've got a whole farmyard in my vehicle.

'Right, I'll do it,' I say. 'But you diggin' us out, Mr Deane, if anything goes wrong.'

More chicken noises come at me over the net.

I ask Mr Deane to get everyone out of the wagon.

The chicken noises stop.

I'm not making a direct, head-on crossing. I don't want to risk putting a track over the edge and a twenty-five-tonne Warrior into the wadi. I decide to cross at a slight angle.

Because the wadi narrows at this point, a part of the vehicle remains in contact with the ground the whole way across.

We make it safely to the other side.

Five minutes later we're at the VCP. We rendezvous with three other vehicles and take up our positions.

VCP work is boring; I try not to fall asleep as I watch the dismounts pull cars to one side of the road and search them for weapons and explosives. Nobody finds anything and the only moment of light relief is when Woody pulls a football out of someone's boot and starts impressing the locals with his skills. He plays centre midfield for the battalion and left midfield for the infantry. In fact he's so good that he plays football not only for the whole army, but for a combined services' team as well.

'Time to go home,' Mr Deane says, as soon as Woody and his dismounts are back on board.

On the way back to camp a black cat crosses in front of us near Blue Five. Mr Deane says this is good luck, but I tell him not where I come from; my gran always used to make the sign of the cross when a black cat crossed the road and, just to be on the safe side, I cross myself now.

As I manoeuvre into a space in the tank park and switch off, people start running for cover.

'*Incoming!*' Mr Deane shouts.

We crouch down beside the vehicle. I feel the pressure wave in my ears as the rounds explode. Two clouds of smoke drift across the perimeter from the north.

'They getting closer,' Sammy says.

Everyone turns and heads for the accommodation block.

'You coming, Bee?' Mr Deane asks.

I tell him I will when I've checked over the vehicle.

'You'll soon be sleeping in that damn thing,' he says.

He looks at the two clouds of smoke drifting towards us. 'Then again, perhaps we all will.'

CHAPTER TWENTY-NINE

'OK, this is it, the moment we've been waiting for,' Mr Deane says, as we gather around our vehicles under the glare of lights in the tank park. 'Operation Pimlico, our chance to take the initiative for a change.'

The plan is for A Company the Royal Welch Fusiliers to go into the housing district just to the north of us, snatch around a dozen people who've been identified as the leaders of the unrest movement and bring them back to Abu Naji for questioning.

We're excited and the boss knows it. At long last we're doing something about all the shit we've been getting since we arrived. The housing district, on the southern edge of Al Amarah, is also the place where most of the rocket and mortar attacks have been coming from. The job of 8 Platoon is to conduct a route clearance for the RWF all the way to the out-skirts of the town, then wait at Broadmoor, just to the south. From there we'll be ready to give assistance to the RWF if they need it.

Although we're not taking a direct role in the arrest op, we're going to have a busy day. When Pimlico is over we must prepare the Warriors for a major re-supply of CIMIC House – food, water, ammunition and personnel; all the things we take for granted in Abu Naji.

Currently 8 Platoon is the Warrior Reserve, which means

we'll remain on standby in the camp, ready to support 7 and 9 Platoons – the units actively involved in the re-supply mission – if we're needed.

It's just starting to get light when we roll out of Abu Naji and turn on to Red Route. We head north in box formation: us and Whisky Two Three, Lewy's vehicle, in front; Whisky Two Two, Broomstick's wagon, and Whisky Two One, Joe Tagica's, bringing up the rear.

From Red Four onwards we move not much faster than walking pace, stopping every fifty metres to scan the route ahead.

In a route clearance a lot of the surveillance task falls on the driver. Using the eight-times magnification of the day sight, we look for anything that could suggest the presence of a roadside bomb – a suspicious-looking car, a newly disturbed pile of sand, even dead animals by the side of the road. If we see something we don't like the look of, we call in the REME.

Apart from a dustbin lid that gets mistaken for a mine, we find nothing to get excited about. The route is clear. Pimlico can begin.

We pull into Broadmoor and park up, listening to our radios as the RWF go into the housing district. They are going in on foot to arrest the suspects and bring them out in Saxons and snatches.

Broadmoor is a strange place. It's a prison that never got finished. There's no light or water in the buildings, and rubble all over the place. Despite the heat, most of us prefer to stay in the vehicles rather than hang around the half-finished cell blocks.

'So how come the army has to go in and arrest these people?' Sammy asks. 'I thought the idea was for the local police to take charge.'

'Can't trust 'em, that's the problem,' Mr Deane says. I can hear him munching on a sandwich he picked up from the cookhouse before we left camp.

'What do you mean, Boss?' I ask.

'More often than not,' he says, 'they're the guys who are shooting at us.'

'This place is totally mash–up,' I say.

'Too fuckin' right,' Sammy adds.

Mr Deane carries on eating. He says nothing.

From the traffic over the net it seems that the insurgency leaders are being rounded up and arms and explosives caches found without a shot being fired – until shortly before 0530, when we hear one of the arrest teams report a contact.

A couple of minutes later there is another contact, and then another. As the call signs report them, we hear gunshots over the radio, then the *crack-crack-crack* of small-arms fire not too far away.

We get the order to go and help the RWF extract back to Abu Naji; we're directed by Zero to a street corner on Red Route where the dismounts are waiting to be picked up. The first time we go down the road we see nothing. Mr Deane orders us to turn around and head back, while he checks with Zero on the radio.

Then suddenly I spot a group of dismounts moving up an alleyway towards us.

Battened down in the Warrior, we don't hear the shots, but I can see them returning fire in the direction they've just come from.

I stamp on the brakes and reverse up to the corner.

We open the door and several of the dismounts pile into the back. I hear Sammy traversing the turret, looking for targets, but whoever's doing the shooting remains well hidden, and when we've picked up as many men as we can carry we close the door and move off.

Whisky Two Two and Whisky Two Three take those we can't fit in. The rest get picked up by Saxons and snatches at RVs where the threat isn't quite as intense.

Back in camp, I check that Whisky Two Zero is topped up with oil, water and fuel, while most of the rest of the company gets briefed and ready for the operation to replenish CIMIC House, scheduled for 1400 hours.

At seven-thirty the sun is already high in the sky and with it comes the heat.

When I'm satisfied that Whisky Two Zero is as fit as she can be for this afternoon's run, I head off to the cookhouse and get some decent food. Instead of the horror bags we can now get proper cooked meals at any time of the day or night.

While I'm in line for bacon and eggs, Broomstick tells me that fourteen suspected insurgent leaders are now under lock and key. After a debrief here they will be sent to Shaiba for interrogation.

'Gleaming,' Broomstick says. 'Abso-fucking-lutely gleaming.'

Sammy and I are waiting by the vehicle a couple of hours later, when Mr Deane appears.

'There've been some developments,' he says. 'And it doesn't look healthy.'

'I thought Pimlico had been a success,' Sammy says. 'Beharry heard they picked up fourteen of the bastards and they on their way to Shaiba.'

'It was a success,' Mr Deane replies. 'So damn successful, in fact, that we've managed to stir up a complete bloody hornet's nest in the process.'

Sammy and I look at each other.

'The Mahdi Army have secured all routes into and out of the city. They've taken some Iraqi policemen hostage and are demanding we release their men in return for their lives. In hindsight, we probably should have re-supplied CIMIC before we went in and did the arrest op.' Mr Deane shakes his head. 'I guess we live and learn.'

'So what goin' to happen, Boss?' I ask.

'The replen of CIMIC House is going to go ahead as planned. We're going to wait here as the reserve, while 7 and 9 Platoons and a couple of RWF Saxons proceed to Blue One, five klicks south of the city. They'll cross the Tigris and approach CIMIC from the east, where intelligence indicates the Mahdi Army's hold on the approach routes is weakest. Meanwhile Y Company is going to send out a couple of multiples from CIMIC to clear a route in for them.'

'We're goin' to sit this one out?' Sammy says.

'I may be wrong,' Mr Deane tells him, 'but I doubt any of us is going to be twiddling our thumbs.'

Shortly after lunch 7 and 9 Platoons, led by Major Coote, leave camp.

We hear over the net that the two Y Company foot patrols, call signs Three Zero Alpha and Three Zero Bravo, have deployed from CIMIC and are fanning out to the east and west of the Majidiya Bridge to secure the main route into the compound.

By turning right out of camp instead of left on to Red Route, Major Coote is hoping to keep the element of surprise on his side for as long as possible.

The problem with Red Route is that it's long and straight and the insurgents can see us coming for miles. A mobile-phone call tips off anybody with an AK or an RPG that we're on our way.

The re-supply convoy will cross the river and hook up with Blue Route several kilometres to the south of camp and go into the town from there, hitting CIMIC from the west.

Hopefully, Mr Deane says, the Mahdi Army won't have any time to prepare a reception committee. He disappears off in the direction of the Ops Room.

The four Warriors of 8 Platoon are lined up facing the gate, engines off but ready to go. Today they are joined by a fifth, Sergeant Major Falconer's. As the CSM, Dave Falconer often accompanies the reserves, especially on supply missions. His vehicle is known by most of the guys as the Millennium Falconer.

Sammy and I head for the QRF (Quick Response Force) Room, a small brick building close to where the Warriors are parked. Another sweltering day – forty-seven degrees in the sun – and any kind of shelter helps.

People are sitting where they can. Some are smoking. Some are reading paperbacks. Some are sleeping. Helmets, body armour, day sacks and SA80s fill most of the spare floor space.

Since the ops are non-stop, sleep is in short supply and we're learning to grab it when we can. If we're lucky we may be able to snatch five or ten minutes before we're summoned to deploy.

There's a small stretch of empty floor next to Big Erv and Woody, who have been assigned to our vehicle again as dismounts. Woody and Erv introduce me to the guy sitting next to them. Private David Clifton is tall, with dark hair and pale skin and looks like he runs and works out a lot. He too has been assigned to Whisky Two Zero.

'Go easy on the throttle, eh, Beharry?' Woody says. 'It's the poor bastard's first trip. He's only been with the battalion a couple of months.'

'Your first trip in a Warrior?'

'Yes, mate,' Clifton says. He sucks thoughtfully on a cigarette. His voice is softer and quieter than I thought it was going to be.

'Where you from?' I ask him.

'New Zealand, mate.' He offers his hand. 'You?'

Grenada, I tell him. We shake and I ask him how come he's not in the New Zealand Army.

'My parents are originally from the UK and both were in the British Army, so I guess I never stood a chance,' he says. 'I'd been planning on joining the army back home, but while I was over in the UK visiting my gran something made me walk into a recruiting office in Croydon and the rest is history.'

'That recruitin' office?' Sammy says, shaking his head. 'That was the place that got me to join. What is it with Croydon and the army?'

'Dunno, mate.' Clifton tosses his cigarette out of the window. 'Maybe it's something in the water.'

Out of the corner of my eye, I catch movement beyond the door.

Others seem to sense it too.

'Oi, oi,' Woody says. 'Something's happening.'

'How do you know?' Clifton asks.

'I just saw the runner.'

Woody gets to his feet. Others get to theirs. The runner is used by the Ops Room to tip off the QRF platoon as soon as something starts to go down.

'Looks like party time,' Woody says. 'Let's go.'

I pick up my helmet and body armour and join the rush for the door.

By the time we get outside, the platoon is swarming around the vehicles. I see Mr Deane lowering himself into the commander's hatch of Whisky Two Zero.

Engines start. Diesel fumes belch into the air. I pull on my body armour, jump up on to the hull of Whisky Two Zero and slide into my seat.

A couple of seconds later I have my helmet on and my radio plugged in.

'Boss, Sammy, can you hear me?'

'Roger,' Mr Deane says.

'Loud and clear,' Sammy says.

I check that my SA80 is where I left it, in the foot well next to my knee. I press the starter button. The CV8 diesel roars into life.

'What's happening, Boss?' I ask.

'We're deploying to Blue One. Things are popping and we need to move our arses. One of the Saxons has broken down, the two Y Company multiples have run into trouble and the OC's taking 7 and 9 Platoons into the town to assist. We'll wait at Blue One and monitor the situation from there.'

He checks in with Broomstick, Lewy, Big Joe and the Millennium Falconer.

'OK, Bee,' he says when all five vehicles are ready. 'Let's roll.'

Soon after we turn out of the gate on to Red Route, we hear a corporal from the Y Company multiple on the east bank, call sign Three Zero Alpha, report that he's holed up in a house between Green Four and Green Nine, surrounded by enemy, with RPG and small-arms fire inbound.

His boss, CSM Norman, is watching the battle from the roof of CIMIC House. The corporal can't see them, but he's got more enemy moving towards his position – at least thirty insurgents armed with AKs, heavy machine-guns and RPGs.

The situation sounds increasingly desperate.

Then we hear a 'zap number' over the net. Somebody is down – shot in the chest at Blue Eleven and in urgent need of a casevac.

We hear Whisky Zero Alpha, the OC, transmit that he's moving up to assist.

The OC is going to lead 7 and 9 Platoons into the city,

come to the aid of the cut-off and pinned-down call signs, dispatch at least one Warrior to bring the casualty back and then drop off the supplies at CIMIC. Two Warriors, meanwhile, are to remain at Blue One to protect the broken-down Saxon.

A couple of minutes later we spot the Saxon and the Warriors and pull on to the side of the road next to them.

Comms on the 'all-inform net', the radio network that is supposed to enable all elements of the battle group to listen and talk to one another, are often patchy; today there are plenty of cut-outs, making it hard to piece together what's happening.

We track the OC's Warrior convoy as it moves north into a housing estate close to the river, where Whisky One Zero reports a direct hit by an RPG.

The shell penetrates the hull and leads to a loss of power, but Second Lieutenant Styler tells Zero that they are able to continue on task.

The net fills with Warrior commanders reporting that they are engaging enemy positions with their chain guns.

Second Lieutenant Plenge reports that Whisky Three Zero has identified the location of the wounded dismount. From his zap number Woody realises it's a mate of his – Lance Corporal Barry Bliss.

Moments later Plenge says they've got Bliss in the back of Whisky Three Zero and are administering first aid, but that his chest wound is serious and he's going downhill fast.

We listen as Plenge sets up a helicopter landing site just down the road from us so they can casevac Bliss to Shaiba.

Mr Deane tells Zero we're moving closer to the action. 'Whisky Two Zero. Blue Five, figures five,' he says, indicating five minutes.

As the reserve force it's our job to be as close to the contact area as is reasonably safe, ready to move in the moment we're needed. Blue Five is right on the edge of the town. We've been at Blue Five no more than a couple of minutes when we hear that the Warriors under the OC's charge have managed to pick up some dismounts and are now offloading them – under fire – along with the food, ammo and water, at CIMIC.

The OC says he's heading back into the contact area to extract the other call signs that are still pinned down. Mr Deane tells Zero that we're moving up into the southern suburbs. 'Whisky Two Zero. Blue Six, figures two . . .'

I slip the vehicle into drive and head for the houses I can see at the edge of the heat haze.

Water bubbles up from a broken main in the middle of the road. The sun is high in the sky and the reek of shit makes me gag. I've decided to drive with the hatch open; as the boss says, you see fuck-all from inside the vehicle.

We pass a cart by the side of the road loaded with water melons. The guy who's selling them waves at me as we drive by. We're on the outskirts of the city, just past Blue Six, and he doesn't seem to have a care in the world.

I take my eye off the road for a fraction of a second and don't see the woman with the bucket on her head until she's almost under our tracks. I brake hard and hear Sammy and Woody swear. The woman just carries on walking; I don't think she realises I'm here, let alone how close I came to killing her. I watch her slip into an alleyway and disappear.

The boss is talking to Zero about trying to follow the OC to Blue Fourteen, but there is nothing wide enough for a Warrior where we are, so we press on to Blue Seven. We can turn right there, but the boss is trying to avoid it as Blue Route north of Blue Seven is a huge boulevard that runs up through the centre of the city, where the Mahdi Army is thickest on the ground.

When the boss isn't talking to the Ops Room, he's giving Woody a running description of the scenery that surrounds us. Every so often he feeds Woody coordinates from his hand-held GPS. I know that Woody is listening hard and following these on his map; he needs to know exactly what to expect in case he, Erv and Clifton suddenly have to jump out of the back.

'We're three hundred metres short of Blue Seven . . . two-fifty . . .' Mr Deane says. 'There's flat-roofed houses on the left, more on the right, some single-, some two-storey, you know the kind, same old same old . . .'

He pauses, then says, 'According to the map, there's a road on the right any moment that looks like it could take us up to Blue Fourteen. I'm going to pop my head out and see if I can get eyes-on.'

I hear him open the hatch.

A motorcycle overtakes us and makes a right down the next street. It catches my attention, because the guy who's riding pillion has an AK slung across his back.

As we approach the turning I see that the bike has turned right round and is now facing us on Blue Route. The passenger has got off and is hanging with five other guys by a lamp-post on the corner. They are dressed in jeans and T-shirts and three of them are holding AKs. They all stare at us as we rumble past.

'Boss, six guys on our right, some of them with AKs . . .'

'Got 'em,' Mr Deane says. 'Don't like the look of 'em much.'

'Isn't that the route up to Blue Fourteen?' I ask.

'Yeah,' he says. 'One of them. Best we keep going.'

He transmits our LOCSTAT to Zero. 'Whisky Two Zero at Red Seven, figures one.'

I see the junction up ahead. In less than a minute the road will veer sharply to the right. Checking my mirror, I see the

four other Warriors in the convoy strung out along the street
to our rear. Whisky Two Two, Broomstick's wagon, is fifty
metres back. The rest are spaced out evenly behind him.
Broomstick's turret is traversing from right to left, gun raised
at an angle towards the rooftops. Apart from Mr Deane and
me, everybody else, as far as I can tell, is battened down.

When I look at the junction again, a voice inside my head
is telling me that something is wrong. I ease off the power and
we start to slow.

'Bee, what is it?' Mr Deane asks. 'Why are you slowing?'

'Somet'ing ain't right, Boss.'

'What isn't right?'

'I dunno, Boss, somet'ing . . .'

I look in the mirror and catch another glimpse of the view
to our rear. The road behind us is as clear of people as the
junction in front, and yet a minute ago – less, maybe – it was
busy, busy, busy . . .

'There's no people, Boss. Look. Front and back. Everybody
fucked off.'

There's a pause, then Mr Deane says, 'Yeah, see what you
mean. Better bring her to a stop. I'll check with Zero.'

After they have held a brief discussion about other route
options for cutting up to Blue Fourteen, Mr Deane decides to
press on.

We move forward again. I spot another street on the right.
It looks wide enough to take us. Dust kicked up from the platoon's tracks makes it difficult to see, but I realise there's
something across it.

As the dust clears I see a low barrier made out of rubble, oil
drums and an old lamp-post.

'Boss, what now?'

It's our last chance to turn right before the big junction at
Blue Seven.

'Can't drive over it,' Mr Deane says. 'There could be an

IED in there.' He pauses. 'Looks like we've got no choice now but to move on up Blue Route. Got that, Bee?'

'Got it.'

I slow down as I approach the junction and the Warriors behind me start to bunch. The street we're in is narrow. Houses rise up on either side of us. I snatch quick, nervous glances, left and right, at their flat roofs. I see nothing, no one. The street remains absolutely deserted.

'Hang a right,' Mr Deane says.

Ahead is a typical Saddam boulevard – two lanes either side of a central reservation, with lamp-posts like palm trees, evenly spaced.

Five-storey tower blocks rise up on both sides of the road between crumbling, one- and two-storey brick houses. Every thirty metres or so alleyways disappear between the buildings.

I start to make the turn. The four lanes of the boulevard disappear into the distance. The heat from the road twists the lamp-posts out of shape. There isn't a single car on the road. As I straighten up I see why. Fifty metres in front of us is another makeshift barrier.

'Boss . . .?'

'I know,' Mr Deane says.

Maybe he's thinking the same thing as me. The first place we want to turn right is blocked by guys on motorcycles. The second has got a barrier across it. We're bunched up on an approach road to a major junction, and now this . . .

'Shit!' I hear Sammy say.

'What?' the Boss says.

'Left-hand side. There's a kid across the street. Eleven, maybe twelve years old. He's holding what looks like a fuckin' RPG!'

I'm turning to look when there is a massive explosion and the vehicle shakes like it's been hit by a tidal wave.

I grab hold of the tiny cross and I do what Auntie I said: I pray to God and all His angels for help.

Even though I'm heads-up, scanning the road through the open hatch, I've seen nothing. The world outside is exactly as it was a moment ago. Al Amarah is still a ghost town. Again I finger the silver chain at my throat and feel droplets of sweat race down my back beneath my battledress.

'Boss . . . what was that?' I try to keep the fear from my voice.

There isn't even a crackle of static in my headphones.

'Boss, what happened?'

Still nothing. Whatever hit us must have mashed up our comms.

I twist and crane my neck, but the turret blocks my view of anything on top of or behind the vehicle, the boss and Sammy included.

Smelling burning, I glance back down the driver's tunnel. Then I hear someone scream.

I've seen this moment many times in my dreams. My thoughts slow and for a split second I see the mess we have stumbled into as if I'm above the street, looking down. I can't reverse up.

Looking for exits ahead, anything that offers protection, I see only the endless boulevard, shimmering in the last of the day's heat.

I know that Whisky Two Zero stands out like a double-decker bus in the glare of the street lights. I reach for the silver chain again, and my fingers find the little cross my Auntie I gave me. I hear her voice inside my head: 'Promise me one thing . . . If ever you find yourself in danger, you hold this close and pray to God for help.'

I hear another voice too, one that tells me RPGs come in threes.

I hit the accelerator, but the power kicks in a fraction too late. The Warrior lurches and a second detonation punches its back end a metre and a half across the road.

The power pack coughs and for a moment I think Whisky Two Zero is going to die on me. But miraculously the revs pick up again. I point her nose towards the open highway and see the barrier – a line of hastily erected breeze blocks – too late to avoid it.

An instant before we crash there is another explosion, even bigger than the last. A pressure wave filled with noise and heat tears past me and out of the hatch. With little forward speed, Whisky Two Zero grinds against the concrete wall. Deafened by the last explosion, I don't hear the tracks spinning uselessly on the road surface, but I can feel them.

I slip the Warrior into reverse and take her back a few metres. Then I edge forward again, this time targeting the right side of the block. We hit it hard and my head almost strikes the rim of the hatch. I increase the revs, knowing that the engine, always Whisky Two Zero's weak point, is losing power.

As I brace myself for another explosion I feel movement from the barrier. Whisky Two Zero begins to force her way through. I shout, urging her on as the gap widens until, with a final push, we manage to squeeze through.

But the men who erected the barrier know what they're doing. They know our routine. They know we're coming. It's as if they've predicted our every move.

Bang in front of me is a small mound of stones with an aerial sticking out of the top: an IED. The mine is big enough to seriously vex a Challenger tank. What will it do to us?

Again, time slows. All I can think of is the battery of RPGs to my rear. I can't go back.

I hear the screaming again. It comes from the back of the vehicle.

I know all too well what an RPG does to the inside of a tank.

First, the fuse activates the shaped charge penetrator of the high-explosive warhead. In a nanosecond the energy of the explosive focuses on a band of copper wrapped around the charge. The explosion builds from the back of the charge, melting the copper and propelling it forward in a pencil-thin jet capable of cutting a hole through ten centimetres of armour – more than enough to penetrate the hull of a Warrior – and bringing a melon-sized chunk of metal with it.

If you're in the path of the jet she'll bore straight through you.

I decide to take my chances with the mine, hoping the power pack alongside me will take the full force of the blast, shielding the men behind me.

I pull the hatch closed and the front of the Warrior passes over the antenna.

I remember what my gran told me all those years ago – my gran who knew the power of dreams. She saw all this. She tried to warn me.

It wasn't just her. My fate, like those of the men behind me, was written years ago – my gran and my aunt both knew it. I can see Auntie I's face. There are tears in her eyes. She gave me the cross because she knew I was going to die here.

The Warrior fills with the stench of burning. There's shouting and screaming from the back and the driver's compartment fills with smoke. It catches in the back of my throat.

I radio the boss several times, requesting status on the vehicle, but I hear nothing. My headphones are dead. Then I hear someone. 'Boss, Boss, you all right?'

The voice reaches me through the driver's tunnel. There's something strange, almost dreamlike about it. It sounds like it's a long way away.

'Boss, Boss . . . Talk to me, for fuck's sake . . .'

Woody.

Outside, I know there are more RPGs waiting for us. I can't go back, because the other four Warriors are directly behind me. All I can do is press on. I have little or no space to manoeuvre; I ease Whisky Two Zero to the right. I want to make sure that when the IED goes off, the power pack will shield us from the worst of the blast. I gun the engine, close my eyes and fumble again for Auntie I's cross.

When I open my eyes again we're ten metres beyond the barrier and there's been no explosion. The smoke filling the driver's compartment makes it difficult for me to breathe. I throw open the hatch again. Bullets hit the front of the vehicle like hailstones and I look up and see gunmen shooting at us from the rooftops.

Then I hear answering fire from the turret – not the *ratatatatat* of the chain gun, but an SA80 on single shot. *Bam, bam, bam* . . .

Sammy.

'*Drive, Paki. For fuck's sake, drive!*' he shouts. 'There's more of 'em lining up with RPGs.'

I tread down on the accelerator, but get very little response from the engine.

'Move, Beharry. *Move, move, move!*' Woody yells.

'I'm trying,' I yell, but there's something wrong. The RPG that singed the back of my head went straight into the engine compartment. I don't know how much life Whisky Two Zero has left in her.

Slowly we start to pick up speed. There's a lot of shouting from the back. Erv is yelling he wants to get out so he can take as many of the bastards down as he can. I can hear Woody trying to calm him down.

Woody calls out to the boss again.

'Stop calling the boss,' Sammy yells. 'The boss is dead! He's fuckin' dead!'

'Dead?' Woody shouts.

'He got hit by the first RPG. He's lying on the floor of the turret. He's a mess, man. A complete fuckin' mess.'

'What about you, Sammy? You hit?' I yell.

'I got burned. It's burnin' in here.'

'Where's the fire?'

'I dunno. Can't see it. Somewhere on the floor of the turret, I think. Just drive, Paki. Fuckin' drive! There's RPGs everywhere, man . . . everywhere!'

A guy wearing Arab dress runs out into the middle of the street and sprays us with his AK47. I hear the strikes pinging off the armour in front of me.

'Use the chain gun, Sammy, for God's sake!' I shout.

'I can't, man, it's jammed! My SA80 got hit. All I got is the boss's weapon . . .'

The guy with the AK just stands there. He's fifty metres away and firing from the hip. Something slams into my helmet and my head is thrown back against the hatch. When I open my eyes the guy with the gun is still there.

'Shoot him, Sammy, shoot him!'

'*Stoppage!*' Sammy screams. 'Fuckin' stoppage!'

The guy keeps firing the AK until the last possible second, then darts into an alleyway as we thunder on down the street.

Black flags hang from the balconies of the houses we pass by. Black flags, a part of me is thinking. What the hell's that all about? Are they for us? Do they know we're going to die here?

A movement in the shadows on the corner of an alleyway catches my eye. A guy steps out. He's wearing a green combat jacket and jeans. He heaves a brown and black tube over his shoulder and fires.

Dust flies into the air from the back-blast as the tube kicks upwards.

I should have yelled 'RPG!' but I can't. I'm hypnotised by the sight of the shell as it heads straight for us. I've been here before. At first it seems frozen in space. Then, as I reach up and grab the hatch, the speed picks up and a millisecond before the round hits us I realise it's coming straight for me.

I duck and pull the hatch down with a crash and then there is an ear-splitting explosion that tears it out of my grip.

A wave of heat and a blast of pressure shoot over my head and on down the tunnel. There's a scream behind me and I realise that Sammy has been caught by the explosion. I sit up and open my eyes. I stare through the day sight but I can't see a thing. The RPG must have exploded against it, destroying it completely.

The engine coughs again and for the first time I feel the heat from the bulkhead between me and the power pack. I throw open the hatch, breathe in a huge lungful of air and press down on the accelerator. Whisky Two Zero judders.

'Sammy!'

Nothing.

I hear the sound of an extinguisher going off. There's more yelling and screaming from the back. And then I remember. The extinguisher isn't meant to be operated when there are people inside the vehicle – it sucks the oxygen out in a heartbeat. No time to think about that now . . .

The road seems to stretch all the way to the horizon. The street lights appear like matchsticks in the distance. I don't see any gunmen, but I can still hear the rain of bullets on the hull. I know I've got to get us out of the killing zone. I know I've got to get us off this road. But which way do I go?

I can't raise the rest of the platoon; our comms are totally mash-up.

All I know is that CIMIC is somewhere at the end of Blue Route and the rest of the company is somewhere near CIMIC. Trouble is, I've never been there before and I don't know the road.

I check the mirror and see the other vehicles. They're

following me and firing back with their chain guns at the gunmen on the roofs. They're following me because they think Mr Deane is still in charge of the platoon; they don't realise he's dead.

Dead. The boss. I can't believe it.

I press my foot to the floor and check the speedo, but we can barely raise thirty-five miles per hour. The heat from the engine compartment is adding to the sweltering conditions inside the Warrior. How much longer can we last before the power pack gives up on us, or just blows up?

Don't go there, Johnson, I tell myself. Just concentrate on getting us out of this mess . . .

I start to weave, left and right, down the boulevard. With our speed dropping off I know we present an easy target for another strike by an RPG. We've been hit by at least four; we can't take another.

A fresh volley of small-arms fire, and this time I see the sparks as the bullets crack and fly off the armour. I can see no end to the killing zone and for the first time I feel real fear. If I fuck up now, it's not just going to be the boss, me, Sammy, Erv, Wood and Clifton that will pay the price. Where I go, the platoon follows.

I hold the little cross by my neck and as I pray again, I hear the words of a song: 'Angels descending bring from above, echoes of mercy, whispers of love . . .'

'Gran,' I whisper. 'Please help me . . .'

There's an opening on the left. I know I have to take it.

I swing Whisky Two Zero into the turn. The street is narrower than I thought. It bunches in front of me. I start to panic again. What if the road runs out? What if we get caught in this rat run?

Sammy starts to scream. The blast from the last RPG must have knocked him out. He's alive, but in terrible pain. From the sound of it, I know he's burning . . .

'Sammy?' I shout. 'Sammy? Can you hear me?'

He doesn't respond.

More shouting from the back. Sammy isn't the only one who's wounded. Someone – it sounds like Erv – is yelling that Clifton has got a huge piece of shrapnel sticking out of his face.

Suddenly another road opens up to the right. It looks wider than the street we're on and I decide to take it. I fire Whisky Two Zero into the turn and check that the others are still behind; they are.

For the moment the shooting has stopped. I gun the engine. It coughs and splutters and I know from the sound she's making that she won't last much longer.

I check that my SA80 is still in the foot well, and am about to yell to Woody that we're probably going to have to get out and fight, when I see another Warrior at the end of the street. It's so unexpected that for a moment I wonder if it's my imagination. I blink, but the Warrior is still there, by a crossroads, angled away from the street we're on. I'm not sure it has seen us.

'Sammy! Woody!' I yell. 'There's a Warrior dead ahead. Hang in there, all right?'

I get no reply.

I daren't take my eyes off the Warrior. Without comms I have no way of attracting its attention.

Stay there. Please. A few seconds longer . . .

We make it.

As I pull up alongside, the hatch opens and the commander's head appears. When he turns my way I realise it's Major Coote, the OC. I can see him talking into his mike, but because my comms are shot I can hear nothing. I look at him, tap my helmet, then jab a thumb behind me in the direction of the turret. I draw a finger across my throat.

The OC hesitates for no more than a second. I'm telling

him Mr Deane is dead and I know how badly this news must hit him.

He touches the top of his head – the signal for me to follow him.

I stick to his tail. The road makes a sweeping turn to the left, hugging a bend in the river.

Suddenly the ground opens up and there's a walled compound on my right, ringed by HESCO barriers of galvanised steel and polypropylene, with a stone-built sangar guard post out front. Beyond the OC's vehicle, in the middle of the open ground, is a Warrior out on its own. Two more are lined up alongside the HESCO barrier. Some dismounts are crouched down by the vehicles and firing at targets to my left. The vehicles' chain guns are shooting in the same direction. More dismounts are chucking boxes over the barrier.

It's chaos, but at least we've made it to CIMIC House.

Major Coote pulls up in front of the Warrior in the middle of the clearing. Bullets spatter the hull of his Warrior. Seconds later I hear them do the same to us.

I pull up a few metres behind the OC's wagon and look to my left. Fifty metres away is the edge of another run-down housing development. Washing lines and TV aerials jut out of an endless sea of flat roofs. The perfect vantage point for enemy snipers.

The barrier to my right marks the edge of the CIMIC compound. Beyond it I can make out palm trees, a large concrete water tower, and in the distance, right by the river, the roof of CIMIC House itself.

The smell of burning is getting stronger. I look down. The heat from the bulkhead wall is so bad that in places I can see it glowing red. As I pull myself out of the hatch four or five rounds ricochet off the front of the Warrior. My God, some bastard is targeting *me*.

I drop back down into my seat. My hands are shaking. My

breath is coming in short gasps. If I sprint through the bullets and throw myself over the barrier, I say to myself, I'll be safe.

What do I do?

The boss is dead.

What do I do?

Sammy, Woody, Erv and Clifton can look after themselves.

What do I do?

'Johnson?'

What do I do?

'Johnson . . .?'

'Yes, Gran . . .'

'I'm here, Johnson . . .'

I close my eyes. My gran is standing on the steps of her little house. She's looking at me and I'm looking at her. It's early morning. There isn't a sound, not a breath of wind in the trees.

I'm asking her about the future and what it holds for me . . .

CHAPTER THIRTY

What do I do, Gran?

'People always has choices,' her voice tells me. 'You'll know what they are right enough when the time come . . .'

Choices.

The boss is dead. Whisky Two Zero is my vehicle; she's my pride and joy.

Sammy, Woody, Erv and Clifton all need my help.

I pull myself out of the hatch. A bullet whines through the air above my head. I crouch down beside the turret.

There's a burst of machine-gun fire from the flat roofs and an answering volley from a chain gun somewhere close by.

I roll on to the turret, hugging the hot metal. The hatch is still open. I smell burning.

Crack!

A bullet hits the turret a foot from my face.

I move closer.

When I lean over the hatch I see Mr Deane slumped across the floor, face down, the back of his head covered by his helmet. There is blood on his seat and the shredded remains of his body armour on the ammunition rack. He must have caught the full blast of the first RPG.

I lean inside and tap the back of his helmet. He doesn't move.

But something in the corner of the turret does. Sammy is hunched, clutching his sides, head lowered. An explosion has ripped the clothes from his upper body. His chest is peppered with burns.

'Sammy, man, it's me.'

He turns towards me and there are burns all over his face as well. When he opens his eyes they are blood-red. I'm not sure he can see me.

'Paki . . .?'

He reaches out for me and I grab him by the wrist. I start to pull him towards me. A bullet hits the hatch. I let go and he falls back. The boss groans.

Jesus Christ, the boss is alive.

I look at Mr Deane and I look at Sammy. Smoke is pouring into the turret from deep inside the vehicle. The heat is unbelievable.

I don't know how long we have before the vehicle blows. All I know is I've got to get the boss out. I reach down, take hold of his shirt and pull. I manage to lift him a little, but he's too heavy and he slips from my grip. I get a picture in my head of the day Big Joe tried to lift me at Lydd and Hythe. I'm half Big Joe's weight and Mr Deane is twice mine. I'm never going to do it.

'Sammy, man, you got to help me lift the boss. I can't lift him on me own.'

Fumbling, Sammy grabs hold of a part of the boss's shirt and pulls. Mr Deane's head comes up a fraction and before Sammy lets go, I grab hold of the boss's helmet. I know I have only one shot at this. I pull with all my might and manage to get the boss into an upright position.

Another bullet cracks off the hatch, but I ignore it. This time I'm not letting go.

I place my feet either side of the hatch and pull. Mr Deane starts to make a terrible choking sound, but his head and upper body are through the mouth of the hatch. If I let go now I'll never get him back up.

A volley of bullets cracks and whines off the side of the vehicle. I'm not letting go.

With a roar, I pull, and as I do I feel the muscles in my back rip in all kinds of places.

I – am – not – letting – go . . .

Mr Deane's body flops out of the hatch on to the top of the turret.

A bullet thuds into the armour a couple of inches from his helmet. I take a deep lungful of air. There's a terrible red welt on the boss's neck where his helmet strap has dug into his skin. But he's breathing, he's alive.

I take hold of one of his arms and drag him on to my shoulders. My back is agony but I'm not letting go. I make my way to the front of the vehicle. I can hear the OC's chain gun providing me with covering fire as I lay Mr Deane's body as gently as I can on the sloping armour. Then I jump down on to the ground, pull the boss more firmly on to my shoulders and carry him as quickly as I can to the back of the OC's vehicle.

The door opens and I hand him over. I don't know who to, and I don't care. Now I have to go and get Sammy.

On my way back to Whisky Two Zero, I see the Millennium Falconer and the other three vehicles of the platoon for the first time. They are parked up next to the HESCO barrier, their chain guns pouring fire into the housing development.

I can see Falconer, the CSM, hurling ammunition boxes over the barrier. The vehicles are too far away for me to be able to get anybody's attention. If I tried to make it over there, I would be cut down by fire from the rooftops. They have their own problems; I have mine. I'm on my own.

Sammy is already halfway out of the commander's hatch when I jump back on to the hull.

'Come on,' I say, grabbing him by the wrist. There's so much blood on his face I'm still not sure he can see.

'What fuckin' happened, man?' he asks.

I don't know, I tell him. And now's not the time to be talking about it.

But the question matters to him and he repeats it, over and over: 'What fuckin' happened, man? What fuckin' happened? What . . .?'

We hear another burst of gunfire from the housing estate and I pull him down below the level of the turret.

A volley of shots rakes the front of the vehicle.

I hop down on to the ground and drag Sammy after me. Then I turn to the OC's wagon.

It's disappeared.

For a moment I'm confused, then just plain angry. Where the fuck's it gone? But then I remember: as the command vehicle, its dismount section is stuffed full of radio kit. There's room in the back for just one person – Mr Deane. And the Warrior he parked next to is still there, its rear door open.

Holding Sammy with one arm, I start to make my way to it. Just before I get there I look up and see the OC's vehicle reversing towards us. It screeches to a halt alongside the other vehicle and starts hammering at the flat roofs fifty metres away with its chain gun.

Sammy groans.

'It's OK,' I tell him. 'You're safe now.'

We make it to the shelter of the Warrior.

I climb in the back and sit him down on one of the bench seats.

'Paki . . .?'

'I can't stay with you, Sammy. I have to go back.'

'*Paki* . . .?'

I turn around and head back towards Whisky Two Zero. Smoke is pouring from the commander's hatch.

I run around to the rear. The door is open a crack. I take hold of it and yank it back.

'Son of a bitch, I'm gonna fuckin' kill you, fuckin' kill you, kill you, you bastard sons of bitches!'

Hearing this, I jump backwards, scared out of my skin. Big Erv is pointing his SA80 at my chest. There's blood on his face and a wild look in his eyes. He's a split second away from pulling the trigger.

'Erv, for fuck's sake, it's Beharry!' Woody appears out of the smoke at the back of the dismount section.

Erv lowers his rifle. He's bleeding from a gaping wound just below one of his knees.

Woody is a mess too. His face is covered in cuts. His helmet has been blown off and he's missing most of his hair.

There's blood on the floor and the walls. I can see daylight through the left-hand wall, where the molten jet of the RPG scythed through the armour and the turret cage.

'Where the fuck's Clifton?'

Woody shrugs. 'What happened?' he asks. 'What fuckin' happened?'

'I don't know, Woody. We got zapped. Where's Clifton? We're still under contact . . .'

He shrugs again. He's in complete shock.

'Erv, where's Clifton?'

Big Erv stares at me vacantly. He's slumped back against the wall of the Warrior, cradling his SA80. 'I dunno, he just . . . went . . .'

I hear something behind me.

I swing round, half-expecting to see an Iraqi with an AK. But I'm confronted by a sergeant, one of the guys from Y Company, based in CIMIC House.

'You lot,' he says, 'fuckin' move, *now*. This wagon is on fuckin' fire!'

'We're missing a man, a dismount,' I tell him.

'Missin' someone?' the sergeant yells, ducking down behind the door for cover.

'Yeah,' I say. 'Clifton. Big guy, got a piece of shrapnel in the face . . .'

'Size of a bloody credit card,' Erv adds.

'What's the size of a credit card?' the sergeant says.

'The shrapnel,' Erv says, 'is sticking out the side of his nose.'

'Oh, him!' the sergeant says. 'I've just seen him. He's inside the compound. Didn't realise he was one of yours . . .'

Clifton, at least, is safe.

The sergeant pulls Woody and Erv out of the back and the four of us rush over to the vehicle I've left Sammy in.

As soon as Erv and Woody are safely in the back, I sprint over to the OC. Major Coote is hunkered down behind the open hatch.

'Sir, what do I . . .?'

My words are drowned by the chatter of his chain gun.

The OC looks at me.

'What do I do now, sir?' I ask.

Bullets ping off the front of Major Coote's vehicle. He cups his hands around his mouth. I can see his lips move, but I can't hear what he's saying.

'Sir?'

'Follow me. We're going to drive out of the contact area.'

Ducking bullets, I'm halfway back to Whisky Two Zero when I realise that the OC doesn't know how badly damaged she is.

I hear the rev of engines as his Warrior and the one with Sammy, Erv and Woody on board get ready to move out. I climb back on to the hull of Whisky Two Zero and drop into the driver's hatch. It's too late to do anything else. Smoke is pouring out of her engine vents, but the power pack is still running – I can feel the pedals vibrate through the soles of my boots.

The two Warriors ahead of me neutral-turn and start to move off, heading back the way we came. I release the hand-brake and pray Whisky Two Zero can still drive. She hops forward, but after less than a hundred metres she starts to judder. The entire bulkhead separating me from the engine compartment is now glowing. The power pack has done all she can. Now she's giving up the ghost.

The OC stops. He knows I'm in trouble.

I coax Whisky Two Zero alongside his vehicle and tell him the problem. Basically, my wagon is fucked; she could blow at any moment.

'Go back to CIMIC and dump it,' he shouts. 'We'll wait for you here.'

On the way back Whisky Two Zero is hit by another volley of shots from the housing estate.

The Millennium Falconer and the three other 8 Platoon wagons are still parked up next to the compound. The guys are still heaving ammunition and food boxes over the wall into CIMIC House.

If Whisky Two Zero blows, she could take them with her. If she doesn't, she could fall into enemy hands.

I'm wondering where I can dump her that's both safe and secure. I see the HESCO barricade that marks CIMIC's outer perimeter. Its concrete blocks will absorb most of the blast if Whisky Two Zero blows.

I drive back into the killing zone and manoeuvre the vehi-cle so that I get the barrier between me and the other wagons. I switch off the engine, reach over to my right and pull the handle that triggers the fire extinguishers. There's a whoosh-ing noise behind the bulkhead and a cloud of white vapour pours out of the vents.

As the life drains out of Whisky Two Zero all I want to do is sit in my vehicle and go to sleep.

'If you sleep here, you die,' my gran says. 'Come on, Johnson, get back on you feet . . .'

I grab my SA80, spare ammo clips and belt kit, clamber out of the driver's hatch and haul myself on to the top of the vehicle. I place the rifle and the belt kit on the hull and ease myself into the turret through the commander's hatch.

Despite his injuries, Sammy has managed to disconnect the chain gun's belt feed.

I turn to the Rarden. The 30mm cannon has a cover that you lift and stow above the breech when you're on operations. Dropping the cover and locking it prevents anyone from loading ammunition into the breech.

The last thing I want is for the enemy to get into Whisky Two Zero and turn her armament on us. I drop and lock the cover. Then I pick up the boss's SA80 and pull myself back out into the open. As I drop to the ground my legs give way and I fall face down into the dirt. I lie there; for a moment I'm on the path up to my gran's house. Then I hear gunfire again and the spatter of bullets nearby. I pull myself back on to my feet.

I stagger around to the back of Whisky Two Zero and pull my day sack from the rack, then Sammy's and the boss's.

Weighed down by three day sacks and two SA80s, I turn and run towards the waiting Warriors.

Sammy and Erv are seated towards the back of the compartment. Woody is sitting by the door. I collapse on the seat opposite him. The door closes. It feels like I've been sealed inside an oven. I try to breathe, but I can't. The vehicle moves and I tip forward, ending up with my head on the floor, alongside Sammy's feet.

'Get his helmet off!' I hear somebody yell.

And then I can't hear or see anything else at all.

★

I'm lying in the semi-darkness. I hear no vehicles, no heli-copters, just the faint sound of the wind shaking the canvas above my bed.

A dim light glows on around twenty other beds. Three of them are occupied. The other patients are sleeping. I can hear the sound of their breathing.

I'm tired too, but I prefer not to sleep. When I close my eyes I see things – RPGs coming at me left, right and centre . . .

I'm in the Med Centre at Abu Naji. Random thoughts run through my head. I'm not sure which are memories and which are dreams. I remember coming to in camp. I remem-ber people ripping my body armour off me and a medic yelling for water, lots of it.

I've dreamed of water too – fetching it for my gran . . . the two of us drinking from the bucket . . . swimming in the pool above Red Mud – only the water there is hot, not cold, and it burns my skin.

At some point I asked one of the medical staff, a female doctor, about my mates. She told me that Sammy, Mr Deane, Woody and Erv were safe. They'd been stabilised in camp, then transferred to the hospital at Shaiba.

She told me that there's nothing wrong with me, either, except heat exhaustion, and that all I need is a lot of rest. I'm supposed to remain here for a few days under observation.

The lights flicker, then go out. In the distance a dog barks. I hear shouting.

Inside the tent the patients stir. Several orderlies rush in, holding torches. One of the beams shines directly into my face.

'Get under your bed,' a voice says. 'Mortar attack, inbound.'

'I ain' movin',' I tell him.

'Get under your bed, *now!*' he yells.

'No way,' I say. I've just been in a major contact with RPGs and bullets all around me, so a mortar that hardly rattles the perimeter wall holds no fears for me.

There's a loud explosion and we get hit by a shockwave that almost flattens the tent.

The orderly dives under the bed beside mine and stays there.

The next morning I get dressed and walk out of the Med Centre. The staff protest; they want to keep me under observation. But they can't keep me in. There's nothing physically wrong with me. They can observe me from a distance.

On the way back to the accommodation block I run into the OC and Falconer.

'Ah, Beharry,' the CSM says, 'we were on our way over to see you.'

'Me, Sarn't Major?'

'Yes, *you*, son.' He holds up a helmet. 'Any idea what this is?'

'She a helmet, Sarn't Major.'

Falconer beams. 'I see a little spell in the Med Centre has done wonders for your IQ,' he says. 'Course it's a frigging helmet, Beharry. More to the point, it's your helmet . . .'

I'm sure he's about to give me a bollocking for leaving my helmet in the back of somebody else's Warrior. Then I look down and see that there's a hole in the top of it and a groove about three inches long. I hear the sound of gunfire in my head; the guy coming out of the shadows, firing an AK from the hip; me shouting at Sammy to use the chain gun, then something slamming into my helmet with such force that my neck snapped back against the hatch . . .

'Beharry,' the OC says, 'are you all right?'

'Yes, sir. I'm fine. Thank you, sir.'

'I want to tell you that what you did yesterday was out-standing,' he says. 'And Richard Deane is going to be just fine, thanks to you.'

'I'm happy he OK, sir. He goin' to be all right?' What am I saying? He just told me that.

The OC nods. 'I spoke to him earlier. He's got the headache from hell and they're still picking bits of RPG out of him, but they think he'll be back inside a week. The same goes for Samuels, Wood and Ervin.'

'What about Clifton?'

'He got so pumped up during your push through the ambush that he leapt out of the wagon the moment you got to CIMIC, ready to stick it to the enemy. Sergeant Cornhill took one look at him and threw him over the wall of the compound.

'Clifton has a shell splinter the size of a credit card sticking out the side of his nose. They don't have the medical expert-ise to remove it at CIMIC, so we're just going to have to wait till the fighting subsides and then get him out to Shaiba. He's not in any immediate danger. In fact they've had trouble trying to stop him going out on ops. He's been taking a full part in the compound's defence.'

'The fighting still goin' on?'

'Yes,' the OC says. 'It's still pretty bad.'

'And Whisky Two Zero?'

'A party went out from CIMIC this morning and removed her ammo, her weapons and her radio – anything, basically, that could still be of any use. As soon as things are a little safer, we'll send in a low-loader and bring her back. But she's a write-off, I'm afraid.'

I raise my eyes to the CSM's. 'So what's with the helmet, Sarn't Major?'

A smile tugs at the corners of Dave Falconer's mouth. 'This,' he says, turning it over. Something is sticking through the lining. 'The round is still in there. Your helmet stopped a 7.62. That's a pretty bloody close shave you had there, Beharry. Well done, son. Well done.'

I take the helmet and look at it. I put my hand up to my throat. Thank God, the little cross is still there.

'Can I keep it, Sarn't Major?'

'Course not, son. That's army property. Go and get yourself another one from stores.'

He takes it back off me and stands there, while the OC looks on.

'But Sarge, I . . .'

'That'll be all, Behappy. Where are you off to now?'

'I'm going to see Lewy,' I tell him. 'I want to get back behind the wheel of a Warrior.'

'Shouldn't you still be in the Med Centre?' the OC says.

'I discharged myself, sir. There's not'ing wrong with me.'

'Glad to hear it, son,' the CSM says. 'I'd hate to think of you off on a skive.'

For a moment I think he's serious. But Falconer's ice-blue eyes are smiling. He gives me a wink and hands me the helmet. 'What you did yesterday, Beharry, was first-fucking-rate, son. The helmet's yours. Something to show the grandkids. Now, fuck off and make yourself useful, before I get you filling sandbags.'

After I've been to stores and got myself a new uniform and helmet, I find Lewy and Broomstick supervising the maintenance of our vehicles.

Although a good many RPG rounds were fired at us, Whisky Two Zero was the only wagon to sustain serious damage. The others are all getting bombed up and refuelled, ready to go out again.

In the tank park all the talk is about what happened on

Blue Route yesterday. Even though we got hammered, the fact that we fought our way through the ambush without any serious casualties has put a smile back on the boys' faces.

'What you did, mate, showed all of us that we don't just have to sit there and take it,' Broomstick says. 'You gave 'em Lennie and Ronnie and no fuckin' mistake, Harry.'

'I was just doin' me job,' I tell him.

I suddenly realise that without my vehicle I feel lost. I hear myself say this to Lewy and Broomstick. Lewy is in charge of the platoon until Mr Deane gets back.

'Listen, mate, you earned yourself a rest for what you did yesterday,' Lewy says. 'Why don't you do yourself a favour and get your head down.'

'But I don't want to get me head down,' I tell him. 'I want to get back out there.'

We're standing under a cloudless blue sky. Lewy is holding a clipboard and ticking things off on a roster. He's busy and I know I'm not helping by hanging around firing questions at him.

'Lewy, please. I need to do this,' I tell him.

He looks up from his clipboard. 'You *need* to?'

'Yeah. I need to.' I produce my old helmet, show him the hole and the bullet in the lining. 'I need to know I can still drive.'

Lewy sighs. He's a corporal doing a sergeant's job, which is not easy. Lewy is the kind of guy who has lived his whole life knowing he's going to join the army – it's the one and only career he's ever set his heart on. I like him because he's fair and a decent bloke. If it hadn't been for him running around shouting, 'What if? What if?' at Lydd and Hythe, a lot of us wouldn't still be standing here.

He squints in the sunlight. 'All right,' he says. 'But there ain't no wagons for you to drive – your replacement vehicle won't be ready for another couple of days. So you'll just have to come along with me as a dismount. Think you can handle that?'

'Yeah,' I tell him. 'I t'ink so.'

He claps me on the shoulder. 'Good lad. It looks like we're going to be having a busy time of it. CIMIC is still under direct contact by mortar fire. It's been raining down on the poor sods ever since we left 'em to it. They're under fucking siege down there. We're going to mount a company-level replen tomorrow morning, only this time we're not dicking around. We're going in with some serious muscle.'

'What kind of muscle?'

'We're going to send some Charlie 2s out in front – see how the bastards like seventy-five tonnes of armour bearing down on 'em.'

He wipes the sweat off his brow and manages a smile. 'Personally I wouldn't miss it for the world, mate, but if you want to change your mind . . .'

I'm not changing my mind, I tell him. I have to do this.

Lewy sticks out his hand. 'Good. I can do with all the help I can get.'

CHAPTER THIRTY-ONE

The next morning we're up at 0300 hours and the sky is as black as ink. I make my way over to the tank park and, after a short briefing from Lewy, clamber into the dismount section of his Warrior. There are two other dismounts in the back with me, Private Chambers and Lance Corporal Parsons. I don't know them that well.

'Glad to have you with us,' Parsons tells me as he plugs his headset into the socket behind him. He sticks his hand out and shakes mine. 'Bloody outstanding thing you did the other day.'

'I heard about the bullet you copped,' Chambers says. 'We could all do with a bit of that charmed bloody life of yours today, I reckon.'

'Charmed life?' I say. 'What's that all about?'

'You, mate. Everyone says that about you. Lucky bloody Beharry. Somebody told me that you once came back from the dead during training.'

That's a bit of an exaggeration, I tell him.

'What about the RPG that bounced off your Warrior during your first bloody contact?' Chambers says. 'I heard about that.'

'The other day we got hit by *four* RPGs on Blue Route,' I say. 'You can't call that lucky.'

'Yeah,' Parsons says. 'But they didn't get you, did they?'

I do up the chinstrap on my new helmet and grit my teeth. It hurts like hell, but I'm determined to keep smiling. The 7.62 round that went through my old one also grazed my scalp. I didn't tell anyone about it in the Med Centre; it didn't seem worth mentioning. But rules is rules, and if Parsons sees me with the strap undone he'll give me a bollocking. Another reason I'm desperate to get back in the driver's seat: up front I can do what I like.

The vehicle starts to move and already I don't like it. It's dark in the back; there's only a tiny window to see out of. I don't know what's going on because I'm not plugged into the net. I think about what Mr Deane calls 'situational awareness'. This doesn't feel right. It's scary.

I know we're sweeping round to re-supply CIMIC from the west, but I've no idea where we are. That frightens me more than anything.

Fifteen minutes after we set out I suddenly hear Lewy shout, 'Incoming!' and seconds afterwards the rattle of our chain gun.

The vehicle stops and I'm waiting for the instruction to move. It doesn't come. I know Chambers is listening to what's happening, but he doesn't pass on any information. Parsons and I are in the dark.

'*RPG!*' Lewy screams.

I pull myself into a ball and wait for the molten jet to punch its way into our compartment. I think of the blood on the floor of Whisky Two Zero, the scorch marks on Woody's face, the gaping hole in the wagon's side where the RPG penetrated and how Clifton must look with a shell fragment the size of a credit card sticking out of his nose.

Bullets ping and ricochet off the side of the vehicle.

I open my eyes. Chambers's face is inches away from mine. 'Beharry!' he yells. 'It's over. We're through.'

I'm still hunched in a ball, waiting for the impact.

'Over?'

'Yeah,' he says. 'We made it. They took one look at the Charlie 2s and fucked off. We're coming into CIMIC now.'

We dismount in the darkness and set up an all-round defence. Apart from the boys hurling ammunition and food boxes over the wall, it's eerily quiet. Either we've caught them by surprise or, as Chambers says, the Charlie 2s really have scared them off.

Back at camp, I tell Lewy that I'm never, ever going in the back of a Warrior again. As soon as a new wagon becomes available I want to go back to driving.

Fortunately a new wagon turns up the next day. Now all I need is a crew.

The night Sammy gets back we talk a little about what happened on Blue Route. He tells me that he, Woody and Erv spent a lot of time in hospital trying to convince Mr Deane that it wasn't his fault. The boss blames himself for leading us into the ambush.

The CO calls it 'calculated risk versus reward' and being in Al Amarah, full stop, is a calculated risk, Sammy says. We were in the wrong place at the wrong time. It was no one's fault, he adds, and I agree.

At two o'clock the following morning we're hauled from our beds and told to assemble in the company briefing room. There the OC briefs us on Operation Waterloo – a battle group 'surge' to re-supply CIMIC, defeat the insurgents in Al Amarah – with what the OC calls 'overwhelming firepower' – and stabilise the city. Mr Deane is sitting at the front of the room taking notes.

The operation is going to take place in two phases. The first will start with C Company's deployment to Sparrowhawk, the military airfield, which we'll use as a forward operating base for our replen mission. This time we're going to approach from the west, up Purple Route, which isn't overlooked by the housing districts that give us such grief when we go up Red, Blue and Yellow. We'll once again be supported by Charlie 2s.

A key part of the plan is securing the junction at Red Eleven, next to the water tower, close to what the OC calls the Mahdi Army's 'centre of gravity' – Yellow 3 and the OMS building, where the CO almost came to grief on our second day here.

For this phase of the operation we'll be supported by air power, in addition to the Charlie 2s.

The idea is for C Company to take control of the western half of the city and for A Company, which has been moved up from Brigade Reserve in Basra, to take the east.

When we assemble in the tank park Mr Deane calls us to a platoon briefing and puts some detail on our part of the operation. From Sparrowhawk we'll shake out into battle formation. The Challengers will lead the way, helping to secure key junctions, allowing the Warriors to push through to CIMIC.

When the replen is over, 8 Platoon's task is to reassemble at Red Eleven and hold it.

'This time,' the boss says, 'we're not going to return to Abu Naji and regroup. We're going to conduct an all-round defence and let the Mahdi Army come to us on the ground of our choosing.'

If they come, he says, our tactics and firepower will beat them. If they don't, they're going to look pathetic and lose face in the eyes of the people they're trying to impress most – the citizens of Al Amarah. It's what the CO calls a win–win situation, so let's make the most of it.

'Point Two. We're going to be joined for the second phase of the operation by an AC-130 Spectre of the US Air Force. The Spectre is a fearsome weapon system. It's armed with two

20mm cannons, one 40mm Bofors gun and a 105mm howitzer, all of which can be trained at night to an accuracy of a
few metres from an altitude of several thousand feet. With any
luck, these jokers are never going to know what hit 'em.'

He pauses to clear his throat. 'One more thing. After the
operation is over we're going to hole up at Coot, the ICDC
police station between Red Eleven and Red Twelve. Chances
are, we're not going to get a whole load of sleep over the next
thirty-six hours, but then again, nor is the enemy. Any
questions?'

'It's good to have you back, Boss,' somebody shouts.

Mr Deane drops his head. For a moment he is lost for
words, and so are we.

'Thanks,' he says simply. Then he sets his jaw, picks up his
helmet, body armour, day sack and rifle and jumps on to the
hull of our new wagon.

'Bee, have you checked out this old crate? How is she?' Mr
Deane says soon after we set out from Sparrowhawk.

She checks out fine, I tell him.

That's good, he says.

A minute passes.

'Sammy?' Mr Deane says.

'Yes, Boss.'

'I've done some thinking.'

'T'inking, Boss?'

'About this whole situation awareness thing. You know
how I hate to be cooped up inside a Warrior . . .'

'Boss, maybe you ought to spend a bit *more* time inside a
Warrior – specially during contact,' Sammy says. 'It supposed
to be safer that way, right?'

Mr Deane laughs. 'Ah, bollocks. You can't see jack through
the piddly little windows in this turret, especially at night.'

'So what is your plan?' I ask.

'My plan', he says, 'is to use the CWS on my SA80 to pick out targets, then designate them with tracer. You can follow my tracer with the chain gun, Sammy, and, hey presto, problem solved . . .'

The Common Weapon Sight has night-vision capability. It's not a bad plan, except for the fact that the boss's upper body is going to be totally exposed to enemy small-arms fire.

Mr Deane has set his mind on it. As soon as he's bombed up with some tracer, he says, he's going to give it a whirl.

As we pass through the western edge of the city, the street lamps flicker, die for a few moments, then come back on again. During the seconds we are in darkness I hear Mr Deane swear.

'What is it, Boss?' I ask.

'Bastards are signalling we're on the way up,' he says. 'They use the lights to tell everybody we're coming.'

But with the Challengers leading the way, we get to the intersection at Red Eleven without incident.

Half an hour later we all move up Red Route and take Red Fourteen.

Too heavy to cross the bridge from Green Five to Green Four, a couple of Charlie 2s are posted in over-watch positions on the northern bank of the Tigris, while a packet of Warriors moves forward to secure the bridge at Green Nine.

We remain at Red Fourteen, listening on the net, ready to push through to CIMIC as soon as the route is clear.

This is the worst part, sitting and waiting in the darkness. For all I know, we're being crept up on by half a dozen guys with RPGs. It's like Mr Deane says: when you're battened down and stationary, knowing those RPGs are out there makes the hairs on the back of your neck stand up.

We hear reports of a contact near Green Four, then, minutes later, a zap number is read out. Somebody has been hit in the throat.

Almost immediately we hear that the Millennium Falconer has deployed to pick up the casualty, but by the time the CSM gets to him 'throat' turns out to be 'foot'.

Not long after this we're told that the route is clear and the OK is given to begin our push through to CIMIC.

I'm relieved to be on the move again.

We pick up some small-arms fire on the way, but nothing like our contact on Blue Route. We all make it to the compound without serious incident.

Half an hour later we're back at Red Eleven, the sky lightening behind us. We stare in the direction of the OMS building, a few blocks to the west.

Overhead I can hear the faint drone of an aircraft. I spend a minute trying to locate it in the blue-black sky and I'm about to give up when there is a flash almost directly above us, followed by a boom and an explosion on the ground just a few hundred metres away.

Seconds later it happens again.

'What the fuck's that?' Sammy shouts.

'That's the Spectre,' Mr Deane says. 'I guarantee you that whatever it's just targeted is now seriously mash-up.'

'You been learnin' Grenadian while you in hospital, Boss?' I say.

'It's cheaper than employing a bloody interpreter,' he says.

When the sun pokes above the horizon the CO gives the order to Major Coote and 9 Platoon to 'go and knock on the door of the OMS'.

A couple of Challengers rumble into position this side of the bridge, then the Warriors go in.

The OC tells us he is outside the building with his Rarden trained on the door, calling for whoever's inside to come out with their hands up.

When they don't take any notice, 9 Platoon, under

Corporal Byles and Lieutenant Plenge, go in and conduct a room-to-room search.

They find no one – just a whole lot of weapons which we round up and dispatch back to camp. The Mahdi Army has fled.

To the west of the OMS building, 9 Platoon find the remains of the target hit by the Spectre's 105mm howitzer – an Iraqi mortar team that had been trying to set up in somebody's back garden. There's virtually nothing left: just scraps of metal and body parts, which ambulances under the direction of the ICDC are sent to recover.

We transfer to Coot, where we'll base ourselves for the rest of Waterloo. The ICDC police station is a shit-hole. All the air-conditioning units stopped working a long time ago, most of the paint has peeled from the walls and the place reeks of raw sewage from the blocked bogs.

We sit in the shade of the vehicles inside its secure compound. The only thing that does work, a thermometer hanging on the wall to the right of the main door, tells us that the temperature in the sunshine is fifty-four degrees. When somebody has the bright idea of putting it in the back of a Warrior, the mercury jumps to seventy-three.

To stay alive in heat like this, Lewy and Broomstick run around like mother hens, checking and double-checking we're drinking enough water. On an average day each of us gets through four litres; here we need twice that. We keep water in the back of our Warriors, but it's not pleasant to drink because it's almost boiling.

The Iraqi policemen who work here watch us with amusement as we fan away the flies. Instead of trying to restore law and order, they've spent the last twelve hours holed up inside. Mr Deane says they're waiting to see which side wins.

They hate us, we hate them and the insurgents don't seem to care who they kill. Smile, shoot, smile went out the window a long time ago.

The RAF flew fighter jets low over the downtown area today, to disperse an angry crowd that had gathered around the OMS building. The fighting has started again tonight and I fall asleep in the driving compartment of our new Warrior to the whine of rifle fire and the thump of blast bombs echoing across the city.

The following morning there's trouble in one of the housing districts on the east bank. We break out of Coot in platoon strength to go and investigate.

We pick up a Challenger 2 on the way, cross the river and sweep down Blue Route.

Here we are again – the big Saddam boulevard, four lanes separated by a central reservation, the lamp-posts that stretch into the distance, alleyways leading off it left and right. The black flags and the barricades are gone, but there's still something in the air – a feeling of threat – especially now, in the middle of Operation Waterloo, as our boys continue, here and in other parts of the city, to flush out the insurgents.

We know that today is going to be a busy one. Seeing a Charlie 2 in my mirror as we drive down the boulevard gives me a feeling of confidence. The locals are paying us more respect too.

We reach our target area, a section of Blue Route near Red Eight. There's no sign of trouble, so we drive on, turn around and swing back. On our second pass I notice a lot more people on the street. The insurgents often use women and children as human shields; when there are people on the streets you can tell from the look on their faces if something is about to go down. Today they look as tired and scared as the rest of us.

'OK,' Mr Deane says to Woody in the dismount compartment, 'we're back where we were. There are more people on the streets. A few bikes and parked cars, alleyways leading into the estate on both sides. Looks like they're setting up some kind of a market here . . .' and a few seconds later, '. . . houses to the left and right, Woody, flat roofs, nobody on 'em . . . OK, we're through now, no sign of trouble, but let's swing round one last time just to be sure.'

The boss leads, Joe Tagica is following in Whisky Two One and the Charlie 2 is behind him. Broomstick in Whisky Two Two and Lewy, his chain gun and Rarden at the ready, bring up the rear. With the Charlie 2 in the middle of our formation it takes time to turn. Fifteen minutes later we're back where we started.

Most of the market stalls have been set out along the side of the road and there's hardly any space for us to pass. Even though there are still a lot of people around, I don't like the look of it. The boss doesn't either; over the mike he says to me, 'Bee, you're on your own.' He is giving me full authority to make my own driving decisions – whether to press on or turn back.

The carriageway has become so tight that I decide I need to get us on to the other side of the central reservation where there aren't so many stalls. I tell Mr Deane this is what I'm going to do and tell him to batten down. The way he's always hanging out the turret makes me nervous.

Now we're hemmed in I can feel a knot in my gut. I close my hatch, then pick out the point where I want to cross the road, but there are people in my way. I rev the engine. The roar of the power pack clears them like magic.

I ease Whisky Two Zero up to the central reservation at an angle, position my left track on the concrete, gently touch the accelerator and we're over it and on to the other side.

In my mirror I see the other vehicles starting to follow.

More market stalls are going up in front of us. The stall-holders work quickly – maybe a little too quickly. Something is going on, but I still can't put my finger on it . . .

Before we get totally wedged in, the boss decides to hang a left at Blue Eight and head up to Yellow Two. He radios the other vehicles.

When we get to the junction I swing out as far as I can to give me the space I need to make the turn. The street we're heading down is narrow – far narrower than one of the carriageways of the boulevard we're now leaving – but at least it's clear of traffic. I press on.

Through the day sight I can see a crumbling balcony on the first floor of the house on the corner.

As we swing into the street my eyes are drawn to a movement in the shadows of the room behind it. I'm about to say something to the boss, when a little kid of five or six appears on the balcony, sticks his head through the railings and waves at us. Seconds later he is joined by another kid – his older brother maybe – and he waves too.

I breathe a sigh of relief. After everything that's happened this week, I'm getting edgy.

I gun the accelerator and move on, keeping one eye on my mirror.

Big Joe makes the turn, but the Charlie 2 is too long and the driver has to reverse to give it another try. The second time he makes it. We start to move forward again.

Broomstick turns into the street and I see Lewy behind him.

Lewy is heads-up, his turret still scanning our rear arc. He passes beneath the balcony. That's when I see something falling, catching the light . . .

A bottle . . .

It shatters on the turret, right beside Lewy's hatch. I see little pieces of glass flying up into the air, liquid spilling everywhere. There's a moment when nothing happens, then a whoosh and the Warrior bursts into flame.

'*Jesus, no, no, no . . .*'

'What the hell?' Mr Deane says.

'What is it, Paki?'

'Whisky Two Three's been petrol-bombed! Lewy's on fire!'

In my rear-view mirror, Lewy's turret disappears in a sea of flame. Seconds pass. I'm totally helpless. All I can do is watch.

A black mushroom cloud rises into the air.

Then, something – a ball of fire – rolls off the turret and lands in a shower of sparks on the road.

Mr Deane throws open his hatch. 'Oh, Christ, no . . .'

In the mirror, the fireball moves. I realise only then that it's Lewy.

'*Get us back there, Bee, fast!*' Mr Deane yells.

I throw us into reverse.

Dust, sparks and smoke rise up into the air as Lewy rolls this way and that, trying to put out the flames.

I see Broomstick clambering out of Whisky Two Two.

In the background, Iraqis scatter for cover.

By the time we reverse, Broomstick has thrown himself across Lewy's body and is smothering the flames with his bare hands.

I throw open my hatch and hear Lewy's screams of agony. Broomstick grabs him and bundles him into the back of Whisky Two Two.

Seconds later Broomstick reappears with a fire extinguisher and leaps into the back of Lewy's vehicle.

Mr Deane is out of our turret and running up the road to Whisky Two Two.

'What fuckin' happened?' Sammy says.

'A kid petrol-bombed Lewy,' I tell him. '*A ten-year-old kid. I seen him do it.*'

'Where?' Sammy says. 'Where?'

I hear him swing the turret.

'*Sammy, no!*'

The chain gun stays silent.

The kid has gone.

Dismounts fan out around the vehicles. All the civvies have fled. Lewy's vehicle is still burning. The flames on the turret have almost gone out, but I can see smoke pouring from the hatch.

Mr Deane reappears and jumps back into the vehicle. His voice shakes with rage.

'Bee, get us back to Coot,' he says. 'Lewy's in a terrible way; they're giving him morphine. Chris Broome's in trouble too. The fire spread to the ammo rack in Lewy's vehicle. Broomstick took a fire extinguisher to it and ended up inhaling the retardant. He's having trouble breathing.'

'Jesus!' Sammy says. 'A kid, a bloody kid.'

Dave Falconer is waiting at Coot when we arrive. He helps to carry Lewy out of the back of Broomstick's vehicle and into the police station.

By the time I make it inside, Lewy is lying on the floor in the reception area and somebody is trying to get a needle into him. It's difficult to find a part of his body that isn't burned. The skin is falling off his arms in sheets.

Another medic is trying to cut off his uniform and Falconer is yelling for water. The only clean water we have is the drinking water we carry in the vehicles and every time the CSM pours it on to him, Lewy screams even louder, because the water's fucking hot.

The boss pulls me to one side. 'The OC's on his way in,' he says. 'I'm going to go and brief him soon as he gets here. Get in the vehicle and stay with it. I'm going to try and set up a helicopter landing site somewhere close for a casevac extraction. When that moment comes, we're going to have to fly like the bloody wind. Have you got that?'

'Yes, Boss.'

Two minutes later the OC's Warrior pulls into the

compound. Major Coote jumps down from the turret, his face like thunder. The boss intercepts him before he can get into the building. I don't hear what they say – it's difficult to lock on to anything except the sound of Lewy's muffled screams – but the look on the OC's face tells me that he wants to go out there and kill somebody.

Falconer appears and the three of them hold a heated discussion. I see the OC heave a deep sigh and head into the building.

Two minutes later the medics bring out Lewy and Broomstick and put them in the back of Whiskys Two Two and Two Three.

The platoon pulls out of Coot and turns on to Red Route, heading north.

As we move up the road people rush out on to the streets and throw stones at us. I can see women and children among them. I don't have to know what they're shouting at us. The hatred is written on their faces.

'Keep going,' Mr Deane says. 'Just keep going.'

We cross over the river and hit the junction at Red Fourteen, a bleak spot on the northern edge of the city where Red and Green Routes meet.

We park up just off the road, not far from where a boy is leading a herd of goats across a patch of scrubland. He's around the same age as the kid who dropped the petrol bomb on Lewy.

The sound of the goat bells reaches me above the noise of our idling power pack. The boy looks at us and moves off towards a housing development a quarter of a mile to our left. I guess he's running to tell someone we're here.

I prepare myself for the thump and whistle of a mortar round.

Instead I hear something else on the wind – the beating of helicopter blades. The noise increases and I see a shadow race across the desert towards us. Seconds later the Chinook appears overhead. It's part of the Immediate Response Team, ready at a moment's notice to casevac casualties to Shaiba.

The Chinook lands. The medics wait for the sand and grit to die down, then run with Lewy and Broomstick up the rear ramp.

As soon as the stretchers are loaded, the engines whine, the rotors pick up, sand flies everywhere again and the Chinook is airborne. Its nose dips towards the desert as its blades struggle for lift. We watch it disappear into the heat haze on the south-east horizon, then we turn around and head back to Coot.

While the boss goes inside to regroup with Major Coote, we find what little shade we can next to our Warriors. The air is thick with the sound of rifle fire and the crump of explosions from blast bombs and detonating mortar rounds. Some of the guys smoke; some sit in small groups talking; some prefer to be on their own. Sammy and I sit with our backs against Whisky Two Zero's road wheels.

We're full of admiration for the people who did what they could for Lewy. Not just Broomstick, but Hughes, Lewy's driver, and Vuetanatokoka and Sewell, two dismounts in the back of Whisky Two Three, who administered first aid on the spot and tried to soothe his pain.

We all thought Lewy was invincible. It has taken a kid with a petrol bomb to prove us wrong.

Mr Deane emerges from the building and makes his way over. He stops and talks to the men from Lewy's vehicle and then the guys in Whisky Two Two.

He asks us to assemble in a small circle next to the vehicles.

Joe Tagica stands next to him. Big Joe is now the platoon's number two.

'I just want to say a few words,' Mr Deane says. 'Because in fifteen minutes we're going to have to go out of those gates and get stuck back in to patrolling the city. In thirty minutes we'll more than likely be passing the place Lewy got zapped. That's not going to be easy. It's going to require every ounce of strength we have. Strength, and restraint . . .'

He pauses for a moment.

'You all know how proud Lewy was of you. You should know too how proud I am of you. The easiest thing right now would be for us to go out there and exact some retribution for what has happened. God knows, it's been on my mind this past hour. But we can't afford to ostracise this whole city because of what one kid has done.

'When you see other kids out there, try and remember this. It's the people who hand them the bombs, the people who make women and children advance under contact as human shields for their ambush activities that we want to remove once and for all from these streets.'

There's a burst of gunfire from the estate on the opposite side of the road.

'Broomstick is going to make a full recovery and will be back with us in a few days. We all know that Lewy isn't going to be that lucky. So let's go out there and make him really proud of us. Let's go out there and do the job we came here to do.'

The boss takes a step back and nods to Big Joe.

Joe asks if we'll bow our heads while he reads a short prayer.

We pray that God will take away Lewy's pain. We pray that Lewy will make a full recovery. We pray for his family and the girlfriend he wanted one day to marry. We pray for the kid who threw the bomb . . .

Big Joe asks us to keep our heads bowed while he reads a short passage from the Old Testament.

'The words of wise men are heard in quiet more than the cry of him that ruleth among fools,' he says. 'Wisdom is better than weapons of war. But one sinner destroyeth much good.'

He closes his Bible and tucks it into his day sack.

Two minutes later we climb back into our vehicles and start engines, ready for whatever the rest of the day will bring.

After four days Operation Waterloo pays off and order is restored to the streets.

As we abandon Coot and return to Abu Naji, we get the good news that Broomstick has recovered and is waiting for us at camp. When we catch up with him I know that he's still trying to get his head around what happened to Lewy.

'It's the time everything takes when your mate is there, screaming in agony and needing your help,' he says. 'Even though we were working as quick as we could, it feels like it could never have been quick enough.'

He's not wrong. None of us can shake the image of Lewy in flames out of our mind.

It took time. Time to get to him. Time to put out the flames. Time to sedate him. Time to get him to Shaiba. Too much *time* . . .

But we couldn't have done it any faster.

I sit in the QRF room, listening to the distant sound of a muezzin's call to prayer. I wonder what today will bring.

It's Friday. Friday is supposed to be a day of peace and rest, but, as ever, we're on standby. Since we got here a month ago there hasn't been a day when we've had any peace or rest, so I've not got a lot of hope for today.

Whiskys Two Two and Two One, Broomstick's multiple, are ten kilometres to the south of us on a QRF task at Red One. They have been sent there to try to catch an enemy mortar team we know to be operating in the area.

Our multiple is on hand to deal with any emergencies closer to home.

Lewy has been replaced in Whisky Two Three by Sergeant Chris Adkins. We all know and respect Adkins – he ran the platoon between Randsy's departure and the arrival of Mr Deane.

The boss is in the Ops Room, listening to developments on the net.

He has been on my case today, because Whisky Two Zero has not been running as she should. Some of the other drivers have said she's exhausting more black smoke than normal, so I've decoked the ports, which usually does the trick, but it's so hot today – the hottest day of the year by far – that even I can't raise much enthusiasm for working on the engine.

When Mr Deane appears everyone shoots to their feet.

'There's something big going down at Danny Boy,' he says. 'Listen up.'

Danny Boy is a VCP fifteen kilometres to the south. It's close to Majar Al-Kabir – Mak – the town where the RMPs got killed last year.

An hour and a half ago, Mr Deane says, a convoy of Land Rovers driven by the Argyll and Sutherland Highlanders got ambushed, but managed to push on through without casualties.

A PWRR Land Rover detachment led by Captain James Passmore deployed to their assistance and also came under fire. Whiskys Three Three and Three One scrambled from Abu Naji around forty-five minutes ago. Along the way they hooked up with Broomstick's two-Warrior multiple at Red One and got ambushed before they even got to Danny Boy. Sergeant Perfect's Warrior got hit by an RPG and set on fire.

Comms are patchy, but the last reports we have are of Broomstick and Big Joe, supported by other C Company Warriors and a lone Charlie 2, mounting a concerted assault on several enemy positions. There could be as many as two hundred insurgents in the ambush, equipped with AKs, heavy machine-guns, RPGs and mortars.

'In short,' Mr Deane says, 'there's a massive bun fight

going on down there and they need our help. I'll update you en route. Let's go.'

Sammy and I run to the vehicle, clutching our rifles, helmets and body armour. I fire up the engine and don't much like what I hear. When I press the accelerator we lurch forward a few yards, then stall.

'Come on, Bee, for Christ's sake,' Mr Deane says, 'let's *go*!'

I try to start her up again, but I know she's not going to work.

'Come *on*, Bee,' Mr Deane says. There's a real edge to his voice.

I lean forward and rest my head on the rim of the hatch. 'Boss,' I say into my mike, 'she ain't going nowhere.'

'What?'

'Engine's fucked, Boss.'

'*What?!*'

I've never seen Mr Deane really lose his rag before, but he loses it now, big time. When I turn around he's halfway out of the turret. He unstraps his helmet and throws it on to the armour. It hits the Rarden and spirals away into the dust.

'I told you to fix it,' he yells.

'I did my best, Boss.'

'Well, you did a piss-poor job.'

He jumps down on to the ground, picks up his helmet and heads for the Ops Room.

'Where are you going?' I shout.

'To try and get us another bloody vehicle,' he shouts back.

I get out of my seat and throw open the engine cover. Because Whisky Two Zero is fucked, Whisky Two Three isn't going anywhere either. No vehicle can deploy on its own; when we move as a multiple we have to move in pairs at the very least. Anything less would be suicide.

No wonder Mr Deane is angry. I daren't even look in Sergeant Adkins's direction.

It takes me about ten minutes to locate the problem. The injectors in the fuel pump are blocked. Some grit has worked its way in there. I clean it out, but it takes a while and by the time I'm finished the battle for Danny Boy is over.

Sammy and I get the low-down from a driver who is one of the first to get back. Some of the guys in camp are already calling it one of the British Army's most decisive battles since the Falklands War.

The enemy were dug in behind a long sand berm parallel with the main road. One group of dismounts led by Woody and another by Corporal Byles had to assault the enemy dugouts frontally, across open terrain, under heavy fire. Broomstick advanced with them in Whisky Two Two, firing his chain gun and Rarden, with support from the other Warriors and the Charlie 2, which were around three hundred metres from the enemy trenches.

When they got to the enemy's network of dugouts, the dismounts had to flush them out with grenades, rifles and bayonets. As soon as one trench fell, another position opened up on them.

Broomstick dismounted alongside the CSM to oversee the taking of prisoners. When they too came under fire, Sergeant Major Falconer, Woody, Byles and the other dismounts had to fix bayonets and charge again. By the time it was all over we had suffered two casualties, neither of them severe. More than sixty of the enemy are dead. Broomstick and the CSM are still out there collecting the bodies.

'Why?' Sammy asks one of the guys who was there. 'Why don't the Iraqis do it? That's their job, ain't it?'

'Word is, some of the insurgents were involved in the killing of those RMPs last year,' the driver says. 'We need to positively identify them.' He goes quiet for a moment. 'When we got to them we discovered that some of them were just kids – teenage bloody kids.'

He wanders off, shaking his head. He has to get his Warrior refuelled and bombed up, ready to redeploy. He is due out on patrol again in an hour.

Five minutes later the remaining wagons roll in through the gates. The only one missing is Sergeant Perfect's, which has badly mash-up gears from the RPG strike and was driven the entire way back from Danny Boy in reverse. It made it to within a few metres of the gate, then the engine blew up. Perfect, covered from head to toe in sweat and dust, and barely able to see past the shit that covers his glasses, strides back in through the gate still clutching the rifle he used to hold off the enemy when his chain gun and Rarden jammed.

The prisoners are handed over to the RSM for an initial interrogation before they're passed on to our intelligence people in Shaiba.

None of us will ever forget the sight of Broomstick jumping down from Whisky Two Two. His battledress is soaked in blood. It takes me a moment to realise it's not his; it's from the bodies he has spent the last hour and a half picking off the battlefield.

He leans against the side of his wagon.

'Broomstick, you OK?' I ask.

'Yeah, gleaming. Thanks, Harry.'

'I'm sorry I wasn't there.'

'Yeah, well, don't be too sorry, mate. Wait till you see what we got in the back of the wagon.'

'What?' Sammy says. 'Bodies?'

'Bits of bodies, mostly. Had to pick 'em up and put 'em in our ponchos. Made me puke.'

He nods towards the rear door of the vehicle.

I turn to see a medic from the Regimental Aid Post trying to open up the rear door. He tells Broomstick it's stuck and Broomstick has a go. But the door won't budge. The electrical activation system must be jammed, Broomstick says. The only other way to open it is manually – from the inside.

Malloy, Broomstick's driver, disappears down the driver's tunnel while medical orderlies and the battalion padre stand by. I know he's working his way past the cage, into the turret, and from there through to the dismount section. I can feel the armoured sides of the vehicle pressing in on him. I can feel them pressing in on me.

We wait, and wait, and wait . . .

Just when I think Malloy is never going to reappear, there's a click, the rear door swings out and an arm, severed at the shoulder, flops on to the ground.

I can see a body inside, propped up like a tailor's dummy. Half his head has been blown away. His one remaining eye stares into space. He is – was – no more than fifteen.

I look down. A river of blood is pouring on to the sand and trickling away under the tracks.

One of the medics catches Malloy as he staggers from the door. His battledress is completely drenched in blood.

'One of them was looking at me, watching me, I swear to God,' Malloy says.

'That's impossible,' the medic says gently, sticking his head around the door and wincing at the smell. 'They're all dead, son.'

Sammy and I watch Malloy head off towards the shower block.

'I couldn't have done that. No way. Not in a million years,' I say.

Sammy says nothing. He doesn't need to.

Maybe Whisky Two Zero's engine problems weren't such a bad thing after all.

Maybe somebody *is* up there, looking after us.

CHAPTER THIRTY-TWO

'Broadmoor . . . Shit!' Sammy says as we drive in through the gates of the former Iraqi prison. 'What've we done to deserve this?'

It's ten days after Danny Boy, eight days after Broomstick's crew managed to wash the last of the blood from the back of Whisky Two Two, and life has returned to normal – as close to normal as it gets in Maysan province.

In the past week Abu Naji has been hit by a stream of mortars and rockets. CIMIC House is being mortared four, sometimes five, times a day; and our patrols are being ambushed every time they go out.

Whisky Two Zero and Whisky Two Two have been deployed to Broadmoor in an attempt to track down the teams responsible for firing the rockets and mortars from the Kadim Al-Mu'allimin housing estate into Abu Naji. Our job is to neutralise the threat.

The other multiple – Whisky Two One and Whisky Two Three – is spending a few days at CIMIC House to lend support to Y Company's foot patrols.

None of us likes Broadmoor. It's in easy range of the enemy's mortars – just a few hundred metres from the southern edge of the city. There's no running water, the electricity generator is completely unreliable and the cells where most people sleep are infested with mosquitoes.

There's a detachment of Royal Welch Fusiliers here, so spare floor space is hard to find. I sleep in the Warrior, which is parked a few yards from the gate, nose to tail with Whisky Two Two.

The Broadmoor compound contains a two-storey prison block, a separate cookhouse and an HQ building, where Mr Deane spends most of his time, monitoring the net for threat activity.

We deploy on patrol soon after midnight. We're tasked with setting up two VCPs, the first one at Purple Two, the second at Purple Six, in the heart of bandit territory – the estates to the west of Red Route, where so much of the trouble begins. On our way up we decide to check out the grid of streets and alleyways that make up the area between Red Eight and Red Nine and Purple Four and Purple Three. Most of the mortar rounds that hit Abu Naji come from this five-hundred-metre by one-kilometre section of the Kadim Al-Mu'allimin estate, immediately to the north of us.

We move up Red Route and enter the grid at Red Nine, moving west towards Purple Three.

The city has been hit by another power cut and this section of the estate has no electric light, but there is a full moon. I can see plenty and we choose to drive with the lights off. The streets are so narrow Mr Deane can almost reach out and touch the houses on either side as we rumble onwards with Whisky Two Two behind us.

Mr Deane and I reckon that being heads-up, having good situational awareness, outweighs the risk of another petrol-bomb attack, so we drive with our hatches open. Broomstick thinks the boss is mad and curses him for not battening down. We get our own back by clucking when Broomstick gets too mother hen on us. Even the boss joins in sometimes.

With the CWS, the night sight on his SA80, Mr Deane scans the alleyways and rooftops. He provides his usual running commentary for Woody. Our other dismounts are Big Erv, now recovered from his leg wound, and a new guy, Jim Cooper.

'Narrow street, mixture of one- and two-storey houses, flat roofs,' Mr Deane says. 'No one around.'

'Alleyways?' Woody asks.

'Everywhere,' the boss says. 'Hang on a moment . . .'

'What is it?' Woody asks.

'Thought I picked up some movement through the CWS. Fifty, maybe sixty metres ahead, on the left-hand side. See anything, Sammy?'

I hear the whine of motors as Sammy rotates the turret.

'Nothing, Boss.'

I look too, but I can't see anything either and we keep going, grinding up the street at walking pace.

I turn my head left and right; I can see eyes staring back at us from the windows. It's the spookiest bloody feeling.

There's a flash on the left-hand side and my night vision goes. I duck instinctively and hear the whoosh of the RPG round as it passes over us. There's an explosion somewhere behind us and I hear Mr Deane's voice, cool as a cucumber, over the radio: 'Whisky Two Zero. Contact. RPG. Purple Three. Wait out.'

Then all hell breaks loose. AKs open up on the roof forty metres in front of us. Bullets ping, sparks fly and the dismounts yell, 'What the fuck's going on?'

'Where are they?' Sammy shouts.

'Follow my tracer!' Mr Deane tells him.

There's a *bam-bam-bam* from above and behind me as tracer, one round in three, zips towards the roof from our turret. Mr Deane is standing up, giving it all he's got with his SA80.

'Got 'em!' Sammy yells and almost immediately there's a *ratatatatat* from his chain gun as he pours fire into the top of the house.

Mr Deane fires off another volley and this time it isn't just Sammy who joins in – I can hear Whisky Two Two's chain gun as Fowler, Broomstick's gunner, follows the pinpoints of orange phosphorus as they home in on the target. Some of the rounds ricochet off the brickwork into the sky.

They continue to pour fire into the top of the building right up to the moment we pass beneath it. There are no further attacks from the rooftops.

'Nice one, Boss!' Sammy says.

'Teamwork,' Mr Deane replies.

Ten minutes later we reach the junction at Purple Two and set up our first VCP. There's little traffic on the road and nothing happens. It's the same at Purple Six.

After an hour Zero orders us to return to Broadmoor. We ask whether we can come back via Purple Three and Red Nine, so we can check out the street where we got contacted.

Zero approves and we head off. It's 1.35 a.m.

'OK,' Mr Deane says, as we turn left at Purple Three and head back into the estate, 'everyone keep a . . .'

He hasn't finished the sentence when there's a flash and a whoosh and an RPG blasts down at us from a rooftop less than thirty metres away. How the guy can miss from that range, I don't know, but he does. The RPG explodes against the wall of the house behind us.

I see flashes of light either side of the launch point and hear the *ping-ping-ping* of bullets striking our armour. Sparks fly where the rounds hit.

Then there's an answering *bam-bam-bam* from Mr Deane's SA80 and I see his tracer shoot towards the rooftops.

'Sammy! Ten o'clock to turret. Three of 'em on the roof. Follow my tracer . . .'

Bam-bam-bam. Then another volley. And another.

The turret swings and the chain gun rakes the top of the building, 7.62 rounds chewing into the bricks and the plasterwork.

Somebody shoots back. The flashes give away his position and Sammy adjusts his aim. The insurgent is halfway through another burst when I see him fall backwards, firing aimlessly into the sky.

'More of 'em. Two o'clock! On the roof!' Mr Deane yells. 'Watch out! RPG!'

The grenade flashes past so close that I drive through its exhaust trail a second later. In the back of my throat I can taste the cordite.

Tracer rounds fly towards the launch point, then Mr Deane is on to the next target – a cluster of gunmen on a balcony on the opposite side of the street.

Sammy swings the turret to the left and the balcony disappears in a cloud of dust.

Then another RPG zeroes in on us, this time from somebody standing in the street forty metres ahead. I guess Sammy is too busy with his demolition work to see the guy who's fired it. The round skims between us and the house on our left and takes out a doorway.

The guy with the launcher scurries away down an alleyway. I shout for Sammy to get his guns to bear as we pass by, but there's too much happening on the other side of the street.

Mr Deane is doing his best to spell out what's happening to Woody. 'Gunmen on both sides of the street, on the roofs. *Jesus!*'

'*What?*' Woody yells.

I know how bloody frightening it is in the back.

'What is it, Boss?' Woody says again.

'They're walking along the rooftops, firing down on us, walking and firing . . . Bastards!'

Bam-bam-bam. I hear Mr Deane's next volley in my head-set. His tracer arcs towards our left and Sammy's chain gun follows it.

Bam-bam-bam . . .

The tracer jumps to the other side of the street. A gunman falls from the roof and thumps on to the balcony below. A second later more plasterwork evaporates as Sammy walks the fire from his chain gun down the wall.

I check my mirror. Whisky Two Two is still there, twenty metres behind us, its chain gun hammering rounds back down the street.

Even though I'm watching the battle, I'm also checking the road ahead, looking for escape routes, just in case.

'I'm out of bullets!' Mr Deane shouts. 'Woody! Chuck us some of your spare magazines, quick!'

Mr Deane keeps six spare clips in the turret. I can't believe how much fire we're pouring at the insurgents – yet they are still out there, still firing at us . . .

'Magazine coming at ya, Boss!' Woody yells. He's passing them up through the cage.

It takes a second for the boss to reload, then he's off again, designating more targets for Sammy.

I reach down to my left and run my hand along the instrument panel where I keep my spare magazines. I grab hold of one and, keeping my eyes on the street, reach back through the tunnel and hit Sammy on the foot with it.

'Another mag for the boss,' I say.

Without taking his finger off the trigger Sammy reaches down and takes it with his free hand.

Another RPG comes at us and in the flash of its ignition I see the guy who fired it behind a low balcony wall running round the first floor of a house sixty metres in front of us, on the right side of the street.

The grenade hits the ground in front of us and explodes.

'Sammy, guy with an RPG, one o'clock to vehicle. On that balcony.'

'*Where*, Paki? Fuckin' balconies everywhere!'

'That one with the low wall.'

'I got the wall . . .'

'The guy's behind it, going for a reload . . .'

'Boss, I need to fire the Rarden,' Sammy says.

'Then fire it!' Mr Deane yells.

The cannon opens up. Thirty-millimetre shells pummel the wall and the balcony disappears. Bricks and plaster tumble into the street. A body falls with it. I hear Sammy bang another three-round clip into the breach.

We rumble on.

When we reach Red Route, a guy runs out of an alley, throws a tube over his shoulder and pulls the trigger.

'RPG!' Sammy shouts, as he fires back.

I watch the grenade streaking towards us and I duck; I know it's going to be close. There's a bang, like somebody's hit us with a crowbar, and Mr Deane curses. Whisky Two Two's chain gun opens up.

'Fucker hit the turret and bounced off,' Mr Deane says. From the tone of his voice I don't know whether he's relieved or angry.

I floor the accelerator, thankful for the tarmac beneath us and the width and space of the four-lane boulevard. I have Whisky Two Zero up to forty in seconds. Two minutes later we're back at Broadmoor.

When we debrief we realise that we have been through five separate enemy positions and survived twelve to fifteen RPG rounds fired at our two vehicles, one of which hit us without going off.

We have no idea how much small-arms ammunition was fired at us; we're talking hundreds, maybe thousands of rounds.

We have fired 486 5.56mm rounds, all from the boss's SA80, six hundred rounds of chain gun 7.62 and nine 30mm HE rounds from our two Rardens.

'I tell you something,' Mr Deane says. 'That target-indication trick worked a bloody treat. I'm looking forward to trying that again sometime, I tell ya.'

Broomstick calls him a mad Irish bastard and we laugh, because we know he's right. But we feel good that we've stuck it to the enemy.

For the first time ever I feel like I'm on the winning team.

Four nights later we're back in the grid, at almost exactly the same spot – the junction at Purple Three, heading up to Red Nine – when we get ambushed again. This time it's guys trying to whack us with small-arms fire, which is a waste of everybody's time, but we identify at least four firing points and return fire with our chain gun, and Mr Deane's SA80 firing tracer one round in three.

We pull back into Broadmoor to catch some rest, but haven't managed more than ten minutes' downtime when somebody lobs a mortar round into the camp and we're scrambled towards the firing point, an area of scrubland on the south-west corner of the Kadim Al-Mu'allimin estate.

Eight hundred metres down the street, between Red Eight and Purple Four, I call the boss to tell him there's an obstruction ahead.

We stand off while Mr Deane checks it out with his CWS and I take a look through the passive night-vision device on the day sight.

'Looks like a pick-up, Boss.'

It's parked on the right side of the street and a sewage channel prevents me going around it.

'What do you want me to do, Boss? Reverse up?'

'The bastards will be long gone by then,' Mr Deane says.

'Plus the fact we're exposing ourselves to ambush,' Broomstick chips in. 'They'll be prepped for us.'

We sit there in the street, engines throbbing, while we decide what to do.

Mr Deane gets on the net to Zero. I hear the calm, reassuring voice of the CO, Colonel Maer. Mr Deane explains the problem – how we're trying to get to the mortar team's firing point, our way is blocked, we don't want to reverse because of the ambush threat, that it might all be a trap . . .

'What do you want to do?' the CO asks.

'Beharry's all for driving over the vehicle,' Mr Deane says.

'Then drive over it,' the CO says.

In case there is an IED either in the pick-up or somewhere close, we batten down. Then I gun the engine.

I've never driven over another vehicle before and I can't quite believe I'm doing it now.

I walk us up to the bonnet, place my right track against the radiator grille and give her lots of power. There's a roar from the CV8 diesel and a slight jolt as the tracks bite into the metal. Glass shatters, metal buckles and the pick-up collapses. It's like treading on a Coke can.

I can't help it. I start to laugh.

'Something tickling you, Beharry?' Mr Deane asks.

'I wanted to do this me whole life, Boss,' I tell him.

'Mad Grenadian bastard,' Mr Deane says.

We get to the end of the street and pause by the junction at Purple Four. I'm just turning left towards Purple Eight when we spot car headlights coming up the road towards us.

'It's three o'clock in the bloody morning,' Mr Deane says. 'So what's that joker doing out and about?'

I edge out into the road. The car screeches to a halt about 150 metres away, does a three-point turn and tears off in the opposite direction.

'Think you can catch him?' Mr Deane says.

I tell him I can give it a try and floor the accelerator.

We shoot off. There's a big shout from the back. If the dismounts aren't strapped in they'll be flattened against the rear door by now.

I watch the speedo climb: thirty . . . forty . . . fifty.

The white saloon is pulling away from us, but then hangs a right into the housing estate opposite the Kadim Al-Mu'allimin grid.

We follow it. The street is hardly any wider than an alleyway. Broomstick, in Whisky Two Two, takes a right on the next street along and we keep in touch on the net. With any luck we'll panic the driver into making another left and flush him straight into Broomstick's path.

I'm throwing Whisky Two Zero around and enjoying myself, but we don't manage to catch the vehicle and reluctantly accept Zero's order to head home.

We decide to go via the street that runs up between Purple Four and Red Eight, the southernmost boundary of the grid.

I hear Mr Deane throw open his hatch.

'Drop your speed, Bee,' he says. 'Let's see what's shaking tonight.'

We get just a hundred metres east of Purple Four when there are multiple flashes on the rooftops ahead of us and I hear bullets pinging off our armour.

'Sammy,' Mr Deane says calmly, 'follow my rounds.'

As Sammy lets fly with a long burst from the chain gun, the rounds punch into the brickwork Mr Deane has just designated with his tracer.

'Nice work,' he says. 'That's two down.'

We move on another hundred metres and get engaged again. Sammy rotates the turret and spots them behind us – two guys on a balcony angling an RPG launcher vertically at Whisky Two Two as it slides by ten feet below.

'Broomstick! RPG!' Sammy yells. 'Above you!'

In my mirror I see the round leave the tube. I brace for the explosion, but it doesn't happen – the range must be too close for the fuse to arm.

Sammy looses off a burst with the chain gun. I see the rounds spatter the balcony and two dark figures flee into the room behind it. Seconds later one of them reappears and fires his AK at us. I stand on the brakes and we rock to a stop. These people are pissing with us.

'Good man, Bee,' Mr Deane says. 'Sammy, engage the balcony with 30mm HE.'

A couple of seconds later there's a *boom-boom-boom* from the Rarden. The first shot blows a hole in the balcony, the second removes it altogether and the third explodes in the room behind, blowing part of the wall out into the street.

Nobody comes back out to have a go at us. We move on.

I'm so used to the sound of bullets striking our armour I don't even bother to duck any more. The way I sit to drive, leaning right back with the hatch cover over my head, gives me room to see and protection from overhead small-arms fire.

As we pass by an alleyway I glance left and see an RPG in flight, heading right for us.

I just manage to scream, 'Boss! RPG! Nine o'clock!' before it whooshes past us. It carries on down the alleyway on the opposite side, cracks into a telegraph pole and bounces off into the night.

'Shit! that was close!' Mr Deane says.

I reverse. Sammy's turret is already turning to engage.

I look left and see a lorry. It's parked up on the right side of the alley, next to a wall, thirty metres from our position. It looks like a water truck.

Pinpoints of light crackle in the darkness; bullets fly at us from the gap between the cab and the bowser.

Sammy lets fly with the chain gun. Bullets thump into the

cab and spatter the wall. Sparks fly off the cab and the bowser, lighting up the alley walls. How can anyone survive that? I wonder. But they do; seconds later the insurgents open up from their same positions.

'Sammy, engage with 30mm HE,' Mr Deane says. 'One round.'

'One round,' Sammy repeats.

The shell flies into the front of the bowser. There's a split-second delay, and then it blows. The blast rocks Whisky Two Zero and bits of shrapnel clatter against our armour.

'Holy shit!' Sammy says. 'Holy *shit . . .*'

'Boss, you all right?' I ask.

There's an unhealthy pause.

'Yeah,' Mr Deane's voice comes back. 'Although I'm still looking for my eyebrows.'

'I thought it was a water truck,' Sammy says.

'So did I,' Mr Deane replies.

The smoke clears. There's nothing left of the truck and the wall that was beside it is completely destroyed.

Silence descends on the street that runs up between Purple Four and Red Eight. Silence descends on the grid.

CHAPTER THIRTY-THREE

Maybe it's the heat or maybe we've been here too long, but tempers are getting frayed and today Sammy does something stupid – he hits Fowler because he thinks he dissed him. It happened in the mess tent at Abu Naji. I don't know what it was about, because I wasn't there and Sammy won't tell me, but it was probably something as stupid as who is the better gunner.

The problem is, this isn't the first time in the past week that Sammy's temper has got the better of him. The other day he threw a punch at Private Consterdine because he took 'his' chair in the mess tent. He's just in a foul mood. When Joe Tagica intervened after the incident with Fowler, Sammy refused to shake hands, so the whole thing has been passed up the chain to Mr Deane. The boss is furious and has told him to get his act together. The next time he hits someone he'll be on a charge.

Sammy is still in a bad mood today. We're on rest cycle; we have three hours' downtime before we deploy again on patrol. Downtime isn't really downtime at all; there are still plenty of things to do, and my responsibility is the vehicle. I have to make sure she's clean, properly maintained, bombed up and full of fuel. Because they are my mates, I invite Sammy and Campbell to help me. It beats sandbagging, which is what the rest of the platoon has to do.

We've finished up and are having a cup of tea, when a runner comes over and tells us we're required for sandbagging duty over by the accommodation area.

'Ah, bollocks to that,' Sammy says, as he drains his cup. 'They'll be finished any moment. Let's go and get somet'ing to eat.'

Ten minutes later we're sitting down, eating a meal in the mess tent, when Mr Deane walks in. His face goes a deep shade of red.

'What the hell do you think you're doing?' he says.

The three of us say nothing.

'You're supposed to be on sandbagging duties. Get over to the accommodation area. *Now.*'

He turns and storms out.

Sammy sits down again. Campbell joins him.

'What you doin'?' I ask them.

'Finishin' my meal,' Sammy says.

'Yeah.' Campbell nods.

'But we're supposed to be . . .'

'Sit down, Paki. Relax,' Sammy says. 'They doin' this to make a point.'

'What you mean?'

'You know how they hate it when they see the three of us together. They think we're plottin' something. So fuck 'em, that's what I say.'

Are they picking on us because they think three black guys hanging together automatically means we've got to be up to something? I don't know, but sometimes it does feel that way, and after all we've been through it suddenly seems as if Sammy has a point. The best way to protest is for the three of us to stick together.

We're leaving the tent when we run slap into Broomstick. The set of his jaw and the look in his eyes tells me that we're in the shit.

'You three!' he storms. 'Fucking hopeless! The entire platoon is sweating its bloody bollocks off and you three no good frigging malingerers – you fucking . . . *skivers* – are swanning around in here like it's the South of fucking France!'

'You can't talk to me like that, Sergeant,' Campbell says.

'Shut the fuck up!' Broomstick yells. 'I can talk to you any fucking way I like. The rest of the platoon is running like clockwork and you three somehow get it into your heads that you can piss about doing any fucking thing you please. In case none of you had noticed, we're fighting the fucking war to end all wars here and I'll do any fucking thing in my power to ensure that a few jack individuals like you don't go wrecking it for the rest of us. Now fall in! The boss wants to see you.'

We line up outside the Ops Room. Mr Deane appears. We stand stiffly to attention.

Mr Deane lays it on the line for us. He's angry, but not in the way Chris Broome is. He tells us that if there's any more disruption, bad behaviour, insolence or skiving, he'll throw the bloody book at us.

As the others leave, the boss calls me back. The anger in his eyes softens.

'Bee,' he says, 'don't you see what's happening here?'

'Happening, Boss?'

'Every man in this platoon has to pull his weight and any man that doesn't is jeopardising what we have built up over the past seven weeks, a *corps d'esprit* that is second to none in the battalion – God knows, maybe in the whole bloody army.'

A helicopter flies low over the camp. Mr Deane waits until he can hear himself speak. 'Whatever Sammy's pissed about, Bee, he's got to work it out for himself. War places unusual stresses on all of us. You can't fight his war for him. Sammy is an outstanding gunner, but I won't tolerate any behaviour that's going to jeopardise the morale of my men.

'Filling sandbags may seem pointless to you, but any man that doesn't muck in here is handing a loaded RPG to those lunatics out there, as far as I'm concerned. A skive here isn't the same as a skive in Tidworth, Bee. Skiving here could mean the difference between life and death for all of us.'

As I walk back to the vehicle I can't shake the look of disappointment in Mr Deane's eyes from my head.

A few days later we're back in Broadmoor, doing what we do best: trying to rat-trap the enemy mortar team that is still chucking rounds at us from the grid bound by Red Eight and Purple Four, and Red Nine and Purple Three.

At one-thirty on the morning of 11 June we're sitting in our vehicles, bombed up and ready to go, when we get scrambled. A mortar has just been fired at Abu Naji from somewhere within the grid. If we're quick we can get them.

Twenty seconds after we turn on to Red Route, Whisky Two Two tucked in behind us, the lights go out. Fuck it, I say to myself, the bastards know we're coming.

There's no moon and we're driving with our lights off and for a moment I can't see a thing. I take my foot off the accelerator and we start to slow.

'Bee, what are you doing?' Mr Deane says. He is tucked down inside the turret, plotting our route to the grid reference that Zero has just sent us.

'I can't see nothing, Boss. I think we're coming up to Red Eight, but I'm not sure. I never known it so dark.'

'OK,' Mr Deane says, 'give us a couple of secs and I'll stand up and take a look through the CWS.'

I hear the clang of the hatch on the turret. I know Mr Deane is up there, scanning through his night sight. The CWS works better than the night-vision setting on the day sight. I flip my hatch down and take a look too.

Ahead the street sparkles in shades of green and black as

my optics struggle to cope with the absence of light. All I see is Red Route disappearing into the distance; open scrub to the right; alleyways leading into the grid between a chequerboard of houses on our left.

'Looks to me like we're around fifty metres short of Red Eight,' Mr Deane says.

I agree. I'm about to set off again, when I see movement at the edge of the day sight's range.

'Boss, what's that?' I ask. 'Something crossing the road. Maybe a hundred metres out.'

There's another pause, then Mr Deane laughs. 'It's a cat, Bee.'

There's relief in his voice.

'What colour?' I ask.

'What do you mean, "what colour"?'

'What colour is the cat?'

'How should I know?' he says. 'What does it matter? Jesus, Bee . . .'

I can see him shaking his head.

It's all right for Mr Deane. Where he comes from, a black cat crossing the road is a good thing, but for me . . .

I throw open the hatch and gently press down on the accelerator.

We edge towards the junction. I'm looking for the turning to Purple Four and cursing the fact it's so dark.

There's a flash off to the left. Mr Deane shouts a warning; Sammy yells my name. I see something out of the corner of my eye. The nose of a shell, flipped-out fins, a plume of smoke . . . less than a Warrior's length away.

There's a flash of light and an unholy crash and something slams into my head. I get a ringing in my ears and a metallic taste in my mouth. I open my eyes but I can't see. I try to remember where I am, what I'm supposed to be doing, but I can't.

Nothing comes to me. Nothing at all.

But then I see something. Gran holding her poultice jar, smiling at me. '*You cut youself,*' she says. '*I make it better for you now.*' She reaches out, but the image crackles and fades.

Then, through the static, I see my dad. He's sitting on the porch of our home in Diego Piece, holding a copy of *Motor*, the one with the Porsche 911 Turbo on the cover.

Daddy?

He starts to flip through the pages. I'm here, I tell him. *I'm here . . .* But he doesn't see me.

What the hell's happening, I say to myself. What's going on?

Bam-bam-bam . . .

I'm driving a Porsche 911 along the road that winds up from the coast to Diego Piece. There's sunlight on my face; wind in my hair.

This is where I want to be.

Bam-bam-bam . . .

I'm on my hands and knees, my fingers raking through the mud. I'm looking for my Auntie Irene's little cross, but I can't find it . . . *I can't find it . . .*

Bam-bam-bam . . .

'Bee?'

Mr Deane is talking to me. He's angry with me. Mustn't disappoint Mr Deane . . .

'Bee, can you hear me?'

'I hear you.'

'Get us the fuck out of here! *Go, go, go!*'

'OK, Boss.'

Mustn't disappoint Mr Deane, I tell myself. Mustn't disappoint . . .

I reach down. Of course. I'm in a Warrior, a Warrior . . .

I slip into reverse and hit the accelerator. We shoot backwards.

'Whoa!' Mr Deane shouts.

'Go, Paki, go!' Sammy yells. 'There's more of 'em out there. They're lining up for another shot!'

More of who? Another shot of what?

RPGs . . . I remember now.

Got to get us out of the kill zone. Got to get us away from here.

Go faster. *Faster* . . .

A flash of tracer . . .

We're not on a road. We're racing backwards across open ground . . .

What am I doing here?

We hit something and stop.

Shouting. Gunfire. Darkness.

Something slides out of the darkness and parks in front of us. Another Warrior.

Broomstick and Mr Deane are talking. Mr Deane is hurt. He's got a cut on his head, but he says he's OK. I've got a cut on mine too. I try to reach up and touch it, but my arm won't move.

In front of me, the Warrior starts to move away.

'Follow him, Bee,' Mr Deane says.

'OK,' I tell him.

But I can't move my foot either.

What's happening to me?

'I got you, mate. You're OK now.'

I look up. Broomstick. Staring down at me.

What's *he* doing here?

He takes hold of one arm. Somebody else grabs the other one. They pull. Lift me out. Next thing I know, I'm in the back of a Warrior.

'*No! Not the back! I can't go in the back!*'

'Shhh! Easy, mate. I got you.'

I open my eyes. Broomstick is still looking down at me. My head is in his lap.

'Stick? That you?'

'Yeah, mate, it's me.'

'What's happening to me?'

'You're going to be all right, Harry. Now hold still, mate, while I put this dressing on you.'

A bandage comes down towards my face.

'*Aaaaaaaarrrrgh!*'

'Harry, what is it?'

'*That hurts! It hurts!*'

'I ain't touched you, mate.'

'*Aaaargh! Me foot, it hurts. Me foot!*'

Suddenly the pain stops.

'Sorry, mate, looks like you got your foot shut in the door.'

'Me foot?'

'Yeah, your foot.' He pauses. 'You're OK now. We're on our way. We'll get you to Broadmoor in a jiffy.'

Tears are rolling down his face. Tears . . .

'Stick?'

'Yeah, mate?'

'Am I dying?'

'Nah, mate, you're not dying.'

'It hurts, Stick. It hurts.'

'Hang in there, Harry, we're bloody nearly there, mate, bloody nearly there . . .'

The door opens. I'm carried into Broadmoor. People stare at me strangely. It's like they've just seen a ghost.

I'm laid out on a stretcher. Straps are placed across my legs and chest.

Radios crackle. Somebody's talking about a helicopter flight.

I try to get up, but I can't. A girl with blonde hair comes up to me and plunges a needle in my leg.

'My head hurts,' I tell her. 'I need to get up, see me gran. She can fix me. She can fix me good.'

You're not going anywhere, she says.

The radio crackles again. IRT Chinook's warming up on the pad at Abu Naji, a voice says.

I feel myself starting to slide.

I'm going on a journey. I wish I knew where.

PART FOUR

Birmingham, 2004

CHAPTER THIRTY-FOUR

Lieutenant Colonel Matt Maer, CO 1PWRR
0800 hours, 12 June 2004

I have been in Basra for the past day and a half, but have been kept in touch with developments on the ground by my team in the Ops Room. Now that I am back in Abu Naji, I need to know exactly what has happened. We have lost two valuable colleagues – Second Lieutenant Richard Deane and his driver, Private Beharry. It has been a very expensive twenty-four hours.

8 Platoon is regrouping at Broadmoor. Sergeants Adkins and Broome, in temporary charge, are among the very best NCOs in the battalion and will be doing their utmost to settle their men.

Inside the Ops Room, the Battalion 2 i/c [second in command], Major Toby Walch, is staring at a large-scale map of Al Amarah while he monitors SITREPs [situation reports] coming in over the radio. 'How's Beharry?' I ask, as he hands me the gen on the contact.

He tells me that it isn't good. His injuries are amongst the worst he has ever seen. Richard Deane has severe shrapnel lacerations to the face. Both men are being treated at the field hospital in Shaiba.

The minutes of the contact report state that in the early hours of yesterday, at 0115, the two Warriors of the Broadmoor-based QRF were moving up Red Route when they were contacted by small-arms and RPG fire.

Whisky Two Zero had slowed almost to a standstill and was approaching Red Eight, an ambush black spot, when it was hit by several RPGs.

One of them struck the strut that holds the driver's hatch in the open position and exploded no more than twelve inches from Beharry's face.

Had it not been for the fact that Beharry is tall and preferred to lean back in his seat while driving, he would almost certainly have been killed outright.

Richard Deane, heads-up, out of the turret, was stunned by the initial impact, but after a few seconds, managed to raise his CWS to his eye. He saw several other insurgents standing in an alleyway, one of whom was preparing to fire another RPG.

Deane emptied his magazine at the enemy position, but soon found it difficult to see because of the blood in his eyes, so told Beharry to get them out of there. Remarkably, Beharry replied in the affirmative. No one knew at this point just how badly he was injured.

Travelling backwards, the Warrior crossed Red Route's central reservation and ploughed across an area of wasteland for two hundred metres until it hit a brick wall.

Still under contact, Deane tried to raise Sergeant Broome in Whisky Two Two, but his radio couldn't send, only receive.

Broome pulled up alongside Whisky Two Zero and the two discussed next steps – getting back to Broadmoor being the priority.

Whisky Two Two moved off. When Deane ordered Beharry to follow, nothing happened. He tried to jump out of the turret to get to his driver, but a Russian-made DShK heavy machine-gun opened up, forcing him to take cover.

Sergeant Broome reversed up, placing Whisky Two Two between the 'Dushka' and Whisky Two Zero.

Deane, meanwhile, had seen more insurgents only sixty or seventy metres away, approaching their position. While he tried to engage them with his SA80, Broome and one of Deane's dismounts, Private

Cooper, now aware that Beharry was seriously injured, started to lift him from the driver's compartment.

Broome carried him into the back of Whisky Two Two and began to administer first aid.

Cooper jumped in the driver's seat and followed Broome back to Broadmoor under Deane's direction. They did well, considering Cooper couldn't drive and Deane couldn't see, but ended up demolishing both pillars as they drove in through the gates.

A medic from the Royal Welch Fusiliers did her best to stabilise Beharry before discharging him in an ambulance back to Abu Naji.

By then, the IRT Chinook was ready to go.

'Makes for pretty sombre reading, doesn't it?' Toby says, as I put down the report. 'How in God's name was he able to drive a Warrior?'

I shake my head. I simply don't know. I have spoken to people who saw Beharry at Broadmoor. Somehow, he remained conscious even then.

'Does he have a wife?' Toby asks.

I nod and look at my watch. By now, she will already have been told what's happened. We will do everything we can to get her out to theatre so that she can be with him in the critical hours ahead.

The radio crackles and I hear the word 'Contact'.

I look at Toby. He says nothing. He doesn't need to. 'Fuck, here we go again,' is written all over his face.

'CIMIC House,' he says. 'Four mortar rounds fired into the compound from the Al Dayya estate. No reports yet of any casualties.'

The Beharrys' world has been turned upside down, but in downtown Al Amarah, it's very much business as usual.

1100 hours, 12 June 2004

I wake up to the sound of a Chinook beating its way into the air on the other side of camp, glance at the clock and realise that I have drifted off. I check with the watch keeper that there have been no key developments in the past two hours, then haul myself out of my chair to make a cup of tea.

When I return, a note on my desk tells me that Beharry has been transferred by helicopter to a civilian hospital in Kuwait City, where doctors are better equipped to cope with his injuries.

At the bottom of the note there's a phone number where I can get updates on his condition.

The only good piece of news is that Captain Chris Wright, the battalion's unit welfare officer, is in Abu Naji on a fact-finding tour. His job is to act as liaison between our soldiers on the front line and their families back in Tidworth. I have given orders for Chris to go to Kuwait, where he is to keep an eye on Beharry and make arrangements for his next of kin to fly out.

We have a mild drama mid-morning, when a number of people in camp report hearing the whistle of a mortar overhead, but no explosion is seen or heard.

In the relative quiet that follows, I phone the hospital and eventually get put through to a Kuwaiti surgeon with a flawless command of English.

'He has a soft tissue injury to the shoulder that we've been able to clean up, but the main problem, of course, is the injury to the head,' he says.

'Just how bad is it?'

'He's got a compound depressed skull fracture involving the frontal bone, orbital roof, frontal air sinus and anterior fossa floor, extending into the ethmoids and . . .'

'Hang on there,' I say. 'You're losing me.'

'I'm sorry, long night,' he replies and I now hear the exhaustion in his voice. 'Private Beharry has suffered a severe brain injury. Basically, the pressure wave from the explosion has caused multiple fractures to his skull. His forehead has been crushed. The X-rays show extensive fracturing of the bone. Imagine what happens to an eggshell when you hit it hard with a spoon; that's what his skull looks like, Colonel Maer. Internally, the scans show that he's got further bone damage in the area of the eye sockets, and that the brain itself has suffered a burst right frontal lobe.'

'How bad is that?' I have a feeling I know the answer.

'The frontal lobe is the part of the brain involved in organising, planning and problem-solving, but is also responsible for some of the more fundamental cognitive aspects of our mental activity. It shapes our personality, essentially, and governs how we behave and react to things. Our emotions, too, stem from the brain functions that occur within the frontal lobe. At this stage, we don't know what the long-term effects of the damage will be. Frankly, Colonel, we are not yet in a position to look that far ahead.'

'Is he going to survive, Doctor?'

There's a long pause. 'We don't know, to tell you the truth. He's in a coma and has a GCS of five. That's a scale we use to determine the severity of a comatose patient. One means there is no discernible brain function at all; fifteen indicates brain pattern activity that is only marginally subnormal. The difficulty we face is that there's extensive intracerebral bleeding and dangerous levels of swelling. We've cleaned and closed the scalp wound as best we can, but we don't have the neurosurgical skills to carry out any further medical intervention.

'What I'm saying, Colonel Maer, is that we've done everything that can be done for him in this hospital. All you – all we – can do now is pray.'

'Pray for what?' I ask.

'That the swelling stops.'

'Because if it doesn't, he'll be brain-damaged?'

'Because if it doesn't, Colonel, he'll die.'

An hour later I get a call from Chris Wright, who's now on his way to Kuwait City from Shaiba Camp.

He tells me that Lynthia will be leaving for Kuwait, along with Beharry's aunt, as soon as the travel and visa arrangements are in place.

I wander out of the Ops Room for a cigarette. I smoked occasionally before we left Tidworth for Iraq. I'm now on thirty a day.

Seconds after I light up, I see the imposing figure of Corporal Joe Tagica jogging through the dust-laden air towards me. He salutes and asks whether there's any news. I tell him what the doctor has just told me.

'Pray for him, Corporal Tagica,' I say. 'Because right now that's all we can do.'

He nods and runs off towards the tank park, where the rest of the platoon is preparing the Warriors for another night on the streets.

CHAPTER THIRTY-FIVE

Captain Chris Wright
1400 hours, 15 June 2004

Beharry's wife and aunt touched down in Kuwait City this morning. They've taken twenty-four hours longer than planned to get here because of visa complications in London.

It is four days since Johnson sustained his injury and he is still in a coma. The good news is that the swelling to his brain has slowed and his GCS level – his comatose state – has stabilised at ten.

He remains, however, in a very critical condition.

I have tried to prepare Lynthia and Irene as best I can for what they will see when they get to the hospital, but however I dress it up, coming face to face with Johnson will come as a profound shock.

He is on a ventilator; there are tubes and drips all over his body and he remains under heavy sedation. His head is the size of a football. He has lacerations and bruising all over his face. Fluids seep from his puffed and swollen eyes.

The medics don't have the equipment to perform what could amount to a life-saving operation here in Kuwait. Johnson is going to have to be transferred to the UK.

The Queen Elizabeth Neuroscience Centre at the University Hospital in Birmingham is on standby. The priority now is to

*continue to reduce the swelling and bring him out of coma. If he trav-
els too soon, minute changes in pressurisation on board the aircraft
could kill him.*

*Though tired, shocked and scared, Lynthia and Irene insist they
want to see Johnson as soon as possible. I take them directly from their
hotel to the hospital's intensive care unit.*

*We meet the medical team and discuss the extent of Johnson's
injuries, then are led to his ward.*

*I pause by the door and ask Lynthia and Irene if they want time
alone at the bedside.*

*Irene takes hold of my hand. 'You have done so much for Johnson
and for us already, Chris. We'd like you there too, if you're OK with
that.'*

'Thank you,' I tell her. 'I don't know what to say.'

*'You are part of his family too,' Irene says. 'He was so proud of his
career in the army. It was me who told him not to join. But he
wouldn't listen. He's so stubborn like that.' She pauses. 'Tell me,
Chris – all the pain, all the suffering . . . Did Johnson's being here
make any difference?'*

*I feel a lump in my throat. What can I tell her? 'Every man in his
platoon is praying for him, Irene. They say he did something special.
Saved a lot of lives. I don't know the exact details, because I wasn't
there. But whatever he did, I know he made a difference.'*

Irene gives me a hug and we enter the room together.

*Johnson is lying in a screened-off section of the ward. There are
tubes coming out of his nose and mouth and drips in his arms. I hear
the rise and fall of the ventilator, the beeps of the monitoring
equipment.*

I wait by the door as they approach the bed.

*Irene places a little teddy bear next to Johnson's pillow. Then she
and Lynthia sit down beside the bed and start to pray.*

*For the rest of the day they take it in turn to talk to Johnson. They
talk about his family. His mother in Grenada; his relatives there.
They talk about Raymond, Irene's husband, and their children,*

Darren and Gavin. Everyone, they say, is thinking about him. Everyone is praying.

Over the next few days a routine is established. We arrive at the hospital early and they talk to him, they read to him, they pray.

On Friday, one week after the action, I force them to take the afternoon off. I tell our driver to take them on a tour of the city, then back to the hotel. What they need is rest. They are physically, mentally and emotionally exhausted.

I have told them I will continue to watch over Johnson and call them if there are any developments.

'Only God knows the true extent of his injuries,' Irene tells me as we say goodbye. 'All we want right now is to be able to take him home.'

Tomorrow, Saturday, is a critical day. The doctors are going to reduce his levels of sedation to see if they can bring him out of coma.

If they succeed, RAF doctors will assess whether he is fit enough to fly back to the UK.

As I maintain my vigil I tell Johnson about recent developments, following my morning briefing from the CO.

Richard Deane discharged himself on Monday from the field hospital in Shaiba and is now back on duty in Whisky Two Zero. Private Aitken is driving for him. In the past few days they have seen further, extensive action – most of it in the form of RPG ambushes in the vicinity of Red Eight.

But maybe, I tell him, all that is in the past.

This morning Colonel Maer managed to negotiate a ceasefire with the OMS.

In return for Al Sadr's promise not to attack British troops, we will not send any more armoured vehicles on to the streets of Al Amarah. The agreement has been read out in all the mosques and, so far, the signs are positive. The ceasefire is holding.

Had it not been for the robust action taken by the battle group in their operations to restore order to the city, it is doubtful whether Al

Sadr, the OMS and the Mahdi Army would have come to the nego-
tiating table.

They do say at some level that Johnson may be able to hear me.
But as I talk to him, studying his face, there is no sign of movement;
no flicker of any acknowledgement that my words are getting through.

CHAPTER THIRTY-SIX

0830 hours, 19 June 2004

I'm lying on a hospital bed with no memory of how I got here. The sheets are clean and cool. The walls are bare, except for a clock above the door. Everything is white – the sheets, the walls, the blinds, the monitoring equipment, even the face of the clock. The only colour in the room is the patterned pink and red top of the woman sitting at the end of the bed. Her head is lowered, so I can't see her face. She seems to be praying.

A man enters the room. He is wearing desert combats. As he approaches the bed I realise that he is someone I know: Captain Wright, the unit welfare officer in Tidworth. Is that where I am? Tidworth?

The woman raises her head.

'Auntie I,' I say. 'What am I doing here? What are *you* doing here?'

She looks at Captain Wright. Then she turns to me. Her eyes are red-rimmed. She dabs at them with a tissue.

'Why are you crying, Auntie I?'

Neither of them acknowledges me. Why can't they hear me? I'm here, I tell them, I'm he . . .

Captain Wright wheels a trolley over to the side of the bed.

He grabs hold of my upper body and Irene takes my feet. They lift me on to the trolley and Captain Wright wheels me towards the door.

'What are you doing?' I ask. 'Where are you taking me?'

The next thing I know, I'm in a field. Long grass brushes my face. Captain Wright has his back to me. He is pulling the trolley.

I start to panic and try to get up, but straps hold me down. I can no longer see the hospital.

'Auntie I? Auntie I, I'm scared. Where am I going?'

But Irene has gone. It's just me and Captain Wright. And he doesn't hear me.

The grass parts and I see a big, slow-moving river. Mist rises from the water. Birds circle above it, snatching insects from the air.

Captain Wright stares out across the river, his back to me. He's smoking a cigarette. Every now and again he looks at his watch. Time passes. The mist begins to clear.

I become aware of something in the river. An island. It has a beach, a jetty and lush, tended gardens with tropical flowers and palm trees. It could be Grenada, except there's a strange-looking building in the middle; a big, red-brick English country house that is also partly a temple.

'What are we waiting for?' I ask Captain Wright.

I'm so frustrated that he can't hear me I'm about to yell at him. Then, across the river, coming towards us, I see a boat that's like no boat I've ever seen. It's big, but has no engine and no sails. The front and back rise up out of the water. They look like fortified watch towers. Just above the waterline are two rows of oars. There's no one on deck. It appears to be steering itself.

Captain Wright throws his cigarette into the water and pushes the trolley into the slow-moving current. The boat coasts through the water towards us . . .

I'm on board, staring at the sky, listening to the oars as they dip in and out of the water.

Captain Wright wheels me off the boat, through the garden and into the big house that is partly a temple.

We enter a huge darkened room filled with candles. A girl approaches us. I think she might be Chinese. She and Captain Wright lift me on to a stretcher. They carry me into the middle of the room. There, on a platform ringed by candlelight, is a bed of nails.

As they lower me on to it, I ask them to be careful of my shoulder, because it's really starting to hurt.

They leave the room. I close my eyes. When I open them again there's an old man with long white hair and a straggly white beard standing next to me. He is very small, but his face is kind and wise. He steps on to the platform and starts to walk up and down my body in his bare feet; up and down, up and down. The nails dig into my back, neck and legs, but I don't feel any pain.

'Why are you doing this?' I ask.

The old man looks at me and smiles. 'It's a test,' he says.

'A test? What for?'

'To see if you're ready to go back.'

'Go back where?'

Tiredness washes over me. I'm struggling to keep my eyes open. 'Where am I going?'

'Try and sleep,' he says, 'because you're going back now.'

'To the hospital?'

The old man says nothing. He turns to go.

'Will it hurt when I go back?'

The old man walks away. I hear a door open. Then a breeze blows through the room and all the candles go out.

'Will it hurt?' I call out. 'Will it hurt?'

But the old man has gone. I'm alone in the darkness, lying on a bed of nails, fighting sleep because I'm afraid of what awaits me when I wake up.

The peace and tranquillity is shattered by the sound of shouting. I try to open my eyes, but I can't. The light that filters through my eyelids is so bright, it's like a laser drilling into my head.

Everything hurts. My body is on fire. My shoulder is killing me. The noise in the room is deafening. I want to get back on the boat.

'He's awake! He's awake!'

'Johnson . . .?'

I know that voice.

'Auntie I . . .?'

That's my voice, but it doesn't sound like me. I try to sit up. My mouth is dry and there's something in my throat. I can't breathe. What's happening to me?

'No, don't do that,' a man says. 'Please, don't do that.' The voice is heavy, accented.

'What's he doing?' the woman who sounds like Auntie I asks.

'He's trying to spit the tubes out.'

Tubes? I try to raise my right arm, but it feels like it's made of lead. If I have tubes in my throat, I need to pull them out.

'Johnson, can you hear me?'

'Auntie I . . .?'

Again I try to open my eyes. Shadows move across the light.

And then I see something familiar.

A clock. A clock with a white face . . .

A white room, with white sheets; white blinds on the window.

I'm in hospital.

'Try not to move, Johnson. You've had an accident.'

'Where am I?'

'You're in Kuwait City. Lynthia's here. I'm here. And Captain Wright from the army . . .'

'Why am I in Kuwait?'

'Shhh, Johnson, no talking now. There'll be time for talking later. Now you've got to rest.'

Somebody touches my face. A light shines in my eye.

'Auntie I, it hurts.'

'What hurts, Johnson?'

'My head, my shoulder . . .'

'I know, Sweetie. But you mustn't talk. You've got to rest.'

'Please, Auntie I; take away the pain.'

'The doctors will take away the pain, Sweetie.'

'You're a nurse. Please . . .'

The tiredness washes over me again and this time I don't fight it.

I want to be back in a world where there is no hurt, no pain. I want to be back in the house with the candles and the old man.

0630 hours, 21 June 2004

Although I'm sedated, I'm aware of what is going on around me; the pain makes sure of that.

Details of the attack have started to filter back: deploying from Broadmoor, slowing down at Red Eight, a flash off to the left, the explosion in front of my face . . . Then nothing until the boat journey with Captain Wright.

Irene tells me it was a dream, but I don't see how it could have been. If it was a dream, how come the room I saw was identical to the room I woke up in?

When I try to talk about it, Irene just gets vex. What I should be doing, she says, is resting, not talking.

My head is so swollen I can hardly open my eyes. When I do I see double.

I'm fitted up to drips that are meant to control the pain, but they don't. I feel like someone's mashing up the front of my head with a sledgehammer.

The priority now, the doctors say, is to get me to the Neuroscience Centre in Birmingham.

Two days after I come out of coma I'm heavily sedated, put into an ambulance and driven to the airport.

I'm airborne on an RAF TriStar. I drift in and out of consciousness until we arrive at RAF Brize Norton. It's a two-hour ride in an ambulance to the University Hospital in Selly Oak, Birmingham.

Over the next three days I'm scanned, X-rayed and visited by consultants. Some of the doctors try to tell me about the operation, but I find it hard to listen. Concentration only makes the pain worse.

I'm in a room by myself. Captain Wright has arranged for the next-door room to be kept for Lynthia and Irene. They have been joined by Darren and Gavin, who are staying in a nearby hotel.

I don't want to see anyone else. I know the operation is risky. I see the look on everyone's face. But right now my head hurts so bad, I don't care whether I live or die. I just want them to take the pain away.

CHAPTER THIRTY-SEVEN

Irene Beharry
7.30 a.m., 24 June 2004

Two hours before Johnson is due to be taken into theatre, the consultant who will lead the operation comes to see me. He takes me into the family room, so we can talk.

I am a nurse. I should be able to take this. I keep telling myself not to cry; that I must be strong for Johnson; that I am lucky. I have my children here. Darren and Gavin are being wonderful – so caring and supportive. Even now, they are at Johnson's bedside.

I take a deep breath and ask the consultant about the procedure.

'Once under general anaesthetic, Johnson will be placed on the operating table in the supine position, his head held by a horseshoe-shaped headrest,' he says.

'His hair will be shaved and his scalp anaesthetised with lignocaine and adrenalin. An incision will be made across the top of his scalp, from one ear to the other, and the coronal flap pulled down in front of his face to expose the compound fracture.

'The X-rays show that he has extensive damage to the forehead, the bones around the airways of his nose, the eye sockets and the part of the skull that supports the frontal lobes. After the impact, the right frontal lobe burst, leading to massive bleeding into his skull cavity.

'Although the surgeons in Kuwait did a remarkable job of cleaning

his wound and closing it up, the scans show that the whole frontal lobe area has been peppered by fragments of bone.

'Any dead tissue has to be cut away and the bone fragments cleaned out. We can then lift the frontal lobes and carry out an inspection of the skull above his eyes; at the very least, there is a bad fracture above the right eye that needs to be repaired.

'We'll also have to rebuild the airways around the nose. As soon as I'm finished on the neurosurgery, my colleague will reset the broken pieces of bone and attach them to his cranium with plates. Then we'll reset the coronal flaps and hold them in place with skin-clips.'

'How long will the whole procedure take?' I ask.

'All in all, he could be in there for up to eight hours – longer if there are complications.

'Mrs Beharry, please, try not to worry. He is in the best possible hands.'

'But cutting away a part of his brain, doctor . . . Even if he survives . . . I mean, what will he be like? Will what's left still be him?'

I can't help myself. I start to cry.

The consultant takes my hand. 'We'll know so much more after the operation, Mrs Beharry. In the meantime, please try and hang on to this: your nephew is young and fit; he doesn't smoke, he doesn't drink and he is strong. Not just physically, but mentally.'

'You know that?' I say.

He smiles. 'I'm a neurosurgeon, Mrs Beharry. With some patients, you can just tell. Besides, Captain Wright has told me about some of the things he has done in Iraq. If anyone can pull through what's ahead, it's Johnson.'

After I have regained my composure I go and pay Johnson one last visit. He is already on the trolley that will take him into theatre. He has been sedated prior to administration of the general anaesthetic. His eyes are closed.

The nurses move around the trolley, checking drips, tubes and monitors.

I take his hand, close my eyes and pray.

When I open them again I'm surprised to see that he is looking at me.

'Auntie I,' he says sleepily, 'you all right?'

I'm fine, I tell him. And you are going to be fine too.

'Don't go blamin' yourself, Auntie I. Sometimes, I know, you think this is all your fault . . .'

I feel the tears coming again. 'That's true,' I say. 'I do.'

'You gave me another life, Auntie I. Joining the army was my decision. I don't regret it. I did what I wanted to do.'

'I know, Sweetie, I know.'

CHAPTER THIRTY-EIGHT

10 a.m, 25 June 2004

I hear the beeps of monitoring equipment, the rustle of curtains opening and closing; people whispering; a phone ringing somewhere . . .

The pain in my head is terrible, but I'm alive.

The first person I see is Irene. She is sitting by the bed, holding my hand. When she sees I'm awake she starts to cry.

Lynthia, Gavin and Darren are there too. It isn't a dream. I close my eyes.

The pain in my head only eases when I sleep. The drugs must be working. I feel myself drifting away.

Sometime later I hear the curtains open. A doctor and a nurse sit me up and shine a light in my eyes. I ask them how long I've been lapsing in and out of consciousness, thinking it's been a week or more, but they tell me it's only the day after the operation. They need to run some tests.

I look to the left and right and then up and down. I follow the beam of light from the torch. They ask me what I see, what I feel. I tell them that I've got a pain in my left eye and that it hurts in my right eye when I look up. The throbbing pain inside my skull is not as bad, but it's there. The double vision has gone.

The doctor scribbles some notes. He tells the nurse I'm

'alert and orientated'. When he's finished she settles me down again and I drift off to sleep.

When I wake the next day the consultant who performed the operation comes to see me.

'You're going to have a bit of a headache over the next few weeks, but otherwise you're in pretty good shape,' he says.

He shakes my hand, tells me I'm doing well and that he'll be back to see me in a few days.

'When do I get out of here?' I ask him.

'Johnson,' he says, 'you've just come out of major surgery. We have to take each day as it comes.'

'Please,' I say, 'just tell me.'

'Well, when you leave rather depends on you,' he says. 'But there's no reason why you shouldn't go home in around three weeks.'

I start to count the days. I hate being ill and I hate being in hospital. I'm determined to leave as soon as I can.

When I tell Darren and Gavin this, they say that I must chill and allow my body whatever time it needs to heal. But as the days pass I become obsessed with discharging myself – and satisfying a strange craving for Kentucky Fried Chicken.

'Gav,' I say one morning, soon as I wake up, 'help me out of here, will you?'

'Johnson, you're not meant to move.'

'I know, but I'm cryin' out for the toilet and if I have to go one more time in that t'ing they gave me, I'm goin' to kill someone.'

'If you've got to get out of bed, I'd rather one of the nurses helped you.'

'I want to show 'em I'm not a cripple. I can walk. I know I can. I just need a bit of help.'

'The doctors said you've got to be real careful of your head.'

'I'll be real careful of my head. I just need you to support me; make sure I don't fall.'

'I ain't holding you on the damn toilet, man.'

'You don't need to. Once I make it to the bathroom I'll be fine.'

He raises an eyebrow, but he's my cousin and he knows that when I make up my mind I'm not going to change it.

'OK,' he says. 'But don't let me down or Mum will kill me.'

It takes about ten minutes to get sat upright on the bed with my feet on the floor.

Gav is terrified that someone is going to walk in and catch us, but no one does and after five minutes of struggle, with Gav holding me and me shuffling, we make it to the toilet across the corridor.

I close the door behind me; my sense of achievement is huge. I take a pee, thank God that I'll never have to relieve myself again in bed and turn around to wash my hands.

What I see when I look up in the mirror is such a shock that I take a step back and have to grab the handrail.

The pain in my head returns with a vengeance. For a minute I don't dare look in the mirror again. Then, slowly, I raise my eyes.

My head is twice its normal size. I have deep bruises around my nose and eyes. It's a wonder I can see at all; my pupils are almost entirely hidden by swollen lids.

There's a bandage on my head, far enough back for me to see where they have shaved me, and the beginnings of a scar running up from one of my ears. There's a line of clips – like big staples – where my face meets my scalp.

I stare at myself, trying to find some part of my face that is recognisable as me. There's a knock on the door and I hear Gav's voice, low and urgent, asking if I'm all right.

I open the door and almost fall into his arms. We hobble

back across the corridor to my room. Gav goes on at me all the way for wanting to run before I can walk.

For once I don't argue with him, and climb back meekly between the sheets.

At night, when I close my eyes, I see a stream of images of Iraq – kids laughing and smiling one moment and throwing petrol bombs the next; Malloy wading through body parts to get to the rear door of his Warrior; alleyways and streets bordered by houses with flat roofs; insurgents running alongside us, firing down at us with AKs . . .

And RPGs. I see RPGs everywhere. Coming at me out of the darkness, so close that I can see every last detail of them in the split second before they explode . . .

My eyes snap open. I look at the clock. It's six-thirty in the morning. I'm not in Iraq. I'm in Selly Oak, Birmingham.

'Johnson? You awake?'

It's Gavin. He and Darren have been taking it in turns to sit with me during the night now that Irene has gone back to work. She drives up to Birmingham most afternoons, stays with me for a few hours, then travels back to London for her night shift. Captain Wright comes and goes with messages of support from my mates in Iraq and asking whether there's anything I need.

Lynthia is staying in a nearby hotel. She spends an hour or two with me every day. I know the sight of me shocks her and now that I've seen myself I'm not surprised. Though I'm on my feet and walking regularly, I've not had the courage to look at myself in the mirror again.

Gav is sitting on a chair by the bed, gazing at a newspaper. He holds up the front page so I can see it. It's the *Sun* and there's a picture of a guy in combats. When I look closer I realise it's me.

'Read the headline,' he says.

'Gav, I can hardly see . . . What's it about?'

'It's about you.'

'Me? Why they writin' about me?'

'Because of what you did. They say you should get the VC.'

'VC? What's the VC?'

'The Victoria Cross. Britain's highest award for gallantry. Even I know that.'

'What does it say?'

'"A squaddie who saved the lives of 30 soldiers during a terrifying firefight in Iraq should be given the Victoria Cross, his comrades said last night . . ." It's all about what you did in Iraq, pulling your commander out of your tank.'

'She's not a tank, Gav. She's an AIFV. An armoured infantry fighting vehicle. A Warrior.'

'Yeah, whatever. What you did was amazing, man . . .'

'I didn't do not'ing, Gav. I was just doin' me duty. Any of me mates would've done the same.'

'Well, officially you're a hero, mate. Even your commanding officer says so. Listen. "The squaddie's overall CO in Iraq, Lieutenant Colonel Matt Maer, paid tribute to him last night. He said, 'To do what he did showed extraordinary courage. Hero is a grossly overused term these days, but he is a true hero.'" See? That's what they're saying about you.'

'Well, I don't feel like a hero,' I tell him. 'I feel like a KFC. I want to get out of here.'

'Then you should try being a little more cooperative. I just spoke to one of the nurses. She told me you're refusing to allow them to take any blood.'

'They don't need to take my blood,' I tell him. 'It's just . . . procedure . . .'

Gavin folds up the newspaper and puts it on my bed. 'That's not true and you know it. What these people have done here is a miracle.'

'Yeah, well, I don't like needles. I seen too many when I was in Iraq.'

'You threatened to punch one of the doctors yesterday.'

'He made me vex.'

'He's doing his job, Johnson. He's trying to make you better.' He pauses. 'Why are you so angry? Why won't you let them help you?'

'I got a pain in me head, Gav, and it won't go away. It's like the worst headache you ever had, on top of an army of ants marchin' around the inside of your skull. It's there. The whole time. And there's not'ing they can do about it. Lyin' here all day only makes it worse. I want to get up. I want to be doin' something. The doctors don't understand.'

'What you want me to do about it?' he asks.

'I need you to help me show these people I can stand on me own two feet.'

'We already shown them that. They know you can walk.'

'I don't mean it like that. I mean, I need to show 'em I can survive on me own, so I can get discharged from here.'

'So how do you intend to do that?'

'I need you to take me somewhere. You and Darren.'

'You mean, out of the hospital?'

'Yeah, out of the hospital.'

'But they'll kill you.'

'Gav, lyin' here is killin' me.'

'So where do you want to go?' he says.

'I was serious about that Kentucky Fried,' I tell him.

I poke my head around the door. Darren is at the end of the corridor, by the swing doors. I check right. Gavin is standing in front of the desk, thirty feet away, flirting with the duty nurse. All he has to do is distract her. He is doing far too good a job.

I glance back at Darren. He beckons me.

I've left a note on my bed saying I need to get some air and I'll be back straight after lunch.

Darren and Gav have bought me a pair of jeans, a T-shirt and some black Nike trainers. I've got a bandage on my head, but the swelling is better. Nobody on the outside, I figure, is going to give me a second glance.

Darren beckons to me again.

I set off, walking stiffly. My balance isn't perfect, but it's slowly getting back to normal.

Five minutes later we're driving out of the car park in Darren's Astra. Gav is in the passenger seat, I'm in the back.

Gav keeps glancing back and asking how I'm doing. I tell him that I'm doing fine, but the truth is, I'm not. The ants are back and all I want to do is plunge the tips of my fingers deep into my skull and squeeze them to death, one by one.

The KFC is on the edge of town with its own parking, so I don't have too far to walk. It's busy, but not packed. We join the shortest queue and talk about what we're going to order.

A little kid is lying on the floor a few feet away, playing with a toy police car while his mother waits to be served in the next line along.

The *nee-naw* noise the kid makes as the car skitters across the floor goes right through my head. I force myself to grin and bear it.

'What you going to have?' the bloke behind the counter asks.

He's black and wears his hair in braids. He gives me a funny look, so I turn away and meet the gaze of the mother of the kid.

She freezes for a moment, then spins around and calls to her child. He takes no notice and carries on playing with the car, so she grabs him by the wrist and drags him to the eating area, as far as it's possible to be from the counter.

'What are we goin' to have?' Darren says.

'The Variety Bucket,' Gavin tells him.

'Is that four chicken pieces or eight?' the bloke with the braids asks.

'Eight,' Gav says.

I nod, then wish I hadn't.

The guy shouts over his shoulder. I wince.

'You all right, mate?' Gav asks quietly.

'Yeah, I'm fine . . .'

'Is he all right?' the guy with the braids asks Darren.

'Yeah, he's fine,' Darren says. He reaches for his wallet. 'How much is that?'

'Ten ninety-nine.' The bloke with the braids glances at me again, then says to Darren, 'What's wrong with him?'

'Who?'

'Your mate.'

'Why don't you ask him yourself?'

He shrugs. 'What happened to you, man?'

'I got shot in the head,' I tell him.

'No shit?' the guy says.

'Yeah, shit,' I tell him.

'What happened?' the guy says.

'You really want to know?'

'Yeah.' He hands Darren his change. 'I really want to know.'

'It happened about a month ago. At night, about 1.30 in the mornin'. I was drivin' along, when suddenly this bloke fires an RPG at me.'

'What's an RPG?' the guy asks.

'Rocket-propelled grenade. It exploded twelve inches from my head.'

'Jesus,' the guy says. He looks at Darren. 'For real?'

'For real,' Darren says.

The guy looks genuinely appalled. 'And this was here, in Birmingham?'

I look at Darren and Gavin. Somehow we manage not to laugh.

'The world's a scary place, man.' Darren grabs the bucket and makes for the door.

'No shit,' the guy with the braids says.

Silence falls on the KFC as we walk out. I swear you could hear a pin drop.

I've lost three and a half stone since my deployment to Iraq and most of it has dropped off me in the past month. I'm weak, but every day I eat a little more, walk a little further and get a little stronger.

Rather than being angry, the doctors are pleased about my trip to the KFC. They say it demonstrates just how much progress I've made and give their permission for me to make other short trips under Darren and Gavin's supervision.

One day I come back from a stroll in the hospital grounds to find a woman in my room. She is staring out of the window, her back to me. I cough lightly and she turns.

'Mummy, what you doin' here?'

'I come to see you,' she says. 'What you think?'

'But how?'

'The army pay. They been real good to us. They take care of everyt'ing.'

I give her a hug. Her eyes fill with tears.

'Oh, Johnson,' she says, touching my cheek, 'what they done to you?'

'I'm goin' to be fine, Mummy. Ask the doctors.'

'It's a miracle you alive an' no mistake,' she says. 'Everybody in the village been sayin' a prayer for you – all you brothers an' sisters, Ena, Nesha, Hammond, Mack an' Joseph an' Westy, Mr Narine . . .'

'And Daddy?'

'Even your father say a special prayer for you – every day.'

I sit down on the end of my bed.

'Everybody so proud of what you done, Johnson, all them t'ings they say about you in the papers. Your gran would 'a been so proud of you too.'

'I didn't do not'ing more than any other man, Mummy.'

I want to tell her about Sammy, Mr Deane, Lewy, Broomstick, Woody, Sergeant Major Falconer . . . All my mates, who are still out there. But where do I begin? How can anyone who wasn't in Iraq ever understand what it was like?

We talk for a while, until the pain in my head gets bad again and my mum has to go.

As she kisses me goodbye she says, 'Johnson, when you goin' to come home?'

'Home, Mummy?'

'To Grenada. To Diego Piece. To your family and friends.'

'It ain't that simple,' I say.

It's not just what happened in Iraq, I tell her. There's all kinds of things I've got to work through. Like me and the army. Whether they want to keep me or whether I'm going to have to leave.

Then there's me and Lynthia. What happened affected her as much as me.

My mother looks at me. I'm not explaining myself well. But I don't want to hurt her either.

Three and a half weeks after the operation, I'm finally discharged. By now I thought that my problems would be over, but adjusting to life in Tidworth, especially with my mates still in Iraq, is difficult. They are not due to return for another two months. In the meantime the garrison is like a ghost town.

I still get pain in the front-right part of my head and sometimes, particularly when I'm tired, the double vision returns. Only now am I beginning to understand how much this injury is going to affect the rest of my life. Even if I make a complete recovery, I can never go back to driving a Warrior, the thing I want to do most in the world, because military rules prohibit a return to front-line duties if you have had any kind of brain injury.

I'm not even allowed to drive my car until the doctors say it's safe. All I can do is sit in the flat, doing what I can to manage the pain in my head, my shoulder and, increasingly, my back. I'm determined to do this without the drugs. The closest thing I take to a painkiller is a Nurofen tablet when the headaches get really bad.

The doctors are hopeful that the pain will ease as soon as I start a course of physiotherapy at the Defence Medical Rehabilitation Centre at Headley Court.

In Tidworth I don't want to see anyone; when the pain's really bad all I want is to be on my own. This makes it difficult for Lynthia, because there's nothing she can do to help.

She says I've changed; that I no longer care about anyone or anything the way I used to.

I don't really know what depression is, but perhaps that is what I have. I don't feel like getting out and doing things or seeing people, but being on my own isn't the answer either. To be able to sleep at all now, I have to stay up as late as I can and then fall into bed when I can't keep my eyes open any longer. Even then, I don't get much more than a couple of hours. Either it's the pain that wakes me or I get a flashback.

At night, in the dead hours, I see wave after wave of RPGs coming at me. Or I'm wading through body parts, like Malloy did, to get to the door-release button in the dismount section of Whisky Two Zero . . . I jump when a door slams. And when I hear a siren wail I'm right back on the streets of Al Amarah.

I wonder if I'll ever get my old life back.

CHAPTER THIRTY-NINE

RAF Headley Court is a big red-brick mansion set in eighty-five acres of landscaped gardens and rolling fields near Leatherhead in Surrey. It's the home of the Defence Services Medical Rehabilitation Unit, a treatment centre for people in the armed forces who have sustained serious spine and limb injuries.

When I go through the gate I feel like I've been here before. At first I don't get it. Then I remember. Headley Court is like the place in my dream. The place where Captain Wright took me. It's the house with the candles, the bed of nails and the old man with the beard.

I've never been to a health farm, but Headley Court is like I imagine a health farm to be. I'm taken on a tour of the building and nurses smile at me as they swish past in white coats. I'm shown the four gyms and the hydro pool and meet some of the eighteen full-time instructors who will work with me over the next three months to get some mobility into my shoulder and rebuild the muscles I damaged in my back when I lifted Mr Deane out of his hatch.

The 'working day' lasts from 0830 to 1630 hours, Monday to Thursday, and 0830 to 1300 hours on Friday.

I'm given an extensive neurological examination. They find nothing wrong with my attention, my concentration, my memory or my reasoning. The bones of my skull are still fragile, but knitting together well. Even my face has returned to pretty much how it looked before the night of 11 June.

The only visible scar is the one across the top of my head.

Most ways you look at it, my recovery is every bit the miracle that Auntie I prayed for.

When I look at some of the other patients here – men and women who are partially or completely paralysed, or have lost arms and legs – I know I've nothing to complain about. I can walk and I can run. And even though part of my brain has been cut away, I can talk and I can think.

It's just the pain. The pain in my shoulder, the pain in my back and the pain in my head . . . The doctors tell me it will go, one day, but I wonder whether they are just saying that to give me hope. I don't think I'll ever get used to it.

In the morning I perform a 'lumbar spine mobility programme', a 'muscle strength programme' and a 'core stability programme', followed by a range of further exercises in the afternoon. They are designed to treat the injuries to my back and shoulder. And while I feel they're doing me good, and my strength is returning, the regime goes on day after day, week after week. It's not like driving a Warrior. I miss life on the front line and I miss my friends more than I can say.

I'm allowed home at weekends, but not for the first two weeks. Darren, Gavin and Irene come and visit when they can, but I get few other visitors.

I've changed, there's no getting away from it. My personality is different. I find it hard to get motivated. I haven't seen Lynthia in a while. Maybe it's easier that way.

My dream, the one about the eggs, now makes perfect sense to me. Part of me died when the RPG slammed into Whisky Two Zero.

Perhaps Gran saw this too, and chose not to tell me.

★

There's a place I go to in Headley Court where I try to make sense of everything that has happened; a little garden, surrounded by a high, carefully trimmed hedge, filled with roses that I can't smell. In the middle of the garden is a bench. I sit here during breaks in my schedule, thinking about the past and the future.

I think about the things I used to build and wonder whether I'll ever be able to build anything again.

I think about Grenada and England and the army and wonder which of them is now my home.

I think about life outside the army, and wonder where my future lies.

I think about Gran.

Little by little, as the summer drifts into autumn, I feel my strength returning. The pain in my head begins to ease too.

Is this because I'm getting better or because I'm getting used to it? I don't know. The doctors don't really know either. With an injury like mine, a lot is down to guesswork.

One warm October morning I'm sitting in the garden, the sun on my face, when my mobile rings.

It's a crackly line. 'Paki? That you?'

'Sammy!' I feel a rush of excitement that I haven't felt for months. 'Where are you?'

'Tidworth. We all are. The battalion's back. We got back this mornin'. How you doing, man?'

'I'm good,' I tell him. 'What's it like to be back?'

'Weird, you know. I been dreamin' of this day for months, but now that it's here, I feel . . . I dunno . . . I can't really explain.'

'Like you don't really belong?'

'Yeah,' he says. 'You read the paper, you watch the TV. Iraq hardly get a mention. It's like nobody even knew we were there. But we were fightin' a war, you know? A full-blown bloody war.'

We talk for half an hour. He asks when I'm next coming back to Tidworth and I tell him that it doesn't figure in my plans any more.

'What about you?' I say. 'What are your plans?'

Sammy tells me the battalion is due a whole load of leave, then it's Christmas, then it's on the move again – to Paderborn in Germany, until March 2006, when it's due to head back to Iraq for another tour of duty.

I know one thing for sure, I tell him. I won't be going with them. The doctors and physiotherapists at Headley Court say that my wounds have made me unfit for military service. I'll be discharged from the army as soon as my course of treatment is over.

One spring morning, shortly after a hydrotherapy session, I get a call from Colonel Maer.

The MoD has arranged for some of the guys in the battalion who fought in Iraq to be interviewed by the media. Apparently I'm one of the ones they want to speak to.

The CO also wants to talk about my future.

Accommodation is being arranged in London. Some of my mates will be there too.

A car comes to pick me up from Headley Court and I rendezvous with Colonel Maer in the lobby of his hotel. He steers me into a small conference room, where we chat about my injuries, and my recovery.

The CO looks at his watch. Almost immediately there's a knock on the door and Mr Deane walks into the room.

'Boss!' I say, jumping to my feet.

'Beharry . . .' He grabs my hand warmly. 'How the hell are you?'

'Good, Boss. You?'

'Oh, fair to bloody,' he says. 'You know how it is.' He's about to clap me on the shoulder, but remembers and stops.

'Good old Whisky Two Zero – she wasn't the same without you.'

I'm so happy to see him. 'You still rather be in a snatch?'

'You know me,' he says with a smile. 'Any day.'

I glance over Mr Deane's shoulder. Sergeant Major Falconer is standing next to the CO. Broomstick is standing beside him.

'Skiving again, I see,' the CSM says. 'How're you doing, Beharry?'

I step forward and shake his hand. 'Good, Sarn't Major.'

'Excellent, son. Glad to hear it. Hurry up and get well, won't you? There's a couple of things of yours I'm holding for safe keeping.'

'T'ings of mine, Sarn't Major?'

'A sodding helmet with a bullet in it, for a start,' he says.

'Anyone ever hand in a little chain with a cross on it?' I ask him.

'Are we talking bling here, Beharry?'

'Special kind of bling, Sarn't Major. She saved my life a couple of times.'

The CSM hasn't seen it, but he says he'll do some asking around.

I turn to Broomstick. For a moment I'm lost for words and so, I think, is he.

'How's your bloody foot, mate?' he says.

'My foot?'

'Last time I saw you I managed to shut it in the door of a Warrior. I never did get a chance to say sorry.'

I smile. 'My foot's fine, Stick.'

'How about the rest of you, mate?'

'Comin' along,' I tell him.

'Gleaming, mate. It's good to see you, Harry. It really is. Hurry on back to us, won't you, mate.'

When we settle down again the CO tells us a little bit

about what we can expect at the Ministry of Defence tomorrow.

There are some awards to be made, some medals to be
handed out later in the year, he says, and the MoD wants to
make sure that the media have everything they need to start
preparing their account of our deployment in Al Amarah.

'I've got to go over there now and prepare some of the
groundwork,' he says, getting to his feet. 'But I'll be back later
to give you an update. In the meantime the bar tab's on me.'

During the afternoon I catch up on what happened to the
BG after I got casevac'd out of theatre.

Captain Wright had told me about the ceasefire. I didn't
know that hostilities had resumed about three weeks later. If
anything, the 'second Sadr uprising' was even more violent
than the first. The enemy stepped up its attacks on our bases
and regained control of the streets, until a second ceasefire was
agreed on 13 August.

'Without you, Bee, I was a bloody liability,' Mr Deane says.

'What you mean, Boss?'

'Got through four more Warriors after you left, didn't I?'
He shakes his head and smiles. 'I'm terrified they're going to
hit me with the bloody bill tomorrow.'

In the evening, when he returns from the MoD, the CO
calls us into a seminar room on the ground floor of the
hotel. He says he has something to tell us. He stares at his
feet for a moment, then looks at us. 'When I took over the
battalion I told you I'd be straight with you. That you'd
always get the truth from me. Well, today, I'm afraid, I broke
that rule.'

I don't know what the CO is talking about. When I look
at Mr Deane, the CSM and Broomstick, I see they don't
either.

'Around a week ago, I was told, under strict instructions

not to tell a living soul, that the battalion would be in line to receive a number of awards for our contribution to Op Telic Four.

'Tomorrow, one day in advance of the announcement, the press is to be pre-briefed on those awards. I'm delighted to inform you that the battalion has done rather well. You, gentlemen, are all among those who are going to be honoured.'

He looks at Mr Deane and Sergeant Major Falconer and says, 'Richard, Sergeant Major, you've both got MCs.'

Mr Deane looks stunned. He stares at the floor and goes very quiet.

'Twice wounded and twice returned to battle,' the CO says. 'Quite outstanding, Richard. Well done.'

Falconer sits there, shaking his head. 'I'm thinking of the blokes, sir. They're the ones who deserve this, not me.'

'Your leadership and courage throughout Telic Four were exemplary,' the CO says. 'As far as I'm concerned, Sergeant Major, they've got it right. I'm proud of you. We all are.'

The CO turns to Broomstick. 'The Conspicuous Gallantry Cross for you, Sergeant Broome. Second only to the Victoria Cross for bravery in the face of the enemy. You're one of only fifteen people to have been awarded the CGC since it was instituted in 1993.'

Broomstick almost falls off his chair. 'Bloody hell,' he says. 'Me? Why me, sir?'

'I can think of any number of reasons,' the CO says. 'But the citation stresses your selfless courage in coming to Sergeant Llewellyn's rescue on 9 May.'

There's a long pause, then the CO looks at me. 'Beharry,' he says, 'this one's rather special. They haven't handed one of these out for quite a while. It gives me the very deepest pleasure to tell you that you are going to receive the Victoria Cross.'

I hear what he says, but it doesn't really register.

I look up and see Broomstick beaming from ear to ear. And I swear I can see tears in his eyes.

The next day we walk on to a stage on the ground floor of the MoD to face a small gathering of TV media.

The Defence Secretary, Geoff Hoon, says a few words, then the CO takes to the podium.

He talks about the honour and privilege of commanding the 1PWRR battle group in Maysan province; the grit and professionalism of the thirteen hundred men and women under his command; the difficulty of the task we faced; and the background to the Al Sadr rebellions that caused us so much trouble.

He takes us back to the time we came to the rescue of his Land Rover group.

'It was day one of the tour,' he says. 'My team had suffered thirty per cent casualties already and we knew it was probably going to be a long summer.'

Over the next six months the BG was to suffer 237 shooting attacks, 51 rocket attacks, 185 RPG launches, 712 mortar rounds and 360 IEDs – over 850 attacks in total, at an average of six a day, every day for five months. At the peak of the fighting there were 109 attacks in one day.

'This was not without cost,' the CO goes on to say. 'The battalion suffered over forty wounded during its time in Iraq. And although today is very much a celebration, it is one when we remember those who were killed.'

He makes special mention of those who lost their lives: Private Chris Rayment and Private Lee O'Callaghan from our battalion and Fusilier Stevie Jones from the Royal Welch Fusiliers.

'Our thoughts today remain with Chris's and Lee's families, and Stevie's young wife,' the CO says. 'In my office, throughout the tour, hung the regimental colours. I drew inspiration from them during some of our darker moments. I drew inspiration from the place names on them and the actions they represented: Anzio, Cassino, Salerno, Normandy, Kohima; back through the Somme and Mons, back more than 350 years ago.

'All we wished to do – what I feel we *did* do – was to keep up the traditions, ethos and example that had been shown to us before.'

In the Q&A session that follows, the media want to know what the VC means to me; what it will mean to my family; whether it will change me; what my plans are; whether I'm staying in the army. The questions come quickly, one on top of the other, and I answer them as best I can, even though they make my head swim. I tell them that I was driven by the need to save my comrades, yet I did no more than any of them would have done.

Honoured as I am to be receiving the medal, there is no way I can conceive of it changing my life. It can't bring me the one thing I want, which is to go back to driving a Warrior, but I hope, perhaps, that it can be a force for good; I want kids like me to know that anything is possible if you set your mind to it.

'What was going through your head during that second engagement?' one journalist asks.

'An RPG,' I say.

Everyone falls about laughing and I realise that this wasn't the answer he was looking for. For the time being, though, it's probably as good as any. My head is starting to kill me again.

After the interviews we head for Stansted and a plane to Paderborn.

The CO wants us all to be together when he tells the rest of the battalion. We're under strict instructions not to breathe a word to anyone. The plan is to assemble everyone in the garrison's cinema at eight the next morning. News of the awards won't hit the streets until lunchtime.

Because everyone is going on leave the day after, the guys will think we're in for the standard pep talk about the dangers of alcohol abuse and the usual gentle reminder of the penalties for returning late when leave is over. All I have to do between now and then is stay out of sight. It's not that Colonel Maer doesn't trust me, but people are going to want to know what I'm doing back in Germany after such a long absence.

'You know,' the CO says, as I wish him goodnight, 'like it or not, Beharry, this medal is going to have a profound impact on your life. All the awards that are going to be announced tomorrow are precious, but the VC is something else again. It will change things – now and for the rest of your life.'

We assemble shortly after breakfast. I enter the auditorium as soon as all eyes are fixed on Colonel Maer and I take my seat, unnoticed, at the back.

He tells everyone to have a good leave and not to overdo things, then says he has a very special announcement to make. He starts to read out the full list of honours and awards, kicking off with the Mentions in Dispatches. Clifton gets one and so does Cooper. There are countless others. Then he reads out the names of those who have won the Military Cross, the Distinguished Service Order that he and Major Coote are to receive, Broomstick's Conspicuous Gallantry Cross and my Victoria Cross.

There is a gasp and a burst of applause.

For all the pride I feel in this moment, I know I'll remember most what happens when the CO is halfway through his list of MCs.

For no particular reason, I'm watching Sammy. He's slouched in his seat, four rows in front of me. I know what that slouch means. It doesn't matter how many honours and awards the battalion is receiving, Sammy is bored and counting the minutes till we break up and go on leave.

Mr Deane's name is read out and then, to everyone's delight, so is Woody's. Suddenly, when we all think that's it, the CO reads out Sammy's name too. There is a moment of silence, then Sammy sits bolt upright.

'Me?' he says. 'An MC? *Fuck!*'

Everyone just collapses.

Just before he lets us go, the CO says he has one further thing he wants to share with us.

'Needless to say, I'm so very proud of you all,' he continues. 'However, as Churchill said, medals shine but they also leave shadows. Today we all rightly take pride in those who have been recognised for their bravery, but what I want us also to remember is that three blokes from the battle group aren't with us today because they gave their lives in Iraq. Their families would give anything – anything, right now – to have them here with us. In the weeks, months and years ahead, when we talk about these awards – who has them and who doesn't – please think of them. In the final analysis a medal means nothing compared with a life that's been given in the line of duty and on the field of battle.

'We will now stand.'

After a short prayer from the chaplain the RSM says that he's throwing open the doors of the sergeants' mess to all ranks.

I put in an appearance, but the talk and the laughter, all the smoke that hangs heavily in the air, starts to do my head in, and so Sammy and I decide we're going to head off to Kevin Campbell's room for a cup of tea.

On the way we pass a lone Warrior that's parked up outside the maintenance sheds. I want to jump in, feel the controls again, start her up. I don't, though. Part of the deal I have made with myself is that from now on I'm going to look forward, not back.

CHAPTER FORTY

Since 1856, 1355 VCs have been awarded – and eleven (not including mine) since the Second World War (six of them posthumously).

The last surviving recipient was Lance Corporal Rambahadur Limbu of the 10th Gurkha Rifles for his action in Sarawak, Borneo, in November 1965. Lieutenant Colonel H. Jones and Sergeant Ian McKay, of the Parachute Regiment, received them posthumously during the Falklands War in 1982.

Four VCs have been awarded to Australians – two of them posthumously – for actions during the Vietnam War.

Fourteen VC holders, including me, are still alive.

I'm beginning to understand what Colonel Maer meant when he said the medal would change my life.

Last night the CO, me, the OC, Broomstick, Mr Deane, Dave Falconer, Sergeant Perfect, Woody and Sammy all stayed at the Wellington Barracks as guests of the Irish Guards.

This morning, as we walk over to Buckingham Palace, the CO tells me about a telephone call he received late yesterday from General Sir Michael Jackson, the Chief of the General Staff – the head of the British Army.

'He's due to come to the Palace today to be made a GCB – a Knight Grand Cross of the Order of the Bath,' the CO says. 'But he asked me if it's OK for him to be there, because he doesn't want his award to clash with yours. This is your day. Yours and the rest of the guys'. How're you feeling?'

I tell him I'm feeling fine. We walk on for a minute or two in the warm April sunshine.

Irene, Raymond and Lynthia are with me. The OC, Mr Deane, Dave Falconer, Sergeant Perfect, Broomstick, Woody, Sammy and their families stroll alongside.

'They'll probably have to rewrite the protocol books,' Colonel Maer says. 'Did you know that everyone in the military – generals, admirals and air vice marshals on down – is obliged to salute you when you're in uniform?'

I tell him I do know this. Sammy and Campbell were pissing themselves with laughter when they told me. They also say I'll get £1495 per year until the day I die.

'It's a pity you don't drink,' the CO says. 'People are going to be lining them up at the bar – not just today, but for the rest of your life.'

I'm figuring I might risk a little champagne today, I tell him. The CO smiles and says it can't hurt.

We're greeted by the Queen's equerry-in-waiting and led through the corridors to the ballroom. As soon as my family are settled one row from the front, I'm directed into a side room to be briefed on the ceremony. I'm the first in line to be decorated; around 150 others will follow.

It all seems straightforward enough. I wait in the wings for the band to strike up the National Anthem on the dot of eleven. Everybody rises as the Queen walks into the ballroom. Before I have time to get nervous, they sit again and my name is called out.

'Private Johnson Beharry, The Princess of Wales's Royal Regiment. For his actions on 1 May and 11 June 2004 in saving the lives of his Warrior crew by dogged and determined perseverance when injured and under sustained enemy attack. The Victoria Cross.'

I keep walking until I'm standing a few short paces from Her Majesty. I look her in the eyes and the corner of her mouth twitches. Is it a smile? Do I smile back?

The Lord Chamberlain, standing to the Queen's right, begins to read my citation.

'Private Beharry carried out two individual acts of great heroism, by which he saved the lives of his comrades. Both were in direct face of the enemy, under intense fire, at great personal risk to himself, one leading to him sustaining very serious injuries. His valour is worthy of the highest recognition . . .'

It takes almost fifteen minutes to read it out, by which time my shoulder and back are killing me.

I step up to receive my medal.

I bow and find myself half a pace away from the Queen. I have so much blood pounding in my ears that I miss the first thing she says to me.

'I'm sorry, Majesty?'

She leans forward and her face breaks into a big smile.

'You're a very special person,' she says, as she pins the medal on to my chest. 'It's been rather a long time since I've awarded one of these.'

'Thank you, Majesty.'

'How are you managing?' she asks. 'You look remarkably well, and yet we have read about the terrible things you have been through.'

'I'm doin' a' right, you know, Majesty, but it's the injuries the doctors can't see that are givin' me the most trouble.'

'They are the ones that take the longest to heal . . .' She says these words with such feeling it's as if she's been with me every step of the way.

She holds out her hand and I shake it. Then I step back, bow, and carry on through to another side room, where I am to collect the real medal. The one that is pinned on my chest is for ceremonial purposes only.

I know that the bronze used for each VC comes from a Russian cannon captured at the end of the Crimean War. The block of metal is held by the 15th Regiment Royal Logistic Corps at Donnington and is so precious that it is only removed from its vault on special occasions. There are 358 ounces of the block left, enough to make only another twelve VCs. Somebody tells me I need to insure mine for a million pounds. I just can't get my head around that.

While I'm receiving the box and being told about the medal, the ceremony continues.

Next up is General Sir Mike Jackson. After him, it's a Grenadian, Sir Royston Hopkin, who receives his knighthood for services to Grenada's tourist industry. I wonder if this is a complete coincidence, two Grenadians being here today. Whatever, it makes me happy, as we are really putting Grenada on the map.

It takes me a while to rejoin the ceremony, because half the royal household ask me for my autograph in the side room. I'm directed to a seat between General Jackson and Dame Ellen MacArthur, the famous yachtswoman.

The proceedings continue for another hour. There are more knighthoods, then a bunch of OBEs.

Finally, 'For Services in Iraq', it's Colonel Maer's turn to go up to receive his DSO, followed closely by Major Coote. Broomstick collects his CGC, then all the MCs are given out. Sammy accepts his and wanders back to his seat beaming from ear to ear. I half expect him to give us all a thumbs-up.

When the ceremony is over we wander outside and take our places in the sunshine. Journalists and photographers swarm around us. They want photos of me and my mates. They want photos of me and Lynthia. They want photos of me and the VC.

In the end Dave Falconer comes to my rescue. 'Easy, son,'

he says in my ear. 'I got you. Probably time we made ourselves scarce, eh?'

My head, shoulder and back feel as if they're on fire. It doesn't much matter whether I stand or sit – being still for an hour and a half is what gets me.

We walk back to Wellington Barracks, where the Irish Guards are holding a small drinks reception in our honour. Upon entering we're led through to the officer's mess, where a colour sergeant major, a huge man with bright-blue eyes, formally welcomes us and directs us towards a guy who's handing out glasses of champagne.

As I enter the room the CSM salutes me and asks if he can shake my hand.

Sure, I say, and we shake warmly.

'Would you mind . . .? I mean . . . would it be all right . . . if I had a look at the medal?'

'No problem.' I reach into my pocket. As I hand over the box I ask him if there's a toilet anywhere near.

He looks a bit surprised and points me back in the direction we have come.

'What about the medal?' he asks after me.

'Why don't you hang on to it till I get back?'

When I reach the gents I close the door behind me and lock it.

My head, shoulder and back are on fire, but I'm beginning to learn how to deal with it. I've got six more months of treatment coming up at Headley Court. My body, slowly but surely, is starting to mend.

There's no talk any more of my leaving the army. Even if I can't drive a Warrior again, there are plenty of things the top brass can find for a VC to do.

I splash some water over my face and stare at my reflection for a moment.

The scar is tucked up into my hairline and barely visible.

The army of ants is still there, but they're a little bit quieter now.

I've been lucky – especially compared with Lewy. He's had multiple skin grafts; he's on the mend, but still in considerable pain. Like me, he will never be able to do the thing he most wants to do – go back on the front line.

I look at the purple ribbon and simple bronze cross on my chest.

Before Iraq, we were a bunch of guys from a hundred different walks of life, doing a job. The day we got to Al Amarah, all that changed. We changed. We looked out for one another. We became family.

How could I not do what I did?

Twenty minutes later, after I've sipped a little champagne and talked to quite a few more people, it's time to leave. We're driving to a place called the Haberdashers' Hall for a lunch in our honour.

As we're leaving I bump into the CSM. 'Thanks,' he says, shaking me warmly by the hand again.

'What for, Sarn't Major?'

'For letting me hang on to the VC – and for so long.'

I pat my pockets. My VC! I'd completely forgotten about it.

The CSM smiles and gives me the box. 'Don't let it change you,' he says.

I smile and thank him, then step into the sunshine, where my family are waiting.

EPILOGUE

Point Salines, Grenada, 18 August 2005

The Virgin Atlantic flight is ten minutes out of Trinidad and Tobago. I get out of my seat and make my way to the back of the cabin, where my dress uniform is hanging.

'How long till we touch down?' I ask the flight attendant.

'Fifteen minutes,' she says. 'We'll be starting our descent any moment now.'

I change quickly in the toilet, and am conscious of the stares I get as I make my way back to my seat. The regiment's blue jacket and trousers with their bright-red trim stand out at the best of times; in an aircraft, at the height of the tourist season, surrounded by passengers in jeans and T-shirts, my uniform is a complete show-stopper.

A middle-aged man, a Grenadian, gets out of his seat as I pass.

'Meetin' you has made me whole day,' he says. 'I recognised you face from the stamp. Welcome home, brother; welcome home.'

For a second I think I must have misheard him. Then I remember. They have issued a five-dollar stamp on the island with my face on it.

'Thanks,' I tell him. 'It's good to be goin' back.'

'I read about you and you wife? I'm sorry. All the pressure, the papers said.'

Yes, I tell him. There's been a lot of pressure.

Other people stop me in the aisle. Children clap and point. A young mother hands me her baby. An old man asks for my signature.

Then the party breaks up. In a few minutes we'll be landing.

As I settle back in my seat I look out of the window and see Grenada.

At first she looks exactly the same – unchanged from the day I flew in for my gran's funeral three years ago. But through a gap in the clouds, I catch sight of the mountains. Thousands upon thousands of trees have been uprooted and scattered across the slopes. Moments later we swoop over a town and I see a church without a roof; houses stripped of their galvanised – evidence of the fury of Ivan and Emily.

On 7 September 2004, for the first time in forty-nine years, Grenada was hit by a Category 4 hurricane, the ninth most powerful in recorded history. Ivan tore across the island, its two-hundred-mile-per-hour winds ripping roofs off houses, pulling trees from the ground and stripping the leaves off those that were left.

In a few hours Ivan destroyed twenty-eight thousand homes, left ninety per cent of the island's houses without roofs and officially killed thirty-nine people. My friends and family say the real toll is more than four times this; the morning after the storm had passed, some of Ivan's victims looked out upon the devastation and simply lost the will to live.

'God is a Grenadian,' they always used to say, as memories of Janet – the last hurricane to hit us – slowly faded. But it seems that a one-degree rise in sea temperature has brought about a change in the Good Lord's attitude towards us. He has shifted the hurricane belt southwards.

Ten months after Ivan, just a few weeks ago, the island was hit again, by Emily.

What Ivan began, Emily finished. Everyone I know has been affected in some way.

When Ivan hit, Jane and Chris grabbed Leesha, Ken and Chunks, abandoned the repair shop and took refuge in an old Dodge bus on the edge of the yard. From there they watched as twister after twister tore across Woodlands and ripped their place apart.

Even though they have lost their house, their business, everything, Jane and Chris are determined to rebuild their lives.

Their attitude to their customers hasn't changed, of course. If you can afford to pay, Chris will take your money; if you can't, never mind. Chris and Jane know you'll pay them when you can.

The money was never important to them; it still isn't.

'It's not the worst thing that could have happened,' Tan Jane told me over the phone. 'Look at us, we're alive, praise God.'

As Ivan passed over Diego Piece he spared Hammond's and Old Man Baptiste's plantations, but went for the buildings instead.

From a back room in his house, Emrol Narine, my teacher, watched as Ivan lifted the roof off the Samaritan Presbyterian School – 150 feet of galvanised steel – carried it over his house and dropped it on the edge of the village. As it fell to the ground it made a noise like a 747 crashing. 'I thought we were all going to die,' he said.

Just before he swept out to sea, Ivan flattened my gran's little house.

Ten months later Emily rooted out everything Ivan had spared.

Grenadians say that Emily must have been his wife; it looked like she was searching for him.

By the time she was done looking, only six of Hammond's

nutmeg trees were left. Old Man Baptiste's weren't any luckier. They have replanted what Emily took, but it will be six more years before the trees bear fruit.

Ninety per cent of Grenada's entire nutmeg crop was destroyed in the two storms. The island's economy is on its knees.

The plane thumps down on the runway and taxies up to the only terminal.

I wait for the other passengers to disembark, adjust my cap and move out on to the steps. There are several official-looking cars below and a sea of faces turned my way. I hear claps and cheers. When I reach the tarmac I'm met by Grenada's glamorous Minister for Communication and Works, Clarice Modeste-Curwen.

'Johnson Beharry, son of the soil, welcome back,' she says, giving me a hug. 'This is such a proud day for us.'

It's thirty-one Celsius, eighty-eight Fahrenheit, outside – cool compared with the inside of a Warrior in Iraq, but in my thick jacket and trousers I'm starting to melt.

The minister's people clear a path and guide me towards the terminal building. As I make my way, people clap me on the back and pump my hand. Hundreds of faces are pressed against a chain-link fence. I wave and they wave back.

I pass beneath a banner that says 'WELCOME HOME, JOHNSON' in huge capital letters.

I'm led into a room filled with people.

'*Johnson!*'

My sister Jemilla elbows her way through the official reception committee and throws herself at me. Moments later I spot the rest of my brothers and sisters. They are all here: Jude, Jill, Jemilla, Jeffrey, Jeffon and Jade. But before I can properly say hello, bodyguards whisk me away and usher me towards a table at the far end of the room, where the Minister of National Security, Senator Einstein Louison, is waiting.

He taps a microphone in front of him to see if it's working. 'The ladies and gentlemen of the media are waiting,' he says.

A Presbyterian minister reads a short prayer, then Mr Louison gets to his feet.

'"Train hard and fight decent" used to be our motto in the army,' he says, as he beams into the cameras, 'but you have brought honour and meaning to this, Johnson Beharry. If the young people of this island will choose you as their role model, then I hope we'll have many more Beharrys in all walks of life. The government of Grenada thanks you and respects you and honours your bravery.'

When he finishes there is a burst of applause.

Minister Modeste-Curwen gets to her feet. 'We are not here to debate the rights and wrongs of war,' she says, 'but to honour the valour and courage of a true son of the soil. Welcome home, Brother Johnson.'

She tells me I'm to be made the island's Ambassador-at-Large, Grenada's representative wherever I go.

After I've said a few words about how grateful I am for this reception, and how happy I am to be back, I'm able to be reunited with my family.

My mother is here, her mother – my other gran – uncles and aunts I never even knew I had, and countless cousins. I hug each and every one, then turn and see my father.

For a second or two we stand there, staring at each other.

My father still drinks and life at home isn't always easy for my mum and my siblings, but I've learned a lot about the fragility of the human mind; I understand the demons that drive my father better than I did before. I step forward and embrace him.

'I am proud of you,' he says quietly.

Just for a moment I am back on the porch, sitting alongside my daddy, looking out at the world.

Five minutes later I head out to a white stretch limo. My

escort opens up the sun roof. I stand up and he hands me a Grenadian flag. I drape it around my shoulders.

With a police car leading the way we drive up to a set of padlocked gates. As a guard fumbles with the key the crowd pushes forward.

'Johnson, welcome home!'

'Beharry! Yes, man!'

Everybody is smiling. Everybody is cheering. People of all ages surge around the car. I reach out and shake as many hands as I can.

Just outside the airport our driver falls into line behind a pick-up truck with a pair of megaphones lashed to the roof.

Behind us are more cars, some official, most of them not. I give up counting when I get to twenty.

As we set off, a voice booms out:

'This is the official motorcade of a son of the soil, Johnson Beharry . . .

'This is the official motorcade of Johnson Beharry, a Grenadian hero, winner of the Victoria Cross . . .

'This is the official motorcade of Johnson Beharry, who saved the lives of his comrades in Iraq and has come back to us . . .'

Horns toot. Crowds wave. Flags fly.

I see people I know. Friends. Cousins. Family. I laugh. I smile. I am so happy. Grenada. It's like a village. Everybody knows everybody. I wave. Everybody waves back.

As we head into St George's every inch of the way is lined with people. I pinch myself. It's like a dream.

'Ladies and gentlemen, this is the official motorcade of Johnson Beharry. Johnson Beharry, our national hero, come back to us . . .'

We drift into the outskirts of the capital. The harbour is on our left. Boats lie smashed on the rocks and upturned on the beach. A bank on my right has had its roof ripped off. There's a guy with a full head of dreads sitting on the balcony, drinking a Carib. He raises his clenched fist in salute as we motor on by. I give him a wave and salute him back.

We move into the town and the motorcade gets bigger. As we loop through the tiny backstreets, the procession snaking this way and that, it becomes so big that we run into the tail end of it as we turn back towards the harbour.

We're circling around towards a hotel in the Grand Anse, where I'll spend the night before making the journey to Diego Piece.

We've been on the road for two hours already and the sun is slipping into the sea.

Darkness falls as we leave the town behind. There are still people lining the roads.

The motorcade slows for a roundabout and I spot a group of small boys standing by the kerb. As our lights play across them, I ask the driver to slow.

One of the kids, a boy of six or seven, steps forward. His T-shirt is torn; his feet are bare.

He stands ramrod straight and snaps a salute.

'Johnson Beharry!' he shouts. 'I want to be you.'

ACKNOWLEDGEMENTS

I'd like to give special thanks to Irene Beharry, who was here for me on day one and who is still here. Thank you, Irene – I love you. I'd also like to reiterate my thanks to Raymond, Gavin and Darren for helping me through some difficult moments. As I hope the book shows, we're definitely getting there.

The same goes to my family and friends, named and unnamed, and to anyone else who hasn't been mentioned either here or directly in the text, but who played their part – my profound thanks and, where appropriate, apologies. I haven't forgotten you and you know that I never will.

A deep, deep debt of thanks goes to the officers and men of the 1st Battalion Princess of Wales's Royal Regiment, especially the guys who served with me in Al Amarah in that sweltering summer of 2004. You know who you are – I certainly do. I will never forget you either.

Another deep debt of thanks goes to Mr Kay and Mr Evans at the Queen Elizabeth Neuroscience Centre and Pam Wells at Headley Court. I would also like to express my lasting gratitude to *all* the doctors and medical staff in Kuwait, Birmingham, Headley Court and Woolwich who helped my recovery.

Further thanks go to Prime Minister Keith Mitchell, Senator Einstein Louison, Minister Clarice Modeste-Curwen and the government of Grenada, and to Captain Chris Wright, Colonel Frances Castle, Colonel Mike Ball, Richard Holmes and the Ministry of Defence, and to Didy Grahame of the VC & GC Association. I am also indebted to Lieutenant Colonel Eric Wilson VC and all the other VC recipients who have shared the benefit of their advice and wisdom with me. It has meant, and continues to mean, so much.

Finally, I would like to thank Nick Cook and Mark Lucas for helping me to tell my story, and Ursula Mackenzie and the entire team at Little, Brown for publishing it.